Richard Parr

RT HON HENRY MCLEISH began his political career as an elected member in local government in 1974, and was leader of Fife Regional Council for five years. In 1987 he was elected as a member of the UK Parliament and acted as Minister for Devolution and Home Affairs in the Labour government from 1997 to 1999. In the first Scottish Parliament he was Minister for Enterprise and Lifelong Learning from 1999, and in 2000 he became First Minister of Scotland until 2001. Retiring from politics in 2003, he is now an adviser, consultant, writer author and broadcaster and lectures in the USA and elsewhere on the European Union and politics.

He chaired the Scottish Prisons Commission, which produced a report into sentencing and the criminal justice system entitled 'Scotland's Choice'. In 2010 he conducted a major report on the state of football in Scotland, which had been commissioned by the Scottish Football Association, and chaired a commission into sport requested by the Scottish government. He is now an honorary professor at Edinburgh University.

D0994429

Luath Press is an independently owned and managed book publishing company based in Scotland, and is not aligned to any political party or grouping. *Viewpoints* is an occasional series exploring issues of current and future relevance.

Rethinking Our Politics

The political and constitutional future
of Scotland and the UK

HENRY McLEISH

Luath Press Limited
EDINBURGH
www.luath.co.uk

First published 2014

ISBN: 978-1-906817-83-1

The paper used in this book is recyclable. It is made from
low chlorine pulps produced in a low energy, low emissions manner
from renewable forests.

Printed and bound by
Bell & Bain Ltd., Glasgow

Typeset in 11 point Sabon
by 3btype.com

Contents

Contents

Acknowledgements

The Author wishes to place on record his thanks to the following for their contribution to the ongoing debate about the political and constitutional future of Scotland and the United Kingdom and in particular the expertise and wisdom they have brought to their work: First, 'The UK's Changing Union' a series of collaborative forums, Wales Governance Centre, Cardiff University and involving Edinburgh University. Second, the Institute for Public Policy Research (IPPR), including, 'The Dog that finally Barked', 'England as an Emerging Political Community' and 'England and its Two Unions'. Third, Linda Colley, Professor of History at Princeton University, and author of, 'Britons-Forging the Nation 1707–1832 and 'Acts of Union and Disunion'. Fourth, Michael Kenny, Professor of Politics at Queen Mary, University of London and his work with, 'The Future of the UK and Scotland' project and the IPPR. Fifth, Vernon Bogdanor, Emeritus Professor of Law, Kings College London and author of, 'The New British Constitution'. Sixth, Will Hutton, Chief Executive the Work Foundation and the *Observer* for two articles on the political evolution of the SNP. Seventh, Michael Keating, Professor of Politics at the University of Aberdeen and along with David McCrone, Emeritus Professor of Sociology, Edinburgh University, 'The Crisis of Social democracy' and along with Malcolm Harvey, Research Assistant, Aberdeen University, 'Small Nations in a big World – What Scotland can Learn'. Eighth, Charlie Jeffery, Professor of Politics at Edinburgh University and Director of the Academy of Government, for his help and advice. Finally, Tom Brown, former editor of the *Daily Record* and source of continuing inspiration and wisdom who co-authored with me three books on Scotland since 2007.

A Progressive Narrative

A Changing World

SCOTLAND IS ENJOYING a summer of sport in 2014 and while sport and politics rarely provide telling insights into the issue of national pride, the World Cup in Brazil and the Commonwealth Games in Glasgow could act as a starting point for our ongoing debate on national identity. Germany, winners of the World Cup for the fourth time in their history, looked disciplined, orderly, confident, sophisticated, focussed, committed, organised, like they wanted to win and played like a team. Germany as a nation state projects a similar sense of purpose, confidence, pride and modernity. This is a country with a complex history: a penchant for militarism as evidenced in 1870, 1914 and 1939; a brutal division of Germany as part of the post-war carving up of Europe; unification after the fall of the Berlin Wall in 1989 and now a successful federalist structure. Now the driving force in the EU and content to cede sovereignty to the states of Germany and to the Eurozone and excelling in the world economy as an exporter and maker of excellent manufacturing products and engineering excellence. No-one suggests that sharing sovereignty with the other 17 countries in the Eurozone makes Germany a lesser nation in either European or World affairs. The United Kingdom, in sharp contrast, looks worryingly inferior. Despite repelling invaders for over 1,000 years, being a union in stages between 1530, 1707 and 1801 and having the benefit of island status, the Union today looks tired, unsettled, unstable, insecure and now bitterly divided. We seem lost in a new world and we are unable to escape the past. Most people when they wake up each morning think it is a new day, but too many parts of the Union, including Westminster, wake up and think it is yesterday. There appears to be a lack of purpose, unity, national focus and pride and a collapse of any sense of collective ambition and endeavour. Britishness and any concept of solidarity are fast disappearing. Faced with this apparent drift and failure of the Union to adapt to a changing world, Scotland and the Scots could be forgiven for thinking there could be a better way to build a new future. History shows that spectacular shocks to nation states can bring about radical change and a desire to correct the wrongs of the past and build a better future. The absence of any shake-up in the fortunes of Britain may have set us on this journey, but could this change if Scotland decides to exit the Union and seek a future of its own control, free from the apathy of the Union and seeking to be more like Germany or the Nordic countries rather than the United States of America? Would the Union see this as a sufficient, albeit dramatic, way to make a point and accept the run-down state we are in? More importantly, would Westminster do something about it? The debate is about Scotland's future in the Union and whether the outcome is YES or NO. But in reality this is primarily about the Union and why it has allowed the conditions to develop in which an independent Scotland is even a serious option. The debate is narrow as the Unionist parties ruled out a second question and the possibility of considering a form of federalism, which is the only serious solution to the problems facing the Union if a NO vote is secured. Scotland could be a serious and successful independent state. That is not the issue. The bigger question is: can the Union survive in its present form regardless of the outcome of the referendum? This book discusses the future of Scotland and the Union and attempts to put into a wider context the challenges facing both. Setting aside the big economic issues, the book concentrates on the political and constitutional issues which do not get the level of debate they deserve in shaping how a nation will vote and a Union will respond.

Why write the book?

After 43 years in the Labour Party, nearly 30 years in elected office and after ten years to reflect on life and politics – a period in which I have gained considerable insight into the challenges and opportunities facing Scotland – I am more and more disappointed about the state of politics in our country, the narrow nature of the referendum campaign, the poverty of political debate, the growing disconnect of the electors from those who govern and seek to govern and the plight of political parties. The Labour Party has enormous potential for positive social, political and economic good but has, in the post-devolution years, lost traction and direction. The SNP, in sharp contrast, has now governed this nation for the last six years during a period of enormous economic difficulty and has captured the imagination of the public through a combination of populism, a broad electoral appeal and the embrace of nationality and identity. Social class is less strongly linked to party allegiance, party membership has collapsed, voter turnout is declining, trust in politicians continues to shrink and people feel disconnected from political parties and disillusioned with all things political.

The Nationalist Party has successfully hijacked the constitutional issue and dominated the debate on Scotland's role in the Union: despite their success, the SNP does not have a distinctive political philosophy and to date cannot be described as a progressive, left-of-centre or social democratic party in Scotland. Instead the SNP, now heading up the YES campaign, combines a broad appeal to nationalist sentiment, populism, competent government, charismatic leadership and a desire to win. Together these qualities have helped to create a formidable political party, which explains in large measure their success since 2007 and 2011: a party on the margins has moved to the mainstream and is now a party of majority government. This has been nothing less than a political earthquake in Scotland, where the seismic impact continues in a series of powerful aftershocks to threaten the very foundations of the political Union of 1707. Again it is hard to understand why this has been allowed to happen. A glance at the traditional Unionist parties in Scotland helps to answer some of the questions. The rise of the SNP has been accompanied by the decline, some might argue the collapse, of Labour as a political force at Holyrood, suffering from being in denial and incapable of learning any lessons of consequence from the SNP rout in 2011. To put it more dramatically, Labour, north and south of the Border, may be judged by history as being a factor responsible for bringing Scotland to the brink and creating the conditions in which Scotland's exit from the Union become a real possibility, maybe not this time but sometime soon. The other central theme of this book is the role a union in decline has played in loosening the bonds between Scotland and the Union, weakening any sense of Britishness and undermining loyalties which have been developed over the last 300 years. To adapt the phrase of James Carville, political adviser in the early '90s to President Bill Clinton, it's the Union, stupid, that lies at the heart of the constitutional and political turmoil that has engulfed Scotland in the post-devolution era. Labour at Westminster has failed to understand what is happening in Scotland since 1998 and ignored at their peril England. Labour in Scotland has failed to respond. This may prove to be the undoing of the Union: the outcome of the vote on 18 September 2014 will answer that question.

Devolution has unleashed a new political landscape in Scotland. The Unionist parties have clearly failed to find any real focus and seem ill at ease with the uncomfortable truth that Scottish politics has changed forever. There will be no going back to the days of a comfortable Union where Westminster; dominated by the myth of absolute parliamentary sovereignty, the philosophy of democratic centralism and a total contempt for genuinely sharing power, as was the political order of the day. The world is changing but the Union of the United Kingdom isn't. A perfect storm of political issues is now brewing in Scotland. Recognising them is one thing, but doing something about them is another. But it might be too late.

This book attempts to set out the issues and ideas that are swirling around the most important debate since 1707, ideas which consciously and unconsciously are being absorbed by Scots and will ultimately decide the outcome of the referendum. There is a new politics in Scotland. But overshadowing all of this is the Union and its main institution, the Westminster Parliament, both of which are in long-term decline and creating the instability, insecurity and threats to the very existence of the Union in its present form as well as the future of Wales, England and Northern Ireland. Is it possible for the Union to embrace change and create a more attractive future for Scotland to be part of or are we now at the point where Scotland will exit, the only doubt remaining being when? There are six principal reasons why the referendum campaign is likely to be closer than was envisaged when David Cameron enthusiastically signed the Edinburgh Agreement. The Prime Minister, frustrated at his failure to dampen the rise of the SNP after he came to office, was motivated to support the referendum in the hope that Salmond, the SNP and Nationalism would be defeated. And in some peoples' eyes Cameron's decision was political and opportunistic and had little to do with securing an imaginative future for Scotland in a new and transformed Union. Instead this was intended to be David Cameron's 'slam dunk' moment, when history would repeat itself, as in 1707, when England wanted more security on its northern flank. Scotland would be brought into line, Scots would vote NO, notions of a new future would be halted and then the nation would await the generosity of Westminster to see what further powers and responsibilities might be handed down. There has never been a hint of humility from the Unionist party leaders that the Union itself might be the cause of Scotland's dissatisfaction with Westminster and the political and constitutional crisis which has worsened under the new virulent strain of conservatism extremism, anti-Europeanism and populism now so attractive to voters in England. This book seeks to go behind the politics of YES and NO to discuss issues of influence and importance, consider a broader sweep of history, wider horizons for the debate and a deeper understanding of what the real and medium term issues are.

First, the steady decline of the Union of Great Britain and Northern Ireland, in particular during the post-war period.

Second, the perfect storm of issues, which have been intensified by the approaching referendum, but have been brewing for some time. These issues will survive a NO vote and continue to haunt Westminster if it fails to undertake the sweeping reforms necessary to save the Union. In the US these issues are described as Wedge issues.

Third, the decline of the Unionist parties in Scotland, especially the Labour party. Uncomfortable with sub-national government or devolution, the interest of the Labour Party has ebbed and flowed, normally in response to the success or otherwise of the SNP. With some exceptions, the Party rarely embraced the spirit of constitutional change and its central importance to political progress in Scotland and the safeguarding of the Union. Post-devolution, post-2007, and post-2011, when the SNP moved from the margins of Scottish politics to the mainstream and then to majority government, Labour has been in denial, lost political traction and found it hard to adjust to the new politics of Scotland. At times it has seemed overwhelmed by the constitutional question. It is a pale shadow of its former self and remains too obsessed with nationalism and less concerned with seeing Scotland as a special political place with distinctive needs which, in or out of the Union, requires new thinking and more imagination. There is clearly evidence to suggest that when a vacuum is created by a political party failing to provide a philosophy, it is often filled by populism and in England more extremism and forms of grudge and grievance politics.

Fourth, Scotland has grown in confidence in the post-devolution period since 1999. Fifteen years have encouraged Scots to respect difference in both outlook and policy and value the responsibility and opportunity to view their politics through a prism reflecting a 'made in Scotland' label. We are less deferential, more confident and less inclined to take matters of history for granted.

Fifth, there is the widespread discontent and disillusionment with the broken nature of British politics and our democracy. While similar experiences exist in Western democracies, Britain has slumped further than most.

We seem to have lost interest in the importance of our democracy and the failing performance of politics, political parties and politicians. Every conceivable measure of the quality of our democracy and political process is on the slide – trust, confidence, election turnout, membership of political parties, political literacy, public discourse, lack of philosophy and ethics, partisanship and tribalism – and since much of the criticism is being levelled at Westminster this dissatisfaction could impact on the campaign, the outcome of the referendum and how the post-referendum debate is framed. In or out, we shouldn't disguise the 'scunnerisation' factor that is all too evident in our politics. Bearing this in mind, the SNP have somehow managed to avoid the political wrath of the people of Scotland and remained reasonably successful for seven years, including the first referendum. There is no doubt that the success of the SNP has been helped enormously by the decline of Labour.

Sixth, the decline of Britishness and the increasing importance of national identity are evident in Wales, Scotland and England. The loyalties of the nations of the Union to the idea of Britishness are changing, with England now embracing a much more decisive sense of Englishness. These changes reflect the wider impact of political, constitutional and governance issues throughout the Union and serve notice that Scotland is not the odd one out. Whether these shifts in attitudes are being promoted positively or negatively, they are giving notice to Westminster and the Union that expectations are being built up which require a response and action.

But linking these factors together provides the most telling feature about the referendum campaign.

There are a number of issues that are inextricably linked – which have for the first time in over a century moved front and centre in British political life. There are good reasons to think that these are just as likely to affect the fortunes of all the political parties in the short and medium term.

They are also likely to weigh heavily on Scots as they consider how they will vote. These are issues which are eating away at the credibility of the Union, highlighting in their different ways aspects of political faith, crucial policy areas, questions of nationality and identity and international developments, which will determine in the short and long term the very nature of the Union, its attractiveness to Scots, who, for the first time for 300 years have a real choice and the means to express this, and a real test of the split political personality of Scotland. These are ostensibly issues of value that are less concerned with the economy or welfare but more about what kind of society we want to live in, what do we value for ourselves and our families and a whole range of ethical and philosophical issues which lie at the heart of a caring, civilised, compassionate and progressive community:

A complex set of factors are now in play and the sum of their respective parts could have a dramatic bearing not only in terms of the September referendum but also in the political and constitutional aftermath of a NO vote. There is no consensus: Scotland is divided and the Union seems, at least at this point, unable to accept responsibility for its part in creating the weak and unbalanced union we have. So Scotland does have a real choice, not just a statement about the Union and 300 years of history, but an opportunity to realise its potential in a different way in a new relationship with the Union, in or out. Underlining the unique opportunity available, whether or not independence wins through this time, notice will have been given that a nation is on a journey and may be content, at this point in time, to be the object of a bidding war by the Unionist parties to 'buy them off' with the least change acceptable to Conservative and Labour MPs at Westminster. But the issue won't go away. This is where the Union will be on trial, with a huge weight of expectancy on it. But, if history is anything to go by, it may be unable or possibly incapable of the transformative work needed to keep the Union intact and retain Scotland's membership. The Union, as a prisoner of its past, may be beyond seeing a different future and having a different and a sensible road map and timescale to get there.

The book finally looks at a possible future for Scotland: a model for the creation of a progressive and positive nation either still in the Union – if transformed – or as an independent country. Either option presents difficult questions for the Labour and Conservative Parties in Scotland, who are reluctant to embrace a federalist structure – supported by the Lib-Dems – and will have to dance to the tunes of their hosts at Westminster. Labour should seize the opportunity to answer their critics as to what they stand for at the start of the 21st century and pursue a platform of unashamedly left-of-centre ideas which embrace 'the common good', thinking through money and the markets and morality and embracing the humanity, happiness and hope agenda of the Nordic countries. This would require an approach which combines social democracy, the Social Investment State and social partnership. This kind of discussion will fill a gaping hole in the middle of the current debate and whatever is likely to happen after the referendum. The SNP or YES campaign is reaching out to the widest possible audience from the extreme left to the extreme right and believers and non-believers in between. Their vision for the future of Scotland is incomplete, but for good practical reasons. Labour in contrast needn't be so hesitant but instead be bold, honest to the founding fathers of the Labour Party and true to the vast majority of Scots who want decent, collective and inspirational answers to some of the burning questions of our times: and this doesn't need Scotland to be in or out of the Union. For Labour it is an approach for both independence and federalism. It would be more difficult in a status quo plus Union, but not impossible. The important point is the need for Labour to waken up to a range of futures and outcomes which all require philosophy, morality, progressive policies, social democracy and self-belief.

My political journey over nearly 44 years has been important in providing insights. I have a breadth of experience that enables me to make sense of my own thinking, the philosophical ideas that party politics should be built on and the political issues that are so important to the people I have represented and the millions of Scots that make up this remarkable country.

Our date with destiny in September 2014 will be one of a whole range of international events being held in Scotland. There is no doubt that whatever the outcome, Scotland will continue to change, develop and seek new constitutional arrangements within the Union. We are on a political and constitutional journey of uncertain destination, but a reasonably clear direction. The elections for Westminster in 2015 and for Holyrood in 2016 may only serve to underline the remarkable volatility, shifting allegiances and unpredictability of the current mood of Scottish electors. One thing is clear: the campaign, despite its many weaknesses, has brought people to meetings throughout Scotland, raised awareness, engaged potential voters young and old, challenged some of the worst aspects of our partisan politics and helped politics be more inclusive. There have also been examples of inspiration and enthusiasm about the Union and Scotland and an attempt to overcome the poverty of our public discourse and the level of our civic literacy. All of this is long overdue.

Pitches, Politics and Pits

Comparing the politics of one generation with another can be misleading, reflecting undue sentiment and a misplaced or distorted sense of how good or bad one period of history was when measured against another. Our history can also be personal and filtered through our experiences. Our memories are not always reliable, some of us often think that the present can never compare with the politics of the '60s or '70s where there was more vision, inspiration and idealism. For the vast majority of people, material prosperity, physical security and social stability have improved enormously. However, many people now feel dissatisfied and disillusioned with modern life and search for some meaning to life amidst the excesses of capitalism, growing inequality, excessive commercialisation and greed invading our public space and undermining any idea of the common good in an increasingly atomised and individualistic society. This is often expressed in the belief that there is something fundamentally wrong with our politics. Politics and political parties are not impacting positively on the way we live, failing to either address or solve enduring problems and allowing unacceptable levels of inequality, the few benefitting at the expense of the many, growing social and economic division and a capitalism which is corroding concern for each other and elevating individualism and shallowness above the common good and solidarity. Many question what political parties stand for. Protests, populism and extremism are all gaining traction at the expense of common sense and fairness, especially in England. People are becoming disconnected and frustrated as their views go unattended. Scotland and the United Kingdom are wealthy beyond anything my grandfather could ever have envisaged in his life of football, mining and serving his country in World War One. Why then does modern politics allow such a poverty of spirit, inspiration and soul to dominate our lives? Why do political parties cling to outdated ideas and lack the courage to do anything about the obscene levels of poverty and the lack of fairness in society? Why are we being conditioned into thinking this is the way it has to be? Our profound lack of confidence in politics and our disillusionment with the lack of solutions to enduring problems is in danger of damaging our democracy, fuelling discontent and forcing many people to seek comfort in the populist and the extremist and those that seek scapegoats rather than solutions. Populism can fill a vacuum created when other political parties run out of ideas, credibility and don't appear to stand for something.

This is the Union of the United Kingdom in 2014. It is also the background against which the referendum will be fought. Do the people reaffirm their commitment to a Union and a political system that is failing, or do they opt instead for the unknown? Whatever their choice, it is a real one. This is what makes this date with destiny so fascinating and so difficult to call. The vote is not just about one geographical entity leaving another. This is about history, a shared sense of sacrifice, post-war achievements and an improved lifestyle for citizens, but now it is also about broken politics, divisive economics, growing inequality, the lack of fairness, new hopes for the future, a rekindled belief in ambition and an increasing weariness about the emptiness and intolerance of much of the political and public discourse. Was it always like this?

Politics and our democracy in crisis

British Politics is going through a period of rapid disintegration. This is putting our democracy at risk. Remarkably, our political parties seem unaware of the scale of this crisis, the urgency needed to address the complex issues involved and the threat to the traditional political system. This crisis has to be viewed against a background of long-term decline in the way we do our politics in Britain and an absolute neglect of ideas, policies and inspiration in terms of looking forward and trying to rescue our democracy and rebuild our politics. Party politics is outdated and structurally antiquated, with little genuine or relevant links to people, who feel disillusioned and alienated from those who seek to represent them. Never in recent history has our politics been so ramshackle and irrelevant to the needs of the vast majority of the population.

The political classes are either unaware of this unfolding crisis, which of course is impossible to believe, or are in a perpetual state of denial. While privately they may acknowledge the seriousness of the problem, there is a worrying paralysis in relation to any serious action or reform. For too long the rules of the political game have favoured the two major parties at Westminster. Despite Labour and the Conservatives losing nearly 20 per cent of their combined vote in General Elections in the last 30 years, new parties emerging and entering Westminster and a dramatic decline in electoral turnout in all kinds of elections over the same period, there has been no real effort to inquire in any systematic way into this crisis. Britain, in consequence, is becoming a much less attractive and less tolerant country to live in and because of the poor levels of public discourse and the pathetic levels of political or civic literacy we are, relative to Western Europe, a declining democracy. The Labour and Conservative Parties have seen a dramatic decline in membership; turnouts in elections are falling; there is a growing divergence in voting numbers between the young and the old, with poll figures for young people worryingly low. Although they are enthused by political issues, they are turned off by politicians and political parties. There is a growing disenfranchisement of the poor as they disconnect from mainstream politics and feel alienated by the often limited response of the Government and institutions to their needs; trust and confidence of the electors in political institutions and politicians has slumped as measured by various surveys; electoral reform is seen as important for European, Devolved and local council elections but not for Westminster; and the recent attempt to move to a form of PR in the recent referendum only showed a massive dislike for a change and a threat to the established hegemony of the two major political parties. For the independence referendum, Scotland will see 16 year olds vote for the first time. But the holding of elections and the actual voting procedures are archaic and anachronistic – electronic tools shift billions of pounds around the world but in the polling station we put x on ballot papers and put them in a box. What about voting on mobile phones, longer election periods, or voting at the weekend? Modernising elections would be a sign that Westminster was serious about the catastrophic decline in turnout – we want more and more people to vote, not less. Statistics abound about the weaknesses and failures of the current system and the serious consequences which follow fewer people voting, especially the poor. In terms of those who actually vote, there is a huge difference between the poor and everyone else.

The Union and Westminster are in a political fix of their own making and to date have been unwilling or uninterested in pursuing reform and modernising. The question is whether there can ever be a mood for a change and then a commitment to radical transformation of our politics and our democracy, but the two main parties show little interest in change. There is a permanent blocking mechanism – mindset, history, sovereignty, preciousness and at times arrogance about the wisdom of doing anything that would blunt the edge of the Conservative and Labour Parties at Westminster. Where does that leave Scots who value their vote and the health of democracy and see no prospect of change at the heart of the Union?

Scotland's independence referendum is unique

For only the fifth time in over 300 years of the Union of Great Britain and Northern Ireland will an issue of such major constitutional and political importance be decided by the electors in Scotland, elevating the sovereignty of the people rather than the sovereignty of Westminster. This historic departure from the conventions of the British State is to be welcomed and may, dependent on the outcome, hasten the end of the absolute sovereignty of Parliament and its role as the guiding principle in our ramshackle constitution. For centuries our unwritten constitution has allowed us to get by and at the same time provided a pretence that our rights and liberties were being valued and protected. Events in the modern era have shown that there is no principle of absolute sovereignty: membership of the European Union, being subject to the jurisdiction of the European Court of Human Rights (ECHR), the holding of binding referendums and the devolution of power to Scotland, Wales and Northern Ireland have driven a coach and horse through the outdated idea that Westminster's power and authority is either credible or relevant to the nations of the Union in the 21st century. Referendums, while being a powerful and useful tool for a modern democracy, are complex and do not usually represent public views or concerns solely on the issue before the people. At a particular moment in time, referendums give people the opportunity to make a judgement or make their views known or express their anger on a single issue, but in doing so they may be using their vote to express their feelings on a whole range of issues which in turn have been framed by a wider set of political, social and economic considerations filtered through their own personal experiences.

Scotland's independence referendum will be no different. When David Cameron signed the Edinburgh Agreement it was clear that, based on a great deal of ignorance of Scotland's history, a sparse knowledge of 14 years of the post-devolution era, confused and wrong intelligence from Unionist parties in Scotland combined with a genuine sense of opportunism, he thought he was calling Alex Salmond's bluff and in doing so looked forward to killing off independence and in the process destroying the SNP. This was to be Cameron's moment where Westminster, after the 18 September, could get back to business as usual and put behind them an uncomfortable distraction which had irritated more than worried the Unionist parties, especially Labour and the Tories. This is likely to represent another Unionist party miscalculation since the SNP came to power in 2007. The subsequent referendum campaign and the clash between 'Better Together' and 'YES for Scotland' has not gone to plan. There is more than a hint of anxiety in what is unfolding and what may be the outcome of the vote, not necessarily about doubting the NO campaign winning, but much more concerned about the margin of that victory and what may happen afterwards. But it could be much worse than that. A victory for the YES Campaign would shatter the confidence and authority of Westminster and be the biggest humiliation suffered by the Union since the US colonies became independent in the 18th century. For Labour this would be a defeat of unimaginable proportions and put the prospect of a Labour victory at Westminster under the present First Past the Post system in some serious doubt. YES for Scotland could accelerate the decline of the Union and undermine the reputation of the rUK (the rest of the UK) in The EU, NATO and the United Nations, where its permanent member status of the Security Council could be at risk. The consequences of defeat for defeat for the Prime Minister could be enormous, and could undoubtedly result in loss of face for The Prime Minister.

We are getting ahead of ourselves in speculating on the outcome of the referendum, but even at this stage searching questions have to be asked.

How have the Unionist parties allowed this to happen?

Why is a victory for the NO vote in danger of turning into a narrow majority or, even worse, a defeat?

Why are Scots so unimpressed by the Union?

Has there been a failure to either understand the Scottish people or the mood of a nation that may simply have had enough of politics and political parties through the prism of Westminster?

Are there other factors at work, some apparent but misunderstood and some less so, swirling around in the political ether, but nonetheless adding to the discontent, frustration and anger that may drive people to vote YES when they would like to vote NO.

Is it 'the Union, stupid' that is the problem and as a result makes it so difficult for the Better Together Campaign to be positive, confident and promote a progressive and positive vision for tomorrow? Is the Union losing its appeal or has it lost it?

Is the YES Campaign just fortunate, despite its obvious strengths, that a perfect storm or powerful cocktail of factors are at work which are weakening the bonds between Scotland and the Union and questioning the historical benefits of a union that has lasted for over 300 years but which now seems incapable of being promoted by its supporters?

Answers to these questions will be discussed in this new book, which unashamedly argues for a better debate than we are currently having and which sets the issues in a broader sweep of history and a deeper understanding of the Union. It is often the nature of our politics to exaggerate the importance of a political event, but we are dealing with a referendum of towering significance to the future of The UK and Scotland. No matter the result, political life will continue after the 18 September and more thought also has to be given to what happens next.

The current debate has been an obvious result of the Labour, Tory and Lib-Dem Parties rejecting a second question on the ballot paper. Without being able to express what a NO vote will mean after the referendum, there is a real danger that voters will feel cheated and opt for a YES despite a real preference to remain in the Union. This raises the issue of how narrow this debate has become: so many ideas, futures and options can't be discussed because they are outwith the narrow parameters of an agreement that had more to do with the narrow and (understandably partisan) views of the major parties than about the Scottish people, who have shown in many opinion polls their desire to stay in the Union, but a very different union with more substantial powers and responsibilities being shared with Scotland. The absence of a second question is putting at risk the outcome of the referendum and may contribute to a diminished NO vote. This was another Unionist miscalculation.

We need a new approach to the problems of 21st-century Scotland and Britain. This book seeks to define and then provide a brief overview of ten of the most important political and constitutional issues facing Scots as they prepare to vote in the independence referendum. These issues lie at the heart of the Union and the political and constitutional questions about its future which remain unanswered. Looking beyond the referendum, regardless of the outcome, all of these issues retain saliency and may in fact become more important as the polling stations close on the 18 September. The real problem is that in the crowded, confused and complex world of politics we often don't have an effective way of addressing the issues that matter to people because they don't fit the soundbite culture, the hard edges of economic policy or the simple in or out rhetoric that this campaign has been subject too. Our politics often seems incapable of finding a deeper seam of wisdom, vision and inspiration to mine. As a result the in or out nature of the debate is narrow, tribalism and partisanship dominate and the key player in all of this, the Union of Great Britain and Northern Ireland, escapes effective scrutiny as to whether or not it is fit for purpose in the 21st century and represents an appropriate arrangement for Scotland to be part of.

We are looking at the past through the prism of the present – often a highly selective version of it – and have little idea of how to predict or understand what might happen in the future. This book, in a very modest way, looks to project a more unified approach not just to the referendum debate and the outcome, but to the long term future of the Union, in the event of a NO vote, or in terms of a YES vote, where the same issues will still have to be faced by the rUK.

We need to explore what kind of Scotland we want and once again this is relevant to the pre- and post-referendum status of our nation as we look at the philosophical, moral, political, international and governance issues that will help shape a different future, regardless of whether Scotland is in or out of the Union: this kind of debate is long overdue and we have neglected for far too long what progressiveness means in the 21st century. We tend to think on highly traditional lines and ignore the fact that new and inspired thinking is needed to deal with complex issues; this referendum has highlighted, especially in relation to the Unionist parties, the vacuum that lies at the heart of our policy making.

In his book *High Noon, 20 Global Problems: 20 Years to Solve Them*, J. F. Richard said:

> Never have there been such massive opportunities for improving the human condition. Yet never has there been such uncertainty about our ability to grasp these opportunities. .

Change the context, from the condition of the planet to the future of Scotland, and his comments have relevance to the plight of our nation. What we need is more imagination and new thinking about how we should be governed. There are unsolved problems that should be at the forefront of this referendum debate and campaign, but they are not. Instead we have the replay of old battles – Scotland v England, Unionism v Nationalism, Independence v some more Devolution, SNP v Labour, Edinburgh v London, Scottish Government v Westminster Government and so it goes on, wrapped up in old style partisanship, served up in fierce tribalism and all delivered to the public through low levels of political literacy, poor quality public discourse and a less than balanced press: not the public's fault, but the result of a lack of interest on the part of the political classes.

Donald Dewar and Scotland's future

But in this introduction let us pause for a moment and look back to someone who made a huge contribution to devolved Government. The late Donald Dewar understood Scotland and the success of our Parliament as based on his White Paper and the referendum held in 1997. Throughout his period in Government he also made some remarkable and insightful comments about what the future might hold. He also reminds us about what this debate is all about.

Speaking at the opening of the Scottish Parliament in 1999, he said:

This is indeed a moment anchored in our history. Today we can reach back to the long haul to win this Parliament, to the struggles of those who brought democracy to Scotland, to that other Parliament dissolved in controversy over 300 years ago.

Today we can look forward to the time when this moment will be seen as a turning point – the day when democracy was renewed in Scotland, when we revitalised our place in this, our United Kingdom.

Distant echoes

The past is part of us, part of every one of us and we respect it. But today there is a new voice in the land, the voice of a democratic Parliament, a voice to shape Scotland, a voice above all for the future.

For me – and I think in this I speak at least for any Scot today – this is a proud moment, a new stage in a journey begun long ago and which has no end. This is a proud day for all of us.

A Scottish Parliament, not an end, but a means to greater ends and these too are part of our Mace. Woven into the symbolic thistles are these four words – wisdom, justice, compassion, integrity.

Burns would have understood that. We've just heard beautifully sung one of his most enduring works, and at the heart of that song is a very Scottish conviction that honesty and simple dignity are priceless virtues not imparted by rank or birth or privilege but part of the soul.

Burns believed that sense of worth ultimately prevails, he believed that was the core of politics and that without it our profession is inevitably impoverished.

The late Donald Dewar in his Spectator Lecture, *Towards a Modern and Flexible Constitution* in November 1998 said:

> For any Scot, today is a proud moment; a new stage on a journey begun long ago and which has no end. A Scottish Parliament. Not an end; a means to greater ends.

Surely this debate can be opened out to include the idea of a more flexible and modernised Union, which sees transferring more power and responsibility not as a sign of weakness, but as strength and confidence in the constituent parts of the UK.

Scotland's date with destiny will be 18 September 2014. The first referendum on independence will take place and we will have a real poll as to where Scots see their country and their own future in the years ahead. History shows that it is given to few politicians to fulfil their destiny. Donald Dewar was without doubt one such politician – and, as with his physical stature, he will stand head and shoulders above others in posterity. John Smith and Robin Cook were also taken early.

Dewar's devolution years should remind us of his insights, often ignored or forgotten, into the significance of devolution, how it was likely to develop in later years and above all else the challenges it would pose to the Labour Party, whose caution, confusion and hesitancy had often threatened to derail the home rule project. Labour's involvement with the constitutional question, leading ultimately to the embrace of devolution, started in the early part of the 20th century. Keir Hardie first pledged the Labour Party's support for Scottish home rule in an election address in 1888 and the Labour Party went in to the General Election of 1918 with Scottish home rule as the third priority in its manifesto, ahead of housing, pensions and education. Labour's engagement with devolution ebbed and flowed, reflecting Scotland's national mood and the varying political fortunes of the SNP.

From 1997 to his untimely death, devolution was Dewar. It is worth noting that without his contribution, we may not be where we are today, where a successful Parliament has positively impacted on the Scottish people, a new and vigorous debate about Scotland's future is in full swing and Labour now appreciate that constitutional change is a 'process not an event'.

Even in 1997, after nearly 100 years of discussing some form of home rule, the Labour Party in Scotland remained uneasy about the constitutional future of Scotland. Devolution was a huge issue in Scotland and Labour now accepted what John Smith had described as 'the settled will of the Scottish People' and 'unfinished business'. In England and Westminster though, there was a feeling of indifference and certainly ambivalence. Devolution had never been part of the DNA or soul of an institution which had ruled without disruption for centuries. This was the context in which Dewar had to win the battle for Scotland.

Being out of politics and able to revisit events more dispassionately has been helpful to me in reappraising the real worth of Donald Dewar's contribution to both the politics and the history of Scotland.

Although we are now 14 years on from the successful establishment of the Scottish Parliament, it is worthwhile to reflect on how and why home rule for Scotland was achieved.

Historical analysis and the reading of Parliamentary reports cannot give the full picture of how one man's sharp intelligence, political skill and sheer grinding hard work helped to make Scotland's dream a reality.

In 1997, when Labour came to power for the first time in 18 years, our Party was in a state of euphoria. We needed time to assume our new responsibilities and become accustomed to our new status as the party of government. It would have been easy to lose focus, but Donald Dewar would not be diverted from the commitments we had made. Throughout that summer, he got down to work to deliver on the promises we had made to Scotland to finally deliver on the home rule campaign that had spanned a controversial century. In doing so, he was responsible for the production of what was generally acknowledged to be one of the most significant White Papers ever presented to parliament and people. It spelled out with clarity and conviction exactly how we would deliver devolution to Scotland, with all the technicalities and procedure for setting up a Scottish Parliament. Many were surprised at how robust it was in relation to Scottish aspirations.

Because of that, and Dewar's advocacy, the White Paper proved popular and largely received cross-party support. The White Paper, the Scotland Act and driving through the devolution programme were, in my view, Donald Dewar's finest moments.

Despite Labour's clear commitment to devolution, there were some in our new Government and Parliament for whom it was a grudging concession. Dewar had to struggle with the big beasts of the political jungle at Westminster and powerful figures within our own party. Yet, throughout the weekly battles within the special Cabinet sub-committee, the Scotland Act emerged unscathed and was massively and triumphantly endorsed in the referendum on 11 September 1997. Returning to Dover House, after long and grueling committee sessions, he would, in that laconic and self-depreciating manner, bemoan how well or otherwise he had done. The civil servants would then arrive to say what another remarkable performance he had turned in to defend Scotland's interest and the integrity of the Scotland White Paper!

That, to me, was Dewar's true legacy: history's verdict will be that Scotland's hopes and future were enshrined in and ensured by that White Paper. He was our nation's trustee and he did not fail his native land, to which he was intellectually and emotionally attached.

Of particular importance in assessing the Dewar legacy are his insights as to how the future of devolution might unfold. These are a sharp reminder to those in the Labour Party today who wish constitutional change to go away and get back to business and politics as usual. Speaking at the Spectator Lecture *Towards a Modern and Flexible Constitution* delivered on 18 November 1998, the day after the passing of the Scotland Act, Dewar insisted:

> Clearly, the debate should not stop when the doors of the Scottish Parliament open. What we have done in Scotland may be a catalyst for further change... what is right for Scotland is not necessarily right for England. There is already innovation in recognising the regional diversity here in England: there are ideas to be assessed, options to be explored. There is time to get it right.

Sadly, Dewar was ahead of his time and the last 14 years have shown the inability of Labour politics to grasp his wider vision and see a different future for the Union. He was also conscious of the role of Scotland in the Union. In the same speech he said:

> It would be absurd to think that the UK is so fragile that any change to the constitutional settlement is bound to result in the fracturing of the whole. It would be even more absurd to believe that the UK can saunter on into the future with precisely the same set of arrangements that have served it in the past.

On this point the Better Together Campaign should take note. Reinforcing his realism and the uncertainty of constitutional politics, Dewar was even more explicit in predicting that devolution would be a process.

There is no doubt that the Holyrood Parliament building will be a source of great pride for our country. It is one of the most iconic Parliament buildings in the world, not only in architecture and design but also as a statement about modern Scotland.

Donald Dewar's political career stretched over four decades, but he was never in government until 1997. In his relatively short period in power, he left a lasting mark and will be remembered as one of Scotland's outstanding statesmen.

It is a profound tragedy that he was not allowed to see the fruits of his labours. In his oft-quoted comment as he read the opening sentence of the Scotland Act – 'There shall be a Scottish Parliament – I like that!' – his real monument is that future generations will look at both Scotland's form of government and its unique home and they, too, will say 'I like that...'

Scotland's first First Minister, had he lived, may have changed the face of post-devolution Scottish politics in so many ways. But sadly, we will never know,

From YES, YES on 11 September 1997, the anniversary of the Battle of Stirling Bridge to a YES or NO on 18 September 2014. Whatever the outcome on that day in the year of the 700th anniversary of the Battle of Bannockburn, Donald Dewar was right. The battle for Scotland's political and constitutional future will go on. John Smith talked about the 'settled will' of the Scottish people. The referendum promises to be the complete antithesis of this. There is no consensus and the nation is bitterly divided. The journey will go on.

Looking back, we can see our constitutional journey through the eyes of a unionist who cares very little about independence but has ended up suggesting a substantial YES vote may well be the only way of shaking up Westminster and forcing them to embark on the radical reforms necessary to make the Union relevant and to more effectively accommodate Scotland's aspirations. Two articles by Will Hutton in the *Observer* in 2002, 'Scottish Independence is a Pipedream' and in 2014, 'Scottish independence: stay united and Scotland could be key to a better, fairer Britain', provide a fascinating insight into the changing fortunes of the politics and the constitution of the Union and illustrate the scale of the SNP journey in the post-devolution period.

His conclusion in 2014 is that the SNP could be a battering ram to create a more federal Britain, with Scotland as the principal beneficiary. His comments provide a valuable insight into what might have been in Scotland if the implications of what looked likely to happen in the post-devolution years had been acknowledged by the Unionist parties. Sadly, the SNP were never seen as opening the political door to a new set of opportunities within the Union but always as a focus of derision and at times hatred as the early successes of the Lib-Lab Coalition at Holyrood lost impact and led the complacent political classes into the first major miscalculation, that it was always going to be business as usual. After being defeated in 2003 at Holyrood, the SNP, who had learned lessons from the devolution years and had started to become a party of civic national-ism, put together a platform of populist but progressive policies and then defied the laws of the new electoral politics in Scotland by becoming a minority party of Government in 2007, a majority party in 2011 and then – the icing on the political cake – they manage to persuade Prime Minister David Cameron to agree to a referendum on rndependence. Of course, this well-respected commentator, like most other Scots, including the Unionist parties, didn't see any of this coming down the track. What Hutton did see that others didn't were the possibilities at that early stage of devolu-tion: of building a more secure future for constitutional change within the Union that would anchor Scotland more positively in a Federalist arrange-ment. Hutton also recognised that without some further thinking, the SNP would create the opportunity to exit the Union. This is now where we are, against all the odds, with poor outcomes in General Elections and despite being in power in Scotland for seven years, the SNP are possibly on the brink of the biggest constitutional upset since the colonies rebelled in the late 18th century and left the Union. The obvious question that still needs an answer is how has this been allowed to happen?

In 'Scottish independence is a Pipedream', Hutton said:

> The English may be indifferent but the SNP remains the animating force in Scottish politics. And if it ever had the chance to push through its programme of an independent Scotland, Britain would be irredeemably changed. It would become Greater England. Its deliberations count. Yet, for the moment, nationalism is stalled.

> But something deeper is going on. The nationalist case is losing its edge. Devolution has opened up two options for Scotland – a future as part of

a more federal Britain or a future as an independent state. It's not obvious that in an era of globalisation there is much point in Scotland adopting the trappings of statehood – its own army, flag, central bank etc. It might not only get all that it wants as part of a more federal Britain; it might also be the cleverest option.

The more the SNP can make its criticisms stick in Scotland, the stronger its position is relative to Labour. The irony does not stop there. To argue for multilateralism is to acknowledge interdependence as the overriding value that must underwrite the relations between states and peoples – and this from a prophet of national independence. The contradiction exposes the dilemma at the heart of the SNP. This is the social democratic party that believes that social democracy can only be achieved in Scotland if it is independent. Its members are the pro-Europeans who believe the cause of European integration is best served if another small state – Scotland – joins the EU. This is the party that argues that Scottish and European values are broadly similar but so different from England's that Scotland must be sovereign. It is the advocate of independence to promote interdependence.

Suddenly, the SNP and its nationalism feel very nineteenth century. Ask why there should be an independent Scotland and the answer is thin. If Scotland's vocation is to build its own distinctive economic and social model, more closely modelled on mainland Europe, then devolved government offers rich possibilities which can be deepened further. And to gain that, it has to recast the British political settlement around a value system of independence in a world where interdependence is the emerging watch-word. Moreover, it has to argue there is so much difference between Scotland and England in terms of core values that the only chance of their expression is through independence.

As I watched Europe take on the US, it drove home to me that Scottish independence is never going to happen. The SNP has discharged its destiny in creating a devolved Scotland which will get ever more power, so paving the way for the same pattern to be copied in Wales and the English regions, an agency for change for which we can all be grateful. But the argument for independence? The world is moving on, with profound implications for nationalists every –where.

These words written 12 years ago are now being put to the test in the Independence referendum!

In his most recent article in 2014, Hutton argues that 'The SNP could be a battering ram to create a more federal Britain with Scotland as the principal beneficiary.' Remaining true to his more radical unionist credentials, Hutton sets out the impact that a YES vote would have on the Union, believing the Union needs another wake-up call:

> The referendum on Scottish independence is an existential political moment. If the YES vote wins, it will mark the end of the arc of modern British history that began its upward trajectory with the Act of Union in 1707. The corresponding fall of the British state that began with decolonisation and deindustrialisation will be complete. It will be RIP to Britain as we have known it.
>
> The English don't begin to recognise the profundity of the consequences. The pretensions and constitutional arrangements of the rump UK will suddenly look very flyblown and pre-modern, thrown into sharp relief as Scotland sets out to write a constitution that reflects the people's 21st-century values and the canons of good government.
>
> Notwithstanding constraints the Scottish National party has yet to recognise, Scotland will be attempting to create the kind of economic and social settlement that has worked in Scandinavia and Germany. Meanwhile, England, perhaps leaving the European Union in a second landmark referendum within three years, will be locked in a diminished future determined by the minority prejudices of a wing of the Conservative party and UKIP.
>
> Whatever else, the putative break-up of the UK could not be described as a success story. Across what remains of the British establishment: are the British state and society safe in the hands of the modern Tory party and its media acolytes?
>
> The fiasco of a Scotland trying to break away, however unsuccessfully, would crystallise concerns, especially if followed by an exit from the EU, about our collective readiness to continue with the decaying state structures and accompanying corrupt political culture that delivers such self-damaging results. The Westminster and Whitehall system, and all that hangs on it, would not survive unreformed for long.
>
> For without Scotland there is no Britain; the country is crucial to these islands' history and destiny. After all, it was Scotland's challenge to Charles I that triggered the collapse of the Stuart kings' attempt to rehabilitate pure monarchical sovereignty, the English civil war and ultimately the compromise settlement between parliament and crown. This was legitimised by Scotland joining the new state in 1707, which in many fundamental ways has survived to this day. Could the SNP and its wily leader, Alex Salmond be about to trigger similar shock waves?

It is an extraordinary achievement to be eight months away from a referendum whose outcome is widely reckoned to be very close run. Increasingly, some of the more reflective and energetic elements in Scottish society want no part of a political order that delivers them too much of Thatcher, Cameron, Osborne and Farage – and too little of politicians and ideas that reflect more mainstream Scottish and European values. The brutally honest account of growing inequality, faltering investment, innovation and exports, detailed in *Building Security and Creating Opportunity*, the report supporting the SNP's case, has to my knowledge never been rivalled by any arm of the British government.

But the SNP lacks the courage of its convictions, which ultimately is likely to cost it the referendum victory it craves. It is ever more obvious that it wants the best of both worlds – to recast its relationship with England in a way that can seem to amount to self-governing powers within a federal Britain, but at the same time to win sufficient autonomy to call itself independent.

If I were a Scot, I would be sorely tempted by the prospect of proper independence but not the damaging halfway house that is on offer, which would leave my country worse off. There is, though, an attractive alternative: to use the SNP as a battering ram to create a more federal Britain with Scotland as the principal beneficiary.

Hutton's political journey over the devolution years raises the intriguing idea that the best outcome would be a narrow NO victory but with a substantial YES vote. Seeking the best of both worlds, Will Hutton exposes the Unionist miscalculation of not providing a second question to ensure a positive outcome and creating a great deal of uncertainty around what a NO vote will mean, in political and constitutional terms, running into a General Election in 2015, a Holyrood election in 2016 and a possible EU referendum in 2017. So will the public vote YES to force the Union into a form of federalism and bring it to its senses, or will the public vote YES for Independence and exit the Union, or will the public just vote NO and then wonder what that could mean?

Better Together Campaign

It is not surprising that the Better Together Campaign has been so relentlessly negative, with the most obvious weakness being its lack of a narrative for the future, and in particular a lack of vision of what continuing membership of the Union would mean for Scotland and the other nations. There is no vision for the future because it would be impossible to construct one. What you have instead is the offer of the past being the future regardless of anything that is taking place in the Union at present. The lack of vision for the Union, and Scotland's role in it, remains the outstanding weakness of the Better Together Campaign: this again is not surprising, as their whole approach is based on four very contestable propositions.

First, the mere fact that the Union has existed for over 300 years is deployed as a convincing reason for its continuation for a few more centuries. The current lack of confidence, purpose and direction of the Union demonstrates a real crisis in the making regardless of what is currently happening in Scotland.

Second, the emphasis has been on the post-war settlement issues and the need for a highly centralised democratic collectivism to deliver. This legacy – the welfare state, the NHS and pension commitments, the interventionist state, social democracy and the embrace of the value of the common good – is now under attack. A combination of extremism and populism in England, the start to privatisation and franchising of the NHS and Education in England provide a real threat to those much cherished ideals and the contribution they have made to the stability, solidarity and social cohesion of Great Britain and Northern Ireland.

Three, the fact that three Unionist parties are seeking to work together in a joint campaign to save the Union and put together a common front on more devolved powers is understandable but unworkable. The politics of Westminster, 100 years of party political strife and the current toxic nature of tribalism and partisanship leave little scope for meaningful constitutional change. A minimum package may be achievable. This may prove to be too little and too late, stopping short of the aspirations of Scots whose expectations have been raised by the referendum campaign and who are anyway increasingly disillusioned by party politics and politics generally. It seems ironic that a NO vote requires Westminster and its political parties to decide what happens next, but a YES vote delivered by the people of Scotland will be binding and sufficient! The Better Together Campaign has been left with the difficult task of explaining what a NO vote will mean. This could have been avoided if there had been a second question on the ballot paper!

Four, the question of the absolute sovereignty of the Westminster Parliament, not necessarily in the real world, where significant constitutional changes have turned this into a complete myth, but in the minds of MPs, members of the House of Lords and the Institution itself. Again, a NO vote could mean that the Houses of Parliament could, in the aftermath of the Referendum battle, settle down on their red and green benches blissfully aware that they are the only power in the land and then subject the outcome of the referendum to a period of unnecessary scrutiny and delay: this may happen anyway as the Westminster parties try to reach a compromise on what could be offered to Scots as the consolation prize. It seems remarkable that after three reported commissions with new schemes for the future of devolution, which started to look like a bidding war, the Lib-Dems came out on top with the most coherent, second were the Conservatives and last was Labour with what was widely agreed to ne the most disappointing and incoherent of the three: this was clearly the triumph of Westminster over the interests of Scotland. After the General Election in 2015, who is to say that any careful agreement arrived at by the Unionist parties in their manifestos will survive and be given the urgency needed to ensure the will of the Scottish people, whatever the vote. A NO vote opens up a risky route to further constitutional change: three political parties, manifestos, elections, composition of the new House of Commons, priorities of the new Parliament, agreement on the details of a further devolution package, the legislative process and while this is taking place there will be the 2016 election for Holyrood! There is never certainty in the political game.

Independence is an attractive scenario which certainly opens up opportunities for political renewal, creating a more informed and inclusive democracy and ultimately helping to realise the potential of a nation. Are we complacent, content with progress and comfortable with our national success, or do we need a major shock to our national psyche that can propel us on to a new and higher trajectory of social, economic and political success as a nation. Certainly Independence would provide that. Independence would be challenging and require Scotland to nation build very quickly, create capacity which currently doesn't exist and negotiate a very difficult and complex process of transitioning to the status of a Nation State. There would be a sense of a dramatic change being experienced on a scale never previously imagined and a compelling need for a new outlook on life. None of this would be beyond our grasp or incapable of being realised, but it would be a very different Scotland needing more ambition, more commitment and a sense of collective resolve probably only ever achieved in times of national crisis or major challenges.

None of this is any longer in doubt. Scotland could be independent with a high standard of living, but the question is, should it be? Scots face a real dilemma which may this time around raise sufficient doubts about the wisdom of voting YES. There is a huge fear factor being promoted by the NO Campaign. Scots by nature are canny, cautious and conservative by instinct and experience. Scots are also divided by age and gender and the prospect of uncertainty and protracted negations are intimidating. The threat to living standards remains the most potent weapon in the arsenal of the NO Campaign. This is the head winning over heart and sees membership of the EU, the Sterling currency union and NATO as important. In reality there is very little the YES Campaign can to do to successfully counter this because despite austerity, cuts, neoliberal economics, threats to the public sector, security of pensions, welfare payments and job security matter to people. If you are trying to create difference, people will be apprehensive about the outcome, but if you are currently in receipt of regular state payments then it will be the devil you know rather than change, despite the fact that currently the major threat to social security benefits comes from Westminster in the form of a Conservative Party much more extreme than Mrs Thatcher ever was.

But we should also acknowledge the incompleteness of the SNP or YES Campaign vision. The emphasis on rebutting the NO case has been given more prominence by the media, and this has meant less coverage for the alternative vision of looking to the Nordic countries rather than embracing the USA.

The question in this debate is why would Scotland want to leave the Union? It would be interesting to ask another question if Scotland was not in the Union – a hypothetical question of course. Would Scots want to join? Would this dramatically alter the dynamic and inevitably result in a resounding NO vote? This would result in the Union having to express what the future might hold and prove its attractiveness. This is not part of the current drama and could certainly lead to a different result.

The future of the Union and Scotland are big issues and we should not underestimate the significance of our date with destiny, and equally important, what happens after that.

This Constitutional issue has dominated the politics of Scotland for nearly two decades and it seems likely this will continue. The big issues at the heart of our politics will not go away. Our lives are inextricably linked to the complex world of political ideas, democratic processes, well-informed discussion, common sense and inspiring leadership. Well, that is what is supposed to happen. The reality is often very different and that is what this part of the book deals with. For thousands of years people have mused over the meaning of life, debated how life should be organised, argued about how our resources should be distributed and priorities identified and worked towards a sense of order and discipline in relation to the relationships between people. Our politics and democracy have evolved to do just that, but today many people now question whether these aims are being fulfilled and why solutions are not being found for the problems of the 21st century. For a growing number of people this represents a crisis of politics.

Scotland is on a constitutional journey with the referendum being the next big test of public opinion. Regardless of the outcome of the vote, the debate about Scotland's future will continue, as will the search for solutions to Scotland's most intractable and enduring problems. The current constitutional, political and democratic setup isn't delivering solutions to urgent issues fast enough, so what other options are there for serious problem solving? A victory for YES or NO in this referendum will inevitably reflect a lack of real consensus about the best way forward, will reinforce deep political divisions within our country, will sharpen tensions between Scotland and the Union, will see unresolved the weaknesses and problems of the Union and is likely to see some really important issues side-stepped or given less priority. This is why it is vital for the constitutional debate to be viewed as part of the wider debate on our politics and our democracy in both Scotland and the UK. For Labour in particular the importance of this cannot be over emphasised. The Union is being severely tested at this point in time, but so is the Labour Party in Scotland. This is a book of reflections. In thinking about the future of Scotland, we need to break free from the current debate and help Scots seize the moment, stir the imagination of what could be and help them shape more effectively their own future and the direction of their country.

Our democracy is fragile and we often take it for granted, but it is worth reminding ourselves that great sacrifices have been made by others to give us the opportunity to debate freely and openly our future. In a year when we commemorate the 100th anniversary of the start of the Great War, we could do no better than combine the sacrifice that was made in the interests of democracy with the powerful sentiment of the sovereignty of the people. In another country and in another era, the Gettysburg Address:

Four score and seven years ago our fathers brought forth on this continent, a new nation, conceived in Liberty, and dedicated to the proposition that all men are created equal.

Now we are engaged in a great civil war, testing whether that nation, or any nation so conceived and so dedicated, can long endure. We are met on a great battle-field of that war. We have come to dedicate a portion of that field, as a final resting place for those who here gave their lives that that nation might live. It is altogether fitting and proper that we should do this.

But, in a larger sense, we cannot dedicate – we cannot consecrate –we cannot hallow – this ground. The brave men, living and dead, who struggled here, have consecrated it, far above our poor power to add or detract. The world will little note, nor long remember what we say here, but it can never forget what they did here. It is for us the living, rather, to be dedicated here to the unfinished work which they who fought here have thus far so nobly advanced. It is rather for us to be here dedicated to the great task remaining before us – that from these honored dead we take increased devotion to that cause for which they gave the last full measure of devotion – that we here highly resolve that these dead shall not have died in vain – that this nation, under God, shall have a new birth of freedom – and that government of the people, by the people, for the people, shall not perish from the earth.

ABRAHAM LINCOLN, November 19, 1863

CHAPTER I

Broken Politics and the Mood
of a Nation

OUR POLITICS ARE broken and this will be the background to our current
and future debates on our constitutional future. An old politics has to be
overlaid with something different, relevant and inspiring. But our politics
did not decline over night and the present crisis will require more than just
tinkering around the edges. The importance of this to the constitutional
debate is obvious. Our attitudes to our politicians, political parties and
political institutions matter and at times when trust and confidence in the
political process is diminishing there is no accounting as to how this could
impact on the four million Scots who will cast a vote in September of
2014. Mood and morale will influence the outcome. Over the next three
years there will be an unprecedented series of tough political tests for the
Scottish electors, including Westminster and Holyrood elections and the
referendum on independence. The importance of these cannot be over-
stated. A series of social, economic, financial, institutional and political
crises over the last five years have not only changed the political landscape,
they have revealed: a Scotland with a split personality; the divergence of
Westminster and Holyrood election results; an electorate increasingly disillusioned and disenchanted with politics and political parties, as evidenced by fewer people voting; declining confidence and trust in our institutions and governance and; a sense of deepening gloom surrounding our
democracy and its ability to deliver progress in a world of massive and
accelerating change. In contrast, the rise of the SNP over the last five years
has captured the imagination of many Scots and has injected some excitement, a sense of purpose and new enthusiasm into what has become a
very traditional and uninspiring political landscape north of the border. The
SNP has won over many Scots to a different kind of politics: by contrast,
the opposition parties have struggled to embrace change and have failed
to write a new narrative for post-devolution Scotland.

The scale of the changes in SNP-Labour politics is dramatically under-
lined by comparisons of the outcomes of the 2010 General Election results
and those of the Holyrood election in 2011. Since 2003 the SNP has steadily

expanded their sphere of electoral influence and now dominate the politics of Holyrood and Scotland. In sharp contrast, indeed a mirror image, Labour has declined and Labour heartlands were the last to go in 2011. This chapter looks at the forthcoming referendum, the state of politics, the political parties and their prospects, and what this means for our democracy, the independence campaign and beyond.

The People's Choice

Election outcomes are decided by the personal choices of nearly four million Scots over the age of 16. What political parties offer on the doorsteps and through the media will influence the choices that people make but so will a large number of other factors, including events, which impact more on the mood and morale of people and their hopes and fears. The referendum on independence is not just another day at the polls. For the first time in recent history a decision will be made which is all embracing in terms of its potential impact on the future of Scotland and the lives of every Scot. This is where the fusion of so many cultural, social, economic, psychological and political factors will have such an impact on how people might vote. So how will Scotland shape up over the next two years? What are the factors that will influence voting intentions? Is our politics broken? Are our political parties up to the challenge of a changing electorate? These are some of the questions this chapter will consider in an attempt to answer the question of whether our politics is fit for purpose. Equally important, what could this mean for the independence referendum? Our politics and the public are changing and political parties should be alert to the implications of this.

Tony Judt, in his remarkable book, *Ill Fares the Land* (2010) published just before his death, said:

> Something is profoundly wrong with the way we live today. For 30 years we have made a virtue out of the pursuit of material self-interest... we know what things cost but have no idea what they are worth... we no longer ask of a judicial ruling or a legislative act: Is it good? Is it just? Is it right? Will it help bring about a better society or better world? Those *used* to be the political questions, even if they invited no easy answers.

Capturing the mood post financial and banking crisis, Tony Judt argues that there is much in society to be angry at: growing inequalities of wealth and opportunity; injustice of class; economic exploitation and corruption, money and privilege damaging democracy. Arguing passionately for change, Judt worries about the age of insecurity we have entered into – physical, economic and political. He argues that insecurity breeds fear, and this is corroding the trust and interdependence on which civil societies rest. This is the state of Scotland and Britain today, where fear of change and mistrust of politics may lead to a growing disconnect between electors and traditional politics, declining numbers of people voting and a growing sense of frustration that our political parties can't deliver in a world where so much power and influence is wielded by unaccountable corporations, global bodies, transnational entities like the EU and the very nature of globalisation itself. For Tony Judt there is a need to dissent from this economically driven way of thinking and return to an 'ethically informed public conversation'. Adam Smith in *The Theory of Moral Sentiments* says:

> The disposition to admire, and almost to worship, the rich and the powerful, and to despise, or, at least, to neglect, persons of poor and mean condition... is... the great and most universal cause of the corruption of moral sentiments.

This drive for community, or solidarity, trust and common purpose has been severely undermined by a series of national events that have shocked the electorate and cast doubt on the credibility of our political parties and democracy itself. What has been accepted as part of the trust factor of the post-war consensus now lies in ruins.

Politics, Government and Democracy

Over the past five years, certain momentous events have led to a breakdown of trust, respect and confidence in our institutions and have created a deep sense of disillusionment and disenchantment among the public. Politics by its very nature requires a set of considerations to be at work in any society if social coherence and solidarity are to be achieved – confidence, purpose, vision, understanding, values, ideas, accepted narrative, nationality, ambition, honesty, identity, trust and principles, and cohesion, substance and direction. Some or all of these have to be part of the political mix. Recent events have only served to reinforce the fragile compact that exists between the elected and the electors. Scots are apprehensive, anxious and uncertain about their future. They are also fearful and, at a time of uncertainty, cautious about the risks involved in change. There are two questions that are increasingly asked. What is the purpose of Britain? And what is the purpose of politics? The global banking and financial mess, the economic crisis and recession, austerity and deficits, the Murdoch press and hacking scandal, cash for questions, honours and access, capitalism in crisis and 'rip off Britain', abuses of older people in private social care and the resentment of the public towards out of control utility companies are all helping to shape a public mood frustrated at the failure of Government and politics to protect their interests within an increasingly fractious and partisan political environment. People are angry and dismayed about the state of society and feel overwhelmed by the failure of politics and politicians to deal with some of this. There is, however, a curious paradox at work here. While dissatisfaction with politics increases, the expectations of the public in relation to Government and politics are also rising. Are unrealistic notions of what politicians and political parties can achieve in the modern world fuelling public anger? Can the gap between expectations and achievements be narrowed? Recent events have brought to the surface anxieties about what kind of Britain we are living in and to what extent our greed, glam, glitz and celebrity cultural obsessions are undermining any notions of ethical values and the common good. Are we in danger of losing the hard won gains of the post-war social consensus in which justice, fairness, liberty, virtue and equality were still on the agenda? Many people are now questioning whether there is any real sense of moral and philosophical purpose behind our politics and our Governments.

The Conservative-led Coalition at Westminster

Scots are being and will be influenced by the politics of the Coalition at Westminster. Austerity Britain and the cuts and deficits agenda are likely to exact a heavy toll from the public and especially those dependent on social welfare and the public sector. No sane person would argue against the idea of balancing our books, but there is anger and resentment about the way this is being done. Recession, austerity, high unemployment and public sector cuts, pensions and jobs will have a disproportionate impact on Scotland. Scots also resent the alien political culture emerging from the Coalition where the Conservatives, helped by the fast fading cloak of Lib-Dem respectability, are trying to tear up the post-war consensus on the NHS,

Europe, Education and the Welfare state and instead risk and wreck hard won achievements by putting ideology before the national interest. This is very reminiscent of the Thatcher era, when Scots lost faith in the Conservatives. This is not Scotland's agenda, but we are influenced by it. While devolution gives us a large measure of protection from right wing politics, again the fear of coalitions and Conservative Governments at Westminster may encourage many Scots to be wary of remaining within a Union which is capable of such excesses.

Why Politics Matters

Politics is about the tough process of arriving at collective decisions out of a bewildering array of multiple and competing interests and opinions. Politics matters because we have different views and perspectives in society about public resources and how they should be used. Politics is essentially about judgement at any point in time and is inextricably linked to the powerful idea of coping with change in an uncertain world.

Against this difficult background, it is little wonder that our politicians and political parties in Scotland find it difficult to anticipate, understand and manage change. Making sense of change and seeking to influence the future rather than be constantly reacting to issues and events is now more important than ever as the accelerating pace of social, financial, economic, technological and environmental change threatens to overwhelm us.

Our political culture in Scotland is uneasy with the idea of change: this could be about a lack of confidence, a deep-seated conservatism and, curiously, a failure to take ourselves more seriously in the post-devolution era. It could also be linked to the fact that the political classes in Scotland, our business community, civic institutions and the well-defined constituencies of interest (including the media) are so closely knitted together that there is no space or political distance between them to enable politicians, Parliament and Government to develop the intellectual, inspirational and enlightened approach for a radical and different look at our future. The soundbite culture and the 'you can never apologise or change your mind' culture are not helpful.

As demographics, globalisation, information technologies and social change crowd in on us, we need a much clearer vision of the future: this can only be achieved if we have a new inspired and informed dialogue.

The weakness of democratic politics and the growing disenchantment of electors has resulted from a number of factors – a profound shift in our society that includes: the dominance of individualism and consumerism; the increasing complexity of globalisation; the collapse of deference and the role of the media in fostering cynicism. These have undoubtedly made governance and political leadership much harder.

This is the view of Gerry Stoker, who, in his book *Why Politics Matters: Making Democracy Work* argues that politics is doomed to disappoint because:

> ... like any centralised collective form of decision making, it requires trade-offs between competing interests, is prone to failures in communication and often produces muddled and messy outcomes.

Democracy as an idea is more popular than ever, but citizens in democracies throughout the world appear disenchanted with the political process. It is important to reflect on this fact as people in North Africa and the Middle East lose their lives trying to vote, while we are losing our interest in voting, as recent elections in both Scotland and the UK have shown. Mass democracy, practised with a universal suffrage, has less than a century's worth of experience. Democracy is a demanding way of doing the politics of compromise and reconciliation because it rests on the fundamental idea that all adult citizens have a right to be involved in matters that affect them.

The future of Scotland is very dependent on retaining our faith, confidence and trust in our politics and our democracy in what is likely to be the most challenging period of elections in a generation. This challenge is captured By Gerry Stoker when he says:

> But it is difficult to escape the idea that the scale and breadth of discontent about politics raises some questions about the long term health of democracy. People perhaps naturally do not trust politicians but more than that, many of the key institutions of democracies – parties, parliament and polls do not command sufficient respect and engagement. Democracy cannot survive if its life blood of politics is seen as a sort of necessary evil – or worse still, a pointless waste of time.

Why has disenchantment grown?

In *Why Politics Matters*, Stoker provides an insightful analysis or framework of explanations for this growing political disenchantment. He puts forward six explanations, two basically blaming politicians, two looking at the changing nature of society and citizens and two looking at the environment for democratic politics which has got much harder and more out of control.

First, the behaviour of politicians, their performance or their economic competence have somehow declined compared to some past 'golden era' and these shifts explain their loss of legitimacy.

Second, there are the issues of truth and power. This argument is based on the notion that politicians are more interested in power than in truth. Worldwide, politicians represent the least trusted occupation and many people think politicians do not tell the truth most of the time.

Third, people are harder to govern and more critical. Citizens are becoming more critical and challenging and as a result are more dissatisfied with the performance of their political systems and the core institutions of representative government.

Fourth, people are more individual and fragmented. This raises the idea that a lack of social cohesion limits the scope of collective decision making.

Fifth, politics is in trouble because issues are moving beyond its control. If globalisation means the world is beyond our collective control or beyond the control of our political institutions then politics runs the danger of becoming more and more irrelevant.

Sixth, there is the growing impact of technological change. The issues of population growth, global warming and biodiversity highlight some of the major issues where science and technology make an impact. These developments create major challenges for politics as they transcend nation state borders and require cooperation and coordination at a global level.

Faced with these challenges, politics will increasingly be a tough and challenging business and will create demands for a different and more intelligent kind of politics. The challenges facing the politicians and political parties are difficult and complex, but if the growing disenchantment and disillusionment are to be reversed then a radical reappraisal of how politics deals with change is long overdue.

Politics – the construction of collective decisions – has lost its grip and that is why increasing numbers people think it no longer matters.

In his book *Defending Politics*, Matthew Flinders reinforces this line of thinking and raises the question of whether elections will be much more difficult to predict in the future as a very different set of social, economic and psychological factors fuse with more traditional considerations to influence the electorate. If democratic politics is deemed to be broken or failing, the reasons for this are systemic in nature, Flinders argues. The great danger of the rise of anti-political sentiment is that it may generate a shift away from collective action towards a more individualised structure that is simply ill-equipped to deal with the major social, economic, and environmental challenges that will shape the 21st century – less equipped in the sense that we will have lost those levers of social trust and social engagement, direction and mutual support that politics delivers. Democratic politics is the politics of life chances, of opportunity and constant renewal. Life politics, by contrast, revolves around individualised responses to social problems. The 'bad faith' model of politics is therefore not only wrong, it also belittles our collective achievements and potential. It glamorises those who heckle from the sidelines and encourages us to despise the very people we vote for. With this in mind, Flinders outlines eight ways in which the nature of political rule has altered during the past 50 years and as a consequence suggests the challenges of governing have become more difficult because of them: the Decline of Deference-less of this and more criticism.

The UK compares very unfavourably in terms of political literacy with some other Western European countries like Sweden. The battle between the State and the market, between public and private and the struggle between the common good and the individual have helped undermine and in some cases destroy the influence of the Church, Trades Unions, the voluntary sector and other institutions, organisations and social networks that don't fit neatly into this struggle between extremes. A vacuum has been created in which many of these trusted organisations have disappeared. Civic culture and working-class culture have been transformed. Philip Blond in his book *Red Tory*, says:

> We are more isolated that at any time in recorded history. Most of us avoid voting at local elections, and little more than half manage to make it to the polls for national ones. We certainly don't join a church or political party and we have fewer friends and social contacts that any British generation for which figures exist.

The atomised society, talked about by Margaret Thatcher in her vision of 'no such thing as society' is fast becoming a reality. Blond, on the theme 'Something is seriously wrong with Britain', continues by arguing that:

> A stronger civic culture would have permitted modernisation and technological development without sacrificing its social foundations. But in Britain we have achieved none of those things; listless and indifferent we

slide into a post-democratic culture of passive consumption and political acquiescence.

Consumers versus Citizens

Robert Reich, one of America's foremost economic and political thinkers and former Labour Secretary in the Clinton administration, provides a new analysis of the competitive economy and its effect on democracy. In *Supercapitalism: the Transformation of Business, Democracy and Everyday Life* (2007) he says:

> A clear separation of politics and capitalism will foster an environment in which both business and government thrive, by putting capitalism in the service of democracy, and not the other way around.

Reich argues that capitalism has become more responsive to what we want as individual purchasers of goods, but democracy has grown less responsive to what we want together as citizens. Much of this new debate is taking place in the United States, but its relevance is particularly appropriate for the UK, where we need to modernise our political systems, re-establish self-belief in our political process and re-invigorate our democracy.

Put simply, the last few decades have involved a shift of power away from us as citizens and towards us as consumers and investors. In this transformation our capacities as consumers have done significantly better, but in our capacities as citizens seeking the common good, we have lost ground. This has enormous implications for our understanding of the current crisis.

Our role as citizens within the democratic process needs to be strengthened. The democratic process itself needs to reflect this new age and assert a new importance. This, in turn, will help revitalise our institutions of Government and Parliament and make them fit for purpose to deal with the challenges of this new form of 'supercapitalism'.

Reich believes that consumers and investors had access to more choices and better deals, but the institutions that had negotiated to spread the wealth and protect what citizens valued in common began to disappear. For this to work, the first and most important step is to have a clear understanding of the appropriate boundary between capitalism and democracy – between the economic game and how its rules are set – so the boundary can be better defended and resist encroachment by business bearing gifts and soothing words.

Reich warns:

> Companies are not citizens. They are bundles of contracts. The purpose
> of companies is to play the economic game as aggressively as possible.
> The challenge for us as citizens is to stop them from setting the rules.
> Keeping supercapitalism from spilling over into democracy is the only
> constructive agenda for change. All else is frolic and detour.

Alice Rivlin of the Brookings Institution warns:

> Market capitalism is a dangerous tool. Like a machine gun or chainsaw or
> a nuclear reactor, it has to be inspected frequently to see that it is working
> properly and used with caution according to carefully thought out rules.

We have to think about the bigger picture. British people are losing confidence in democracy, as are many inhabitants of other democracies. There is a pattern of declining trust, respect and confidence in Government. The current financial crisis and recession provides the opportunity for this to change.

Reich argues the first step in turning democracy and capitalism right side-up 'is to understand what is real and what is make believe'. This should have a particular resonance in Britain today: the cure for our hangover headache is to get real.

Michael J Sandel in his book *What Money Can't Buy: The Moral Limit of Markets* says:

> Is there something wrong with a world in which everything is for sale? If
> so, how can we prevent market values reaching into spheres of life where
> they don't belong? What are the moral limits of markets?

Sandel argues that we have drifted from having a market economy to being a market society and asks: is this where we want to be?

The atomisation of society and the growth of selfishness, not self-interest, pose real challenges to those who want politics to be based on progressive and ethical thinking. There is a move away from collective ways of distributing resources and opportunities: this core idea is at the heart of our changing society and a major threat to our politics and democracy

The contemporary climate of anti-politics is arguably rooted in a generation that has become complacent. We have forgotten the alternatives to democracy which are found elsewhere in the world. We have created little more than a political marketplace in which there are few incentives for politicians to be transparent, and too many people who take for granted democratic politics and what it delivers. The currency of politics is being devalued, we have allowed political standards to drop and far too often seem content with the lowest common denominator.

The root of political disengagement is an 'expectations gap'. Closing this gap is as much to do with reducing demand as with increasing supply. But in order to reduce demand we must rediscover and treasure the basic spirit of politics and broker a meaningful debate about our collective future. We need to challenge the 'bad faith' model of politics by showing that democratic politics matters because on the whole it delivers far more than most people recognise, and the alternatives are far worse.

Powerful Forces at Work

In his book *Post Democracy*, Colin Crouch argues that changes in our society are having a profound effect on our politics and democracy due to consistent pressure for state policy to favour the interests of the wealthy. Nothing was emerging within the body politic to replace the challenge to the wealthy and socially advantaged that had been presented for most of the 20th century to the organised manual working class: the commercialisation or marketisation of the public services market intrusion. This represents an assault on politics and democracy: citizens to consumers, now part of the threat; declining capacity of politicians to act because their legitimacy was increasingly in doubt; politics is being shaped in private by the interaction of government and elites that overwhelmingly represent business interests; there is little hope for an agenda of strong egalitarian policies for the redistribution of power and wealth, or for the restraint of powerful interests; there is a crisis of egalitarian politics and a trivialisation of democracy happening at the same time; there are two different conceptions of citizen's rights. Positive rights stress citizens' abilities to participate in tier polity; the right to vote, to form and join organisations, to receive accurate information. Negative rights are those which protect the individual against others, especially against the state: rights to sue, rights to property.

The contributions of Stoker, Flinders, Reich, Sandel and Crouch are all concerned with the undermining of our democracy and our politics. Each, in their different ways, has expressed their concerns about how societies are changing and how this influences how people vote and if indeed they vote at all.

The Role of the Media

A certain level of credibility is central to the operation of politics. The role of the media in that becomes crucial. Bearing in mind the importance of understanding politics and the issues surrounding political and civic literacy, future elections in Scotland will have to be fought with a greater understanding of the citizen and the consequences of change. These include a new understanding of politics in the modern era; the nature of individualism; the spread of market based consumerism; and the changing nature of citizenship. politics should be about collective debate not individual choice; the search for solutions and the potential to disappoint; politics exist to manage conflict, not surprising that outcomes are messy; politics is driven by complex communication that is demanding and prone to failure; there is much self-interest generated by the nature of the environment we operate; communications and dialogue are crucial; political decisions results in messy outcomes and a complex distribution of costs and benefits; understanding complexity and delivering coordination are key.

There is a great deal of support for the idea that the media in both its message and manner of coverage has encouraged a relationship between politics and citizen that often feeds cynicism, when there should be an emphasis on support. How does this impact on the coverage of politics and the involvement of the citizen? The literature on this issue suggests that much of the media hinders both the effective functioning of both our politics and our democracy. The issues are; it can dumb down the coverage of news and political issues. Second, the cycle of 24 hour news coverage: politics can quickly become a matter of opinion with no resort to evidence or argument – entitled to your own opinion but not your own facts; the conclusion that politics is all a bit pointless; low level of political literacy which allows this kind of material to go unchallenged.

Third, certain parts of the media have spread a culture of contempt for politics, because ownership issues, paper values and ideology

Fourth, media outlets constantly imply that politicians are inept, and though similar cynicism is applied to most professions, for politicians it is the most extreme.

Reflecting on these issues, Gerry Stoker in *Why Politics Matters* concludes by saying:

The political discourse reacts and responds to all of this and starts to fit the frame being created by the media. Their representation starts to become a reality and reinforces the negative frame being adopted by the listeners and viewers-the purpose has been achieved and a wholly defensive approach is adopted-evasive, hesitant, lacking in confidence, shady, concealing, secretive, patronising protective-not admitting mistakes, errors, procrastinating and reinforcing the negative image. In this sense politics and the process becomes its own worst enemy. Journalists see themselves as the holders and definers of the truth. This in turn leads to the accusation against the media that they place themselves above politicians and in the end above democracy-claiming the position of supreme arbiter and judge and sometimes executioner! Tabloid journalist politics becomes a form of sport, a game-ridiculing, undermining, demonising, attacking, and patronising. The quality of journalism itself has declined-faced with competition from new platforms this is likely to get worse. The Facebook world – one slip one word, one error – in the public domain for eternity!

What is vital in this comment on the media is the impact all of this is likely to have on the mood of the electors and the nation in the run up to the referendum and in future elections: in terms of pessimism, cynicism and lack of ambition; the manner in which the fear factor steps in and politicians become overcautious and concerned about what they say; the way it erodes our democracy in other ways by frightening off people who might want to pursue a career in public life... the very same media that berates politicians often complains about the failure of political parties to attract higher quality candidates. We need to be sharply aware of the politics and value base of certain newspapers and groups, who, alongside other institutions in society, weave a web of right-wing ideas, ideology served as common sense and a coherent set of particular lines on what in the us would be described as 'family values' or 'identity issues' or people not voting their economic interests. And we need to be aware of the new opportunities which are emerging in the new media and in particular the opportunity of parties and politicians to reach a mass audience directly without the filter of current media

Stoker argues that there is a need for a fair and balanced approach and that the media should be part of strengthening our democracy and our politics, not undermining it. There has to be recognition that the media is not always some value free, objective distributor of information and knowledge, standing up for the public interest and the interest of ordinary citizens.

Instead it represents a bewildering mix of news information entertainment and editorial and while it remains a key component of our system of checks and balances in our society it has in recent times been less effective at what it should be doing. There are a number of excesses which are helping to undermine the credibility of the printed media. But this has to be about developing political literacy as part of our drive to build a stronger base for our democracy. It may, however, be easier to embrace the Facebook/ electronic platform new media than it will be to reform the old media. There will be arguments about, competing for readers but does that have to mean a rush to the bottom of what passes for good, interesting, inform-ative, inspiring and professional journalism: that's what the readers want, but are we absolutely convinced about that: we reflect the views of our readers is another weak defence: what about the freedom of the press, again freedom is not a license to print what you want – everyone is entitled to their opinions but not their own facts, and that includes newspapers. One thing is certain: progressive politics, informed citizenry, inspired politics and a stronger democracy require a fair and balanced media. This requires more emphasis on political literacy and the quality of public discourse.

The Consequences of Disillusionment and the State of our Democracy

There are a number of important consequences that flow from our growing distrust of politicians, our disenchantment with politics and the under-mining of our democracy. People appear to like the idea of democracy, but not like the politics that goes along with it. There is a real danger that if the slide in our politics continues and we lose faith in the system, we also lose our ability to change it. So why should we be concerned? And how will this impact on Scottish Politics and the forthcoming referendum?

There is a breakdown in party loyalties and allegiances and as a result there is far more volatility in our voting patterns. People are less inclined to vote their economic interests but instead vote their values, which in a referendum debate about the future of Scotland could be significant. What is also significant is the collapse of membership of the Conservative and Labour Parties in the UK, where figures produced by the House of Commons Library show that the Conservative Party has between 130,000 and 170,000 members now, compared with nearly three million in the early '50s; Labour has about 193,000 members compared with nearly a million members in the '50s. These figures compare badly with many social democratic countries in Western Europe. Then there has been the rise of the multi-party system, which has happened at a time when the two major parties in the UK have seen their total share of the UK vote decline from 98 per cent of the total vote to 68 per cent in recent elections. Despite these changes, they still retain an iron grip on Westminster. The rise of UKIP in England may further erode the support of both parties as the political landscape in England changes.

Election Turnout

Overshadowing many of the party performances in recent elections has been the shocking overall turn out. The local council elections in 2012 had a turnout of 39 per cent. Many seats had turnouts where nearly 70 per cent of electors didn't vote and only two councils out of 32 managed to attract more than 50 per cent of the voters. Our forefathers campaigned in this country to win the right to vote. But we are losing interest in voting. What is the point of having elections if there aren't any voters? This is not just an issue for council elections.

Holyrood's figure was 50 per cent in 2011 compared to 51.72 per cent in 2007, 49.2 per cent in 2003 and 58.16 per cent in 1999.

Turnout figures for Westminster elections were 63.85 per cent in 2010, compared to 60.8 per cent in 2005, 58. 2 per cent in 2001 compared with 71.3 percent in 1997 and nearly 80 per cent in 1974. The high point for General election turnout in Scotland was in 1832, the year of the Great Reform Act, when the turnout was 85 per cent and the electorate was only 64,447! The other noteworthy election was 1910 when the turnout was 84.7 per cent. In more recent times, 75.1 per cent was recorded in 1955 when the Conservative Party in Scotland had the highest percentage share of the poll ever of any party in Scotland. How things have changed!

The European elections in 2014 had a 32 per cent poll compared with 30 per cent in 2004, 28 per cent in 2009, and 24.7 per cent in 1999, 38.3 per cent in 1994 and 40 per cent in 1989.

The Council elections in 2012 had a 39 per cent poll compared with 45 per cent in 2003, 59 per cent in 1999 and 44 per cent in 1995.

Averaged out over the years and the different types of elections, at least 50 per cent or one in two of the eligible electors don't see any merit in our system of representative democracy: four in ten stay away in General elections, five in ten stay away in Scottish elections, nearly seven in ten stay away in European Elections and six in ten stay away in council elections. These are overall turnout figures: even more depressing are the figures for 18–25 year olds. Our lack of interest in the ballot box casts a long shadow over our democracy and our politics. Society is changing, as we have discussed earlier, and there is a growing body of thinking which suggests that, without a major rethink of how our politics serves our democracy, there will be fewer people engaging in elections and if this happens, we devalue the process and the product.

Poverty and Disenfranchisement

A look at the turnout in 2011 Holyrood election reveals the true extent of the problem. There was a marked difference in turnout between Edinburgh (highest) and Glasgow (lowest). As a percentage share of the vote, nearly twice as many voted in Eastwood, 62.8 per cent, the highest, than in Glasgow Provan, 34.5 per cent, the lowest. The best seat had nearly 40 per cent not voting, which is depressing in itself, but when measured against the five lowest seats of Glasgow Kelvin, Pollock, Shettleston, Maryhill/Springburn and Provan, we see an even more alarming outcome of between 60 per cent and 65 per cent not bothering to vote! Elections without electors just don't make sense. This level of disenfranchisement, the volatility of electors, the changing nature of society and the low levels of trust and confidence in political parties and politicians raises real fears about the future of our politics and the impact this will have on the outcome of elections in next few years. If our politics are broken, we need to fix them.

A Lack of Trust

This is another area where politicians and politics are losing the confidence of the public. *The survey of public attitudes towards conduct in public life in 2010* was conducted about 18 months after the height of the MPs expenses scandal, nearly 10 months after the 2010 General Election. The evidence collected shows a long-term decline in public confidence in those holding public office between 2004 and 2010. On many issues the 2010 results show a steeper decline than in the previous period. It was not possible to identify with certainty the cause of peoples' declining confidence, but it is possible that the expenses scandal has had an impact on people's views and appear to have fed into and exacerbated the long run trend of increasingly negative evaluations of politicians.

Key findings were that people rated standards of conduct less positively in 2010 than in previous years. In 2004–2008 at least four in ten (44 per cent) people rated standards as very high or quite high, but by 2010 only about three in ten (33 per cent) people rated them as such. In addition, 15 per cent of respondents rated standards as very low compared to only five per cent in 2004: public satisfaction with conduct of MPs has declined on every measure since the last survey was conducted. Most worryingly, between 2008 and 2010 the proportion thinking that most MPs are dedicated to doing a good job for the public fell by 20 per cent (from 46 to 26 per cent); the proportion thinking that most MPs are competent at their jobs fell by ten per cent (from 36 to 26 per cent); there was a 14 per cent drop in the proportion thinking that most MPs are in touch with what the public thinks is important (from 29 per cent to only 15 per cent); there were also large drops in the proportion thinking that most MPs set a good example in their private lives (from 36 per cent to 22 per cent), make sure money is used wisely (from 28 per cent to 18 per cent) and that they all tell the truth (from 26 per cent to 20 per cent).

The state of politics in Scotland and the UK has consequences. Turnout is dramatically down. Trust in politicians, and political parties, is at a low point. Party membership has slumped. Political or civic literacy remain at low levels. Young people remain uninspired by our politics and shun the polls. People, especially the young, have embraced issue-based politics at the expense of traditional politics and especially political parties. Inequality in Scotland has pushed the poorest in our communities to be even more dismissive of elections than the rest of the population and where disenfranchisement is at record low levels. Inspiration and vision are lacking as austerity undermines confidence and creates resentment and disinterest. Add to all of this a deafening silence from our political parties and politicians. The referendum may ignite interest among those who rarely vote. If this was to happen then the outcome may be less predictable than seems to be the case.

Politics is an activity from which the people engage or disengage according to their circumstances that are confronting them. What they lack is any sense of sustained engagement with political institutions and the political system. The picture is one of many citizens alienated from formal politics and trying as best they can to cope with the world of politics and government, but only when they have to because of some pressing need. Maybe the future of their country is such a pressing need.

The public are not to blame. Our politics is letting people down. They are disillusioned and disenchanted and increasingly disconnected from a world which seems remote and irrelevant. They now question the relevance of what parties and politicians are supposed to be doing on their behalf. This is a crisis that needs a response.

Our politics once again needs to inspire, enthuse, educate and be relevant to the needs and aspirations of the public and reconnect with the values that underpin our society. We have to move away from the mindless tribalism and partisanship that too often dominates much of what passes as political debate.

We have become better consumers but poorer citizens. We get a wake-up call at every election, but no one seems to be listening.

The referendum in 2014 may be a simple single question, but how and why people vote and what they vote for will be complex and reflect a bewildering mix of factors, influences and considerations. This volatility, uncertainty and unpredictability could create a few shocks in the autumn of 2014. The future of Scotland will be centre stage, but so will our democracy.

CHAPTER TWO

A Union in Decline

IT IS NOT SURPRISING that the Better Together Campaign has been so relentlessly negative, the most obvious weakness being its lack of narrative for the future, and in particular a lack of vision for the Union and what continuing membership of the Union will mean for Scotland and the other nations. Books proliferate about declining nation states in the US and Europe and 'declinology' has become a national pastime. In a recent article in the *Guardian*, 'Britain must Decline Gracefully', Madeline Bunting sets out neatly some of the categories used to define nation sates in decline. First, there are books which employ the doom theme with endless misery, wondering whether nations or the planet can survive because time is running out and tough and hard decisions have to be made. Second, there are economists and foreign policy experts who are matter of fact and speculate whether Europe or Britain is relative or absolute decline relative to power and influence in the world. Third, Bunting suggests that neither of these points gets much of an airing in politics, where national decline is a no go area and politicians as part of their job description are unable to either reflect or speculate about the state of the Union of Great Britain and Northern Ireland. In its conclusion, the article state:

> Decline and democracy have never yet had an easy relationship. Much of democratic politics is premised on promising the electorate their dreams. Britain is resuming, after a generation of illusions, one of the preoccupations of post war politics: is there a way to decline gracefully? How does a political leader reconcile a country to modesty about its place in the world, making room for the new ambitions of other countries – indeed parts of their own country – authors words – while shaping a future prosperity? Politicians may be reluctant to discuss this kind of thing, but no one else is.

Her comments are thought provoking and capture a modern truth about the United Kingdom. The Union is in decline but we should be careful about describing each of the four nations that have formed this enduring alliance, for over 300 years, in the same way. This independence referendum debate is about the Union and Scotland's role within it. The Union should be more than the sum of its constituent parts, if not then there seems little point in being part of something that does not add much value. The mere existence of the Union is not really a benefit in itself. If on the other hand there is added value and benefits to be gained by membership, then what is the problem with the Union today that is generating much internal stress and conflict, seems incapable as part of the Better Together Campaign to articulate a vision for the future which would spell out a positive case for Scotland to stay and where arguments are cloaked in defensiveness, threats or negativity. Regardless of the outcome of the referendum vote, the Union has its critics and historians in particular seem agreed that in the post-war decades and in so many facets of life, the Union is in decline. Equally important is the assumption that the Union created in 1707 was always an incorporation of nations into an English Parliament with a structure being imposed on Scotland, Wales and Ireland to form an alliance of common interests. Indeed, we tend to talk about English history as if it was British history, and at that point shared aspirations about the Protestant faith, the threats from France and the internal security issues that created, and finally the Empire. Scotland retained much of the fabric of a nation, including law, schools and church, which, along with other national characteristics, were never extinguished. The sense of Britishness that emerged after the Union was created was not guarnteed to last. Today we are probably witnessing Scotland the nation on the move again, restless with its current role within the Union, more Scottish than previously, less impressed with what the Union is now offering, more confident about itself and seeing reignited the fire of nationhood that was never extinguished. In her book *Britons: Forging the Nation 1707–1837* (1992), Linda Colley described the Union as a State Nation. In a wide ranging account of the Union from 1707–1837, Colley describes how a new British nation was invented in the wake of the Act of Union between Scotland, Wales and England in 1707:

> [This book examines] how a succession of major wars with Catholic France – culminating in the epic conflict with Napoleon – served as both a threat and a tonic, forcing the diverse peoples of this deeply Protestant culture into a closer union and reminding them of what they had in common... The worldwide empire which was the prize of so much successful warfare gave men and women from different ethnic and social backgrounds a powerful incentive to be British... How an overarching British identity came to be superimposed on to much older regional and national identities... and

why these same older identities – be it Scottish or Welshness or English-ness or regionalism of one kind or another – have re-emerged and become far more important in the late 20th century.

Nearly a quarter of a century since the book was written, these themes have even more resonance as the independence referendum puts to test the identity question and asks whether this 'invented nation' can survive.

> Virtually every major European state is currently under pressure from a resurgence of small nationalities which one acquiesced in being a compo-nent part of a greater whole. So calls for the break up of Britain should not be viewed as exclusively British. But we can understand the nature of the present crisis only if we recognise that the factors that provided for the forging of a British nation in the past have largely ceased to operate.

There is no disputing the fact that the Welsh, Scottish and English remain distinctive peoples. Colley argues that the sense of identity that emerged post 1707:

> ... did not come into being, then, because of integration and homogeni-sation of disparate cultures. Instead Britishness was superimposed over an array of internal differences in response to contact with the 'Other'– the French and other foreign countries – and above all in response to conflict with the 'Other'.

Accepting the idea of an invented nation, then it is not surprising that in 2014 the conditions which created the Union and that sense of British identity no longer exist. The Union was created out of necessity, based on 'policy rather than affection' and it is easy to understand why, after many decades of decline, there is intense political interest on the part of the Unionist parties at Westminster to revisit Britishness and make a case for a Union very much at risk. The importance of the Protestant faith and culture, the threat and in some respects the challenge of recurrent wars, especially with the French, and the success of empire all contributes to a better understanding of why today the Union and Britishness are less attractive to the four nations of the UK. Colley argues:

> Protestantism is now only a residual part of its culture, so it can no longer define itself against a predominantly Catholic Europe. Indeed now that it is part of the European Economic Community, Britain can no longer com-fortably define itself against the European powers at all. Whether it likes it or not, it is fast becoming part of an increasingly federal Europe, though the agonies that British politicians and voters of all partisan persuasions

so plainly experience in coming to terms with Brussels and its dictates show just how rooted the perceptions of Continental Europe as the 'Other' still is.

The powerful concept of an invented nation, the superimposition of a Britishness on diverse cultures, a Union forged on the back of faith, wars and empire and the retained identities of the incorporated nations explains why the people of these islands developed a sense of British identity but also illustrates the fragility of Union and the repercussions which are evident today. The history of Britain over the last 300 years suggests the issue of national identities was never subdued and was a frequent, if not always talked about, influence on the way each of the nations has develo-ped. Post-war and with the demise of Empire, the glue holding the nations together has weakened and this is certain to continue. Over the past three decades, the issues of devolution, deindustrialisation and political divisions have ignited a new sense of urgency about identity and the role of the nations in the future of an uncertain Union. Today the independ-ence debate in Scotland embraces the idea of a different future for Scotland and in a curious way we are revisiting arguments, ideas and controversies that have never really gone away since 1707. Unfortunately the current referendum debate has failed at times to embrace the broader sweep of history and the deeper, but relevant, under currents of identity, nationality and common purpose that so many of our politicians find it hard to talk about. Linda Colley says:

> ... the re-emergence of Welsh, Scottish and English nationalism which has been so marked in recent decades can be seen not just as the natural outcome of cultural diversity, but as a response to a broader loss of national, in the sense of British identity.

Colley revisits many of her 'Britons' themes in *Acts of Union and Disunion* (2014). This book formed the basis of a BBC radio series. What is fasci-nating is that a quarter of a century on, Colley has sharpened her views on the current state of the Union – understandable in the context of the massive changes that have taken place in the intervening period. Any nation state, state nation, nation or region is a complex mix of identities, values and principles which change over time, shaping and influencing how we live and determining how our lives and wellbeing work out. These are the human issues that will determine the future of Scotland.

There are certain conclusions emerging from the various studies of the Union since 1707. The United Kingdom has experienced considerable success and there have been long periods in which a common purpose, common interests and (too often) shared sacrifices have been evident in wars, protecting faith and building an Empire. In the post-war period this unity of purpose has produced a lasting social, health and welfare settlement, now a consistent and enduring feature of our national life and one that generates great pride. Unlike many other European States, the UK has never been invaded and in consequence there have been no severe shocks to the system that have occasioned a new start, new institutions and often massive renewal of the social and institutional fabric in these countries. Our politics and our constitution have largely reflected this lack of upheaval and therefore look tired, jaded and in need of a makeover. There is also something to regret about our failure to embrace Europe after the War and join Continental Europe in the great European adventure, which culminated in the creation of the EEC in 1958. Churchill set the tone for this in his famous speech in Zurich in 1946 when he said he wished his European colleagues well, but wouldn't be joining them. He would remain a cheerleader on the sidelines and would seek the help of his mighty Empire Russia and the US to help Europe. Instead Britain would look to the USA. This ambivalence and, at times, hostility since then has ensured the French would have little faith in our European credentials and as a result we had to wait until 1973 to join. Britain's post-war delusion about still being a great power influenced our world view and the rejection of Europe has in Colley's eyes:

> ... developed into the European Union has proved one of the biggest sources of disunion in post war British political life , and a cause of disagreement between different parts of the United Kingdom.

Taking stock of the UK today, Colley has three suggestions: an English Parliament, a form of federalism and a written constitution. Much of this in the broadest terms makes sense. An historian's perspective of the Union, covering two books over 25 years, has shown how relevant a broad consideration of history can be in linking what happened in the past with the challenges and problems of the present.

Of course, history can never be the sole predictor of the future. But a careful look at the political and constitutional reasons for the Union coming into being, its development since then and the current realities of post-devolution Britain do provide a useful pointer to what might happen in both the immediate future and in the longer term. The state of the Union today poses a number of questions about why in the post-war period little consideration has been given to the political and constitutional issues. In the immediate aftermath of victory in 1945, Britain looked to a new future and the Labour landslide in 1945 was a reflection of the mood of the people. The Beveridge report heralded a new social, health and pensions settlement, which remains one of the great new society initiatives. The War and the new Beveridge era boosted that sense of solidarity and Britishness. A combination of the shared sacrifice in war and the prospect of social change for the many was a boost for the existing social and political order. The loss of Empire that followed had a bearing on our role in the world and the question of Britain's relationship with Europe emerged in 1958 with the setting of European Economic Community, now the European Union. Joining the EEC 1973 probably ended a hectic and soul searching period in which the future of Britain looked less assured, the credibility of the Union was diminishing and Britishness was declining. The consequences for stability, solidarity and social coherence were less obvious then, but after joining the EEC, the attractions of the Union were less clear and doubts were emerging again about this 'invented nation'. Over the past three or four decades there has been a diminishing sense of Britishness and in the post-devolution era the identities of the Scotland, England and Wales have eclipsed Britishness. Despite this reasonably long-term decline, the political classes seemed unwilling or incapable of looking at this broad sweep of history and deducing that the political and constitutional foundations of post-war Britain were under some threat. A new and more imaginative view was required of the four nations that made up the Union as well as a rethink of Britain's role in the world, particularly in relation to Europe and the competing option of Atlanticism involving the US. These questions have never been resolved and we now have a precarious relationship with Europe, a declining relationship with the US and a political and constitutional union which is literally falling apart with pressure from the nations and inaction and indifference from Westminster.

Scotland, England and Wales in their different ways are moving forward, but Westminster seems in denial. For far too long Westminster and establishment elites have cornered the political and constitutional marketplace to the detriment of the Union and the good governance of Great Britain and Northern Ireland. Scotland is currently in the vanguard of this assault on the Union, but its success so far has been largely due the incompetence and indifference of Westminster and the myth of absolute sovereignty of Parliament that pervades their every thought. The absolute sovereignty of the people is the new power in the Union but with the Unionist parties and Westminster denying this reality, it will be left to each of the nations of the Union to evolve in a disorderly and divisive way. It has been left to Scotland to win success and decisively break the mould of Union politics. Regardless of the referendum result, Scotland is also giving Westminster anther wake up call. But is anyone listening beyond offering Scotland the minimum of change to secure a NO vote in what can only be described as a referendum bidding war?

Globalisation is clearly linked to a range of identity issues and have resulted in immigration, technology, nationalism and national sovereignty changing people's perceptions of politics and the way they think and vote.

Europe provides another layer of uncertainty, which is polarising public opinion and creating bitter divisions around the core EU issue of the Single Market, the free movement of goods, services, finance and people. The increasingly hostile attitude towards the EU could be linked to our wars with the French and our now continental neighbours. But as opinion polls and academic surveys show, opinions on the EU vary widely within the Union, and once again the issue of English problems being construed as British problems raises its head. Colley states that GB and the UK:

> ... are comparatively recent and synthetic constructs that have often been contested in the past and now. Every state has multiple fault lines – ethnic, religious, linguistic, cultural and territorial... many states have been composites... so we are hardly exceptional.

Since the Treaty of Union in 1707, the Union has exhibited all of these characteristics. But despite that, the political and governing classes seem unwilling to address the consequences and as a result we have become so obsessed with the economy that we have ignored how important democratic, political and constitutional issues are to a harmonious, tolerant and inclusive Union. What's the purpose of the Union in the 21st century? During the referendum campaign, this question has rarely been asked. Despite its importance, the question seems too difficult for the traditional Unionist parties to answer.

In *Acts of Union and Disunion*, Colley notes that a State Nation or composite state should operate at two levels. First, the partial autonomy and separate rights and culture of the Union's nations and regions should be protected. Second, the Union has to create, sustain and nurture a sense of belonging and allegiance with regard to the larger political entity. So a successful State Nation has to have a well thought out and steady commitment to the whole and a vision of what that is, as well as a recognition of and concessions to the component parts. The Union, its key institutions and the old Unionist parties may be guilty on both counts of neglecting difference and failing to respect the autonomy of our nations whilst at the same time failing to create enough sense of belonging and allegiance to the larger political entity. This rather simple analysis may explain the crisis that is engulfing the Union as it attempts to keep Scotland in the Union:

> Looking at the span of human history, it is indeed not so much the break-up of some state nations that is remarkable, but rather the degree to which some have managed, at least for a time persisted and cohere.

Colley's incisive comment allows us to see ourselves in a broader sweep of history and politics.

The broader sweep of history essentially looking at the notion that the Union is in decline and now offers a much less attractive place to be and as a consequence regardless of the outcome of the Independence referendum the union has major weaknesses, internal strains and tensions and lacks the integrity, imagination and inspiration to sustain stability, solidarity or social coherence.

Borrowing the work of key historians such as Linda Colley and Tom Nairn, we get a sense that the Union was shaped by a number of external forces and factors and that the pressures that helped create a sense of Britishness and brought considerable economic and political success. But by the very nature of these factors becoming less important over time, there is now a realisation that the original imperfections of the Union – no real national blend created, Scotland in particular retaining substantial institutions and the authority of church, law and education, take over rather merger and being incorporated into an essentially English Parliament – are now playing a part in its undoing and its difficulty in dealing with change. A relationship of convenience is unravelling and without a radical reappraisal of the Union taking place, there is every likelihood that Scotland will over time see a very different future for itself and decide to exit. It may not be this referendum that provides the popular consent, but the weaknesses of the Union, its failure to see a coherent future and vision for a multi-national and multi-cultural entity, the increasing confidence of

Scotland post-devolution and the deepening disillusionment of the public in traditional unionist politics will accelerate further decline and the inevitable breakup of Great Britain and Northern Ireland. The decline of Britishness and the rise of national identity in the four nations of the Union are loosening the ties that bound the Union and are putting at risk the shared solidarity that probably reached its peak in the immediate postwar period and has been declining ever since.

In summary, and drawing on the remarkable work of Colley, the early sense of Britishness is easy to understand. The incentives to be British after 1707 involved a number of major wars over a long period of time, the tussle with Catholic France, the nurturing and protection of the Protestant faith and the success of a worldwide empire, all contributing to a sense of Britishness. Less what people had in common, more to do with what they were against.

> An overarching British identity came to be superimposed on to a much older regional and national identity. It is these identities that have re-emerged and have become far more important in the early 21st century.

> In addition Britain had a Massive military machine, never experienced a major invasion – unlike most European countries. Military glory was achieved without ever having to pay the price of civilian casualties and large scale domestic destruction. Britain in support of the Stuart dynasty always a threat to the security of the Protestant settlement. Great Britain was an invented nation. Absorbed not blended, forged by war. British nationality was shaped by external threats. Define your enemy the tried and tested way achieving internal unity

All of this provides context and helps to explain some of Britain's current difficulties. The conditions that created the Union no longer exist and as a consequence there is a very obvious breakdown being manifest in a variety of ways.

This was how it was with the British after 1707. Britons came to define themselves as a single people not because of any political or cultural consensus at home, but rather in reaction to the other beyond their shores. So what is the glue – if any – that currently binds them together? If the glue is weak, can the Union remain, at least in its present form? If not, what can be done to strengthen all the nations of the Union? Britain is now under enormous pressure. Recent events have only served to reinforce the threats and challenges to the nation, posing searching questions of its future intentions and prompting an examination of whether it has a vision around which a failing consensus could be reinvigorated.

Colley sums this up as such:

> A union of policy not affection for the majority of Scots at this early stage of the Union was only of marginal importance. Looked at in this way Great Britain in 1707 was much less a trinity of three self-contained and self-conscious nations than a patchwork in which uncertain areas of Welsh, Scottish and English were cut across by strong regional attachments. Great Britain was infinitely diverse in terms of custom and cultures. The simple fact was that Britain was an island. War played a vital part in the invention of a British nation after 1707. In a broad sense Protestantism lay at the core of British national identity. Religion was the crucial unifying force in most nations within Europe. Britain was an invented nation.

The resulting doubt and disarray have taken many forms –

> On the one hand, now that so many of the components of Britishness have faded, there have been predictable calls for a revival of other older loyalties – a return to Scottishness, or Englishness and Welshness.

The state of the Union is the driving force behind much of the discord, alienation and desire for something different, but is the Union capable of providing this?

Scotland aspiring and the Union declining are inextricably linked as they move in their different directions. This has been insufficiently covered in the debate and explains part of the reason why the revival of national identities has accelerated in Scotland. The Union in its current form is in terminal decline.

The conditions for a great deal of soul searching are being shaped by a collapse of confidence and trust in politics, politicians, political parties and their institutions. There is a perfect storm of issues and influences shaping this independence referendum.

This is a time of unrest, deepening anxieties and fears about the future, which have only been intensified by the banking and financial crisis over the past four years. There is national uncertainty and insecurity. There are fears in England about membership of the EU. The Germans and French are more confident of their identity and direction. The British are inclined to see Europe as a threat. British insularity is explained by their doubts about who they are.

To retain any sense of structure and national cohesion and reward the four nations of the Union with respect and the sharing and pooling of sovereignty, more federal Britain in some form will have to emerge.

Scotland's incorporation into the Union has been discussed and argued over for centuries, and most Scots are familiar with the claims and counter claims about both the thinking and the reasons for our accession, and the protagonists and early politicians who argued the merits or otherwise of such ceding of power to another Parliament, not to mention how all of this has played into the folklore, myths and memories of Scottish history. We are now approaching our date with destiny, which may result in Scotland leaving the Union to begin a journey that was interrupted 307 years ago. Or, at this point in time, there may be a NO vote leading to our continuing membership of the Union, but by all accounts – social, historical, economic, political and constitutional – we will remain in the same Union and without its radical renewal and reconstruction, Scotland will likely revisit the same issues and discontent in the near future.

The journey Scotland is on will not be halted by a conclusion to the bidding wars of the Unionist parties in offering more powers and more tax discretion. All of this may be too little and too late. The state of the Union, its continuing decline and lack of attractiveness requires major surgery. For some it may be too late and we are left with the prospect of Scotland taking the step to build a new future over which it would have more control – accepting that in our modern world some aspects of globalisation, the work of the EU and whatever accommodation Scotland has with rUK there is no complete independence.

The key problem or tactical weakness of the NO Campaign has been the relentless negativity, the complacency and at times the threatening and insensitive behaviour. Many commentators have remarked on the NO Campaign and its lack of vision for the future regardless of time scale. The reason may be straightforward. The NO Campaign cannot provide a vision because the future is so uncertain and in its current form the Union has been in long term decline. Faced with this uncomfortable dilemma, the past has to be sold as the expected future, the mere existence of the Union for over 300 years is testament to its success and should be the basis on which Scots would buy into it for another 300 years. Although this touches a slightly cynical note, it nevertheless fits the current circumstances. In addition, we have been subject to a series of threats that started off as irritating, then became insulting and finally had most Scots thinking how incredulous this approach was. Not content with these stern messages,

Scotland then endured an endless stream of visitors threatening plagues of locusts, visits from aliens, famines and floods if Scotland failed to get the message over on such issues as the Sterling currency union, accession to the EU and membership of NATO. This was a serious attempt to inject fear and scares into the campaign and it remains to be seen if this has been successful. On another front there were threats regarding the BBC, research monies would dry up, border posts would be set up to keep foreign immigrants out of England. The poverty of material being used by the NO Campaign does raise serious doubts about what the Union stands for and what it could offer Scots and indeed the rest of the UK in the future.

So what is it that makes it so difficult for the Union to move beyond the notion of a future which is a straight extrapolation of the past? In the new politics of England there can be no guarantees that the future will look like the past. This of course raises the issue of the Labour Party and its ability to offer a more inspired social democratic vision for the future that retains the ethics and values of the majority of Scots for decent public services and universal provision, free at the point of need. More importantly, can Labour win the General Election in 2015 and start to reverse the damage being done by the Coalition, reject neoliberal economic and social thinking and waken up to the new realities emerging in each nation of the Union? The answers to these questions are vital, as reassurances will be needed to persuade Scots before the referendum vote that a change at Westminster is likely, with significantly different outcomes for a Scotland that still sees the merits of social democracy and retains a healthy dislike of extremism. Different political cultures are developing in England and Scotland with a growing divide that becomes more difficult to bridge.

What are the most recent signs of a Union in decline?

What would be attractive about populism competing with neoliberalism for the votes of England, and in the process creating social division, intolerance and a harrowing environment for a whole range of people?

What would be attractive about a multi-nation, multi-cultural, multi ethnic and multi-racial Union being neglected from the centre?

What would be attractive about abandoning any serious commitment to a fairer society and a more equal society at a time when the gap between rich and poor is growing and there are massive inequalities blighting every aspect of our lives?

What would be attractive about leaving the European Union and the jurisdiction of the European Court of Human Rights and the European

Convention when a cheap and contrived patriotism and the delusional behaviour of the right are seeking to damage Britain for narrow political and ideological interests?

What would be attractive about an England with 50 million people becoming more politically fragile and anxious, being pushed further to the right and intensifying their discontent about devolved government because it is unfair to England? This is happening and the Unionist parties are refusing to confront these concerns, which are often negative and based on grudge and grievance, but do raise some serious and legitimate questions to be answered.

What would be attractive about the Westminster parties, who show little interest in devolving power to the nations of the Union, seem to have learned very little in the 15 post-devolution years and have been sleeping on the job in relation to the rise of the SNP in Scotland and UKIP in England? For the Unionist parties there is denial, but also a sense of entitlement born of decades of not taking seriously the political and constitutional changes and a steady decline in public trust and confidence in failing institutions and political parties. We haven't had the earthquake, but the tremors are growing more intense.

Unlike the other nations of the Union, Scotland has a choice. A YES vote would secure an exit for Scotland, but our relationship post-independence with the rest of the UK would still be subject to the various weaknesses that hastened our decision to leave in the first place. A NO vote would still see Scotland subject to a Union, unsure of itself, lacking focus and direction, a politically volatile England and lacking the urgency, confidence and inspiration to change. Either way, the future composition of the Union – whatever it is – will be more and more influenced by England and the election battle between UKIP and the Conservatives. The role of the Labour Party is vital and the perception of its prospects in 2015 could have a bearing on how Scots vote in the referendum. There remains a real objection in Scotland to the type of conservatism now so evident at Westminster and alien to a more socially democratic Scotland. The prospect of victory for Labour would be one element of reassurance for Scots, but what they would do in Government is also exercising the minds of Scots who remain unconvinced about what the party stands for, what manifesto commitments will they offer and what kind of improved Scottish Parliament will they offer. Acknowledging their Devolution Commission findings were the weakest and least ambitious of the three Unionist parties and in all there policy deliberations there are hardly any references to the constitution or sub-national government, instead localism and cities are their priorities. Worth noting is their total failure to engage in any consideration of the England question and their ambivalence to the findings of the McKay Commission, looking in to English Votes for English Laws.

What should a more attractive Union look like and how can it come about? We need to build the foundations for creating a new Union capable of addressing the deep-seated problems of our long-term decline in the post-war period. These should really be the terms and conditions for voting NO, for without these safeguards, rejecting YES would result in business as usual after the next election with some minimum improvements for the Scottish Parliament, and a neglect of the political and constitutional changes required to make the UK fit for purpose in the 21st century. Of course there isn't, based on recent evidence, any possibility of any of the traditional Unionist political parties, with the exception of the Lib-Dems, being remotely interested in this platform for saving the Union. Rejection of such ideas could however in the medium term lead to a change in political thinking and the demise of political parties in their present form: realignment could be the order of the day with a more modern style of European politics where manifestos in their current form are abandoned and instead we have broader policy statements of intent around which we can build progressive and inclusive platforms for change. A System of PR for Westminster would accelerate this process and create something more in line with the thinking of citizens in each of the four nations of the Union. For the referendum, Scots might use this as a useful way of putting the Union to the test, with a number of questions which need answered before electors would vote NO. Without responses to these big issues a NO vote may end up being of no help in changing an ailing Union and will only help to underscore the idea that a YES vote carries with it a degree of confidence that Scotland can make it on its own, but also a real sadness that the parties of the Union couldn't raise their game and take Scotland and the Union seriously. We need to be clear on what a NO vote means or what price a NO vote.

First, there has to be a new narrative written for the Union, based on a national conversation and shaped by a new Constitutional Convention of all the nations, with a time scale and certainly within the lifetime of the next Westminster, Scottish, Welsh and Irish Parliamentary cycles, effectively reporting, consulting and legislating by 2020.

Second, the convention needs to be informed by the expertise, experience and the collective wisdom of all of the Union and needs to be inspired by recalling the great political and constitutional reforms that underpin our democracy, but also enthused about a new world of opportunity that is all around us.

Third, we need to learn from other countries, including Europe, and escape this mindset of insularity and exclusivity that shapes so much of our thinking. Europe has much to offer, in terms of large and successful countries such as Germany and smaller but still successful countries like the Nordic nations – we need to explore what insights they could provide for Scotland, Wales and Northern Ireland. For example, federalism makes sense of Nation States that are large but require a way of governing that offers shared, not devolved, power, solidarity, social cohesion and stability and where the sovereignty of the people trump outdated notions of absolute sovereignty. The European Union provides one idea of a model where nations come together sharing power and ceding sovereignty. The UK could easily replicate such an idea. There could be a continuing process of self-determination for each of the nations and regions of the UK, developing at different times, and at different speeds and dependent on difference, diversity, problems and challenges and social and economic conditions in each part of the Union.

Fourth, there has to be a written, codified constitution in the UK which captures how we are governed, offers protection and safeguards for freedoms and rights of citizens and provides access in the form of a single, accessible and easily understood document. The absolute sovereignty of Westminster no longer exists in any form, except in the minds of MPs and in the institution itself. The broader Union requires this be dropped to ensure the other nations are offered some protection from the influence of England and Westminster; devolved power is retained power, instead we need to share power.

Fifth, there is no unity of purpose to be gained by pursuing a referendum on the European Union. This is likely to be divisive and corrosive of four nation politics. So far no case has been made for change. Instead we have UKIP, the Conservative Party and certain sections of the press indulging in 'distraction therapy' where immigrants, foreigners and bureaucrats are singled out for special abuse to create a distraction from the real problems of a declining Union. Unless there are major treaty changes or more powers being transferred to the EU, then this kind of political opportunism should be resisted. Our relationship with the EU and the relationships between the four nations should be incorporated in the new Constitution.

Sixth, if the notion of the absolute sovereignty of Parliament is of little consequence in the real world, it would be a mistake to use this as the pretext of removing the UK from the jurisdiction of the European Court of Human Rights and the influence of the European Convention, which would result in being thrown out of the Council of Europe, joining the likes of Belarus and Kazakhstan. We should also consider Britain's opt out of the Charter of Fundamental Rights, which most other countries in the EU have signed up for. There has to be a debate around why other successful European countries can deal with progressive policies and modern concepts but the UK can't. UKIP and the Conservative party are perpetrating a con on the electorate, especially in England, by pretending all of this is about national sovereignty when in fact, it is about the threat posed by progressive policies and modern ideas, to neoliberalism and unfettered markets. Again arrangements with the ECHR should be included in a new Constitution.

Seventh, the devolved legislation for Scotland, England and Northern Ireland and possibly England in the future, has to be included in any new constitution, providing protection from Westminster and the absurdity of a majority of one in the House of Commons in a single line Bill abolishing the Scottish Parliament!

Eighth, the saga of the House of Lords affords an opportunity for a reform which could bring the four nations into a new revising chamber, bringing to an end an undemocratic, unelected and ancient relic of an institution which, despite its changing composition, is the antithesis of what a modern parliament should represent. Having elected representatives from the nations and regions of the Union will be a statement that the future of the Union is more important than preserving privilege and living in the past.

Ninth, we need to embrace the approach envisaged by Gordon Brown in 2007 when he talked about building trust of the British people in our democracy and said: 'We need a shared national consensus for a programme of constitutional reform.' This didn't happen. Over the last four years the Coalition has abandoned any efforts at constitutional or political reform and renewal and in the process destroyed hopes of political change by mishandling and finally destroying the Alternative Vote referendum. Brown's ambition chimes with today's needs, if we peer in to the future and look closely at the current constitutional setup and within that the needs of Scotland. Without this wider perspective of reform, the case for the Union is weakened and the prospects of further political discontent are guaranteed. This should have been the point of engagement for the Unionist parties at Westminster, especially Labour, who have the most to gain from a solution which tackles seriously the settled will of the Scottish people and makes long-term sense for the Union and Westminster. To date this hasn't happened.

There are signs to suggest that this central point has neither been listened to nor understood. The longer Scotland is out there on its own, the greater the danger that Scotland will have no other option than to exit. This is why a bigger politics, a deeper understanding of the issues and a wider perspective have to be part of this referendum debate, but also a part of whatever happens afterwards. Gordon Brown talked about building the trust of the British people in our democracy. It was an inspiring thought then, but it is much more important now.

Tenth, there is a growing imperative for the traditional unionist political parties to start to take seriously the ideas of political and constitutional change. For far too long this has been seen as a distraction from the 'real issues' and the preserve of a handful of political, academic and constitutional elites whose good work often never sees the light of day. At a time when the Union has no real direction, purpose or strength and there is no compelling narrative for the future, this is the opportunity for the political parties to connect with issues. The UK is at a strategic tipping point that demands a new approach. Without change the Union will decline. The four nations will become increasingly restless and a new round of constitutional and political demands will come to the fore. At what point do the Unionist parties and Westminster concede the obvious: that the Union in its current form isn't working and will continue to decline. For those who support a Union, it has to be reinvented. Anything less will have serious consequences.

These positive suggestions are a response to a catalogue of major issues, which spell out the accumulated inheritance of a declining Union and the failure over the years of Westminster to take the issues seriously and now being compounded by an uninspiring Better Together Campaign.

The issue is not whether Scotland could be independent, but whether it *should* be independent. A soulless, emotionless, bureaucratic, managerial approach has led to a near contempt for the idea that Scotland should seek to consolidate difference in the form of a new constitutional settlement.

The Better Together Campaign has overplayed every hand they have in the Westminster pack: Europe, currency, immigration and US sentiment. These are real and substantial issues, but their significance has been undermined by their approach. In some respects they have actually strengthened the YES vote, where Scots have felt irritated by the arrogance of Westminster.

There is no recognition that the Union and Westminster are in need of any change: blundering through the second decade of the 21st century, there is little hint of humility, weakness or an acceptance that it is the depressing state of the Union that needs urgent attention.

A NO vote could mean that the Houses of Parliament could, in the aftermath of the Referendum battle, settle down on their red and green benches blissfully aware that they are the only power in the land and subject the outcome of the referendum to a period of unnecessary scrutiny and delay. After the General Election in 2015, who is to say that any careful agreement arrived at by the Unionist parties in their manifestos will survive and be given the urgency needed to ensure the will of the Scottish people, whatever the vote, is delivered. A NO vote opens up a risky route to further constitutional change: three political parties, manifestos, elections, composition of the new House of Commons, priorities of the new Parliament, agreement on the further devolution package, the legislative process and while this is taking place there is the 2016 election for Holyrood! There is never certainty in the political game.

David Marquand, writing in the *Guardian* on the State of the Nation in July 1962, talked about how in the last few years what the early Victorians used to call the 'Condition of England Question' has once again become a central topic of political and literary discussion.

> During the intervening century, however, the question has changed its nature. The problems of early Victorian England were the problems of exuberant growth. Ours are the problems of relative decline. The loss of empire and the social changes of the last 20 years have provoked a fumbling, incoherent search for national identity. Acknowledged or not, that search must be one of the major themes of any serious attempt to understand Britain today.

Gordon Brown has articulated the case for the Union more eloquently than most, but his commitment to the post-war settlement of Beveridge, the idea that scale provides the basis for redistribution of wealth and income based on justice and fairness and that all of this will carry on as before, are entirely dependent on politics and the constitution and what is likely to happen in England. On the substance of this there can be very little disagreement. But this is history. The really difficult question is whether this settlement, which is at risk, can be continued into the future. These are not questions of economics but of politics, and the future constitution of the Union, which are now being influenced by the rise of the right and populism and overwhelmingly in England. So the essence of the Union offer is that the past will be the future with little acknowledgement of the present and the darker forces at work who do not share progressive ideas and are not committed to the ideals of the welfare state.

Great Britain as an invented nation superimposed, if only for a while, onto much older alignments and loyalties

Scotland aspiring and the Union declining are inextricably linked as they move in their different directions. This has been insufficiently covered in the debate and explains part of the reason why the revival of national identities has accelerated in Scotland. The Union in its current form is in terminal decline.

The conditions for a great deal of soul searching are being shaped by a collapse of confidence and trust in politics, politicians, political parties and their institutions. There is a perfect storm of issues and influences shaping this independence referendum. The SNP has become the major force in Scottish politics since 2007, but even that level of political success would not have propelled them to their current level of polling in the independence referendum without something spectacular taking place. The long term decline of the Union, a constitutional and political crisis facing Westminster, a perfect storm of difficult issues and the near collapse of the unionist parties in Scotland have largely created the conditions in which the YES vote has gained enormous traction, possibly not enough for victory this time, but laying down a marker to Westminster and the Union that unless they totally transform their thinking and approach they will be the cause of the break- up of Britain, not Scotland or England or Wales or Northern Ireland. It is the Union stupid that is creating the conditions in which consciously and unconsciously the people of these islands are thinking the unthinkable!

CHAPTER THREE

The Constitution of the United Kingdom

THE BRITISH CONSTITUTION or, more to the point, our uncodified constitution, has been the source of endless curiosity, fulsome praise (which at times bordered on adulation from the legal and political establishment, especially in the 19th century). And now serious and concerned criticism that, despite a series of piecemeal changes in the Blair years, this so called constitution is not fit for purpose and is undermining the stability, credibility and attractiveness of the Union of Great Britain and Northern Ireland. The lack of a serious, written and codified constitution has implications for the Independence referendum and for the future of the Union regardless of the outcome: the lack of a modern constitution is creating the conditions in which disillusionment with Westminster, the lack of trust in the Unionist political parties, the myth of the absolute sovereignty of Parliament and the lack of an overarching narrative for the future governance of these islands and the protection of the liberty, freedom and rights of our citizens could lead to chaos and crisis in the immediate future. Successive UK parliaments, our legal system and the wider establishment have linked the success of Britain over the centuries with the fact that we had no written or codified constitution. This allowed Westminster, with few exceptions, to literally make it up as the institution evolved and adapt to events of history and political change. This now ramshackle collection of laws, conventions and legal decisions we call a constitutional framework, from the Magna Carta to the legislation for the devolved parliaments and assemblies, now needs structure, order and modernity to have relevance to the people it purports to serve. Despite the fact that we have written a great number of constitutions for other countries the UK, along with New Zealand and Israel, are the only countries without some form of codified constitution. Unlike the oft-quoted constitution of the United States of America, which is founded on its Declaration of Independence, a Constitution incorporating amendments and a Bill of Rights, Britain has muddled through, despite attempts by Gordon Brown when he was Prime Minister to put the idea of a codified constitution on the political agenda. This has been ignored by the Conservative and Lib-Dem Coalition. In quieter constitutional times, this arrogance and exceptional ambivalence of Westminster had few consequences. Today we live in a far more precarious and volatile political and constitutional landscape with not only the Independence referendum in Scotland, but a whole host of territorial stirrings in the nations of the UK, real and growing fears about the expanding tentacles of the state in the cyber age undermining hard won freedoms, liberties and rights. We are also witnessing a breakdown of trust between the elected and those who elect them. Some order has to be superimposed on this chaos and in doing so our political classes have to accept that this has to be an inclusive process where the sovereignty of the people has to emerge as the basis upon which we transform and operate our constitution. Arguments such as the public are not interested in 'constitutional stuff' – flexibility is the order of the day/ we don't want to be bound by history/ we have continuity on our side/ no major interruptions to our 1,000 years of history/ these are matters best left to a privileged establishment elite – are self-serving and complacent at a point of real peril for the Union. Why should the people of the Union be denied an accessible, written, codified constitution in a single document? Justifying Britain's disinterest in such matters, the lack of a major shock to the way we are governed and our enduring institutions is often cited. Germany, France and the USA, at different moments in history, are dramatic examples of how seismic change created the need and the conditions for a new start. Again this makes little sense. Wales and England coming together in 1536, Scotland joining both countries in the Act of Union in 1707, Ireland becoming part of the Union in 1801, part of Ireland leaving the Union in 1922, gaining membership of the EU in 1973, accepting the jurisdiction of the European Court of Human Rights post-war and devolved government in 1999 were all significant events which needed to be given context, coherence and credibility as part of a single continuous narrative of the unfolding history, politics and constitution of the UK. But it has not happened, and since the Blair Government in 1997, we have had a number of piecemeal constitutional changes which have never been seen by successive governments as part of a vision or a blueprint for strengthening our democracy. The significance for Scotland is real and immediate. The Scotland Act 1999 is not part of any codified constitution and could be repealed by Westminster. Although this is unlikely to happen, it illustrates the absolute stranglehold Parliament has on the existence and operation of the devolved settlement and the Scottish Parliament. The argument for entrenchment – removing the idea of devolved power is power retained – is overwhelming, and Former Prime Minister Gordon Brown has been vocal in his support. But how could this happen when the absolute sovereignty of the Westminster Parliament is the complete antithesis of shared power and will always seek to have the ultimate control and authority? In the event of a NO vote and with the promise of more policy and tax powers being offered by the three Unionist parties, will Westminster abandon its current power and, short of a codified and written constitution, acknowledge the sovereignty of the Scottish people as a higher and more democratic authority that an outdated historical convention of Westminster? These are vitally important constitutional issues that can only be dealt with if we create a more inclusive conversation and a constitutional framework within which we can arrive at a fairer way of distributing power in the UK, therefore ending the absolute authority of Westminster. Such a move would require a form of federalism and a codified constitution, which now looks like the only way forward for Scotland, short of Independence. The bidding war between the Unionist parties of who can offer the most powers and most tax concessions may be too little and too late. Indeed, the debate may have moved beyond this minimalist set of offerings and the limited thinking of the Unionist parties. If there is to be a new future for Scotland within the Union – assuming a NO vote in the referendum – this will require a radical shift in thinking and a move towards a new constitutional settlement for the whole of the UK. At the present time, achieving these changes looks well outside the political comfort zone of the Westminster parties and if history is a guide to what might happen in the future, nothing significant will happen and Scotland will drift further away from the Union and exit will loom large over the next few years.

But constitutional matters have always been the preserve of the political and legislating classes and have never been the subject of a serious dialogue with the people, who have never been asked whether or not they would like to have as central to their role as citizens a single, accessible, reliable and codified document providing a well-crafted corpus of how our governments should work and what our rights, freedoms and liberties are. Following our successful history from 1707, through economic achievements, the remarkable days of Empire and victories in two World Wars, subjects have become citizens, but it is hard to avoid the hint of feudalism and elitism that, at least in spirit, still stalks our land. On that point, certain elements of the Conservative Government and the backbench extremism now gaining traction in England seem ready to move from subjects to citizens and then to clients and consumers where money and markets triumph over moral issues and citizen rights! In sharp contrast to the lack of interest in constitutional renewal and codification, the YES Campaign have set out plans for a new codified constitution for an Independent Scotland. Better Together is silent on the issue, but for silence we must read 'not interested'. In the event of a NO vote, the Scottish Government could still push ahead and create a codified constitution which would build on political difference, distance ourselves further from the Westminster neglect of this issues and move our thinking towards a Nordic mindset more in tune with the 21st century.

Despite the changes introduced by the Blair Government from 1997, these were never conceived as part of a grand constitutional reform strategy but were seen as answers to a range of different questions. They were significant but piecemeal, and were never designed to be part of renewing our democracy, which in recent years has reflected our broken politics and the public's growing frustration and anger about political parties and politicians. This was a lost opportunity, and since then there is overwhelming evidence to suggest that our politics, our democracy and our rights, freedoms and liberties as citizens are at risk and being undermined year after year.

The introduction of devolved government also provided a valuable insight into how Westminster oversees our uncodified constitution and initiates change within their unique 'absolute sovereignty of Parliament' convention: acknowledging there is no greater power than the two Houses of Parliament at Westminster which can legislate or not on any matter, does not have to account for its decisions between five-year election periods and has a House of Lords (which is the complete antithesis of the democratic principle, being both unelected and over which the sovereignty of the people has no influence or control whatsoever). In this context the Referendum has entered the life of our legislators. Used first in 1975 to reaffirm our membership of the European Economic Community (now the EU), the referendum has been used on five occasions since then: devolution in 1979, devolution three times in 1997 and the alternative vote fiasco in 2011. The Independence referendum to be held in September and an EU referendum promised by David Cameron for 2017 will bring the use of referenda to a total of eight in modern times. Some scholars have argued that a referendum is, in the context of the absolute sovereignty of Parliament, unconstitutional. This merely illustrates the absurdity of our current confusion. Westminster can do anything it wishes predicated on the point that is elected by the people and it is sovereign: we end up having a number of referendums on constitutional issues, but only if Westminster decides. But if there was an accessible and codified constitution – agreed by an inclusive and representative group – the people or citizens would know what issues would be the subject of referenda and this allows the sovereignty of the people to curb excesses of governments, agree to the terms and conditions in which governments operate and to know, contestable in a court of law, how their freedoms, liberties and rights are to be nurtured and protected. Equally important, the Houses of Parliament would have no automatic or absolute right to change or amend the constitution, which would be subject to institutions sharing power with them, a second chamber of elected members, as in modern Europe, representing the nations of the Union and the regions of England and clear and unambiguous protocols for our arrangements with the European Union and the European Court of Human Rights: this would reflect a modern and mature approach to supranational organisations and would hopefully avoid the nonsense, lies and myths that surround such institutions and the role they play in our lives. So far in the history of Britain, elites have handled what are ostensibly matters for democratic debate and oversight, so it is vital for the interests of democracy for our engagement with the EU and the ECHR to be open, transparent and the subject of serious debate in this country. This would be the first and obvious step to deal with controversial issues in our political process and enlist the public in creating a sensible conversation about institutions that play an important and vital part in our lives: these issues are too important to be left exclusively to Westminster and the press.

The often cited reason for not having a codified constitution – 'the absolute sovereignty of Parliament' argument – allows the political classes, especially right-wing Conservative MPs, to offer this as the perfect excuse: we simply don't need one. This has endured for centuries and in the context of the modern world is ludicrous. The absolute sovereignty of Westminster means that there is no higher authority than Government, so we remain in this remarkable situation of the Mother of Parliaments being able to legislate on any matter with none of the checks or balances you would expect to find in a modern Nation State or expect to find in the constitution of every democratic country in the world except New Zealand and Israel!

At the heart of Westminster Parliament there are no real checks on the Executive, normally formed from the majority party. The Executive sits in the House of Commons and, if to a much lesser extent, in the House of Lords, which is itself anachronistic and undemocratic. Lord Hailsham once described this setup as an 'Elective Dictatorship', capturing the idea that the ruling party is all-encompassing and powerful. Gordon Brown as Prime Minister published a Green Paper with the intention of strengthening the role of Parliament in relation to the power of the Executive; this was abandoned by the Conservative-Lib-Dem Coalition in 2010. In modern Britain the operation of Westminster doesn't make sense, and despite a compelling case for reform, MPs and Ministers cling to the myth of absolute sovereignty despite the reality of our membership of the EU, the Devolution of power to Wales, Scotland and Northern Ireland, and being within the jurisdiction of the European Court of Human Rights and subject to the European Convention, which have driven a coach and horses through this archaic thinking. For MPs, this is their link with the past, where everything was easier and less complex. What is perplexing and dangerous is that despite all the changes in society, the decline of public trust and confidence in what MPs do and the archaic procedures used to run our democracy and create our laws, politicians, political parties and successive governments have ignored all demands for change and instead are content to put the 'business as usual sign' on the door that Black Rod knocks three times at the annual opening of Parliament.

While most of the western European countries within the EU have signed up for the Charter of Fundamental Right, the UK has not and has negotiated an opt-out. This Charter complements and adds to the rights contained within the European Chapter on Human Rights and provides for added protection in the workplace and in other important areas of society. Instead of this being an issue of practical importance to millions of people, it has disappeared, like so many other innovative and useful ideas from Europe, from the public debate. In sharp contrast, David Cameron wants to elevate the 800th anniversary of the signing of the Magna Carta into a national celebration of what is precious and unique to Britain, symbolic of our important freedoms and liberty secured through struggle over centuries. Much of this couldn't be further from the truth. What it does illustrate is that:

... over time, its true origins and meaning have become obscured by myths and misunderstandings about its content and significance as it has come to symbolise principles which played little part in its creation.

This was the judgement of Claire Breahy in a slim volume published by the British Library in 2002, *Magna Carta: Manuscripts and Myths*. The author suggests that the statements of rights and justice contained in the document, which lies at the root of its fame today, were not in fact central to its original purpose. She adds:

> ... the Magna Carta was not intended to be a lasting declaration of legal principle or theory. It was a practical solution to a political crisis between King John and his baronial opponents. The 63 clauses of the charter imposed constraints on royal authority. Despite all the claims which have been made for it since, the charter was not intended to be the cornerstone of English Democracy, still less the foundation of a code of human rights.

The people of Britain are so excluded from the political and constitutional debates that have shaped both Scotland and the other four nations over the centuries that we can be treated to such myth-making. It seeks to extract political benefit and reinforce that sense of Englishness and Parliamentary superiority that is now at the heart of the political crisis, and ultimately could result in Scotland exiting the UK. It is difficult to capture how removed from reality the Westminster Parliament can be! Again this is a story that is important for the Independence referendum. Scots who attach some importance to constitutional issues – or at least appreciate that our democracy can only work if our institutions have the capacity to adapt and modify – should be shocked by the inability of their Parliament at Westminster, so wrapped up in the past, to be concerned with their futures: even worse, that we have reached a point where party politics have their own internal dynamic and may have, at least in their current form and purpose, reached their sell-by date.

Compounding the political and constitutional crisis in the UK is the growing political divide between Scotland and England and the rise of the political right of the Conservative Party and the populism of UKIP, which is a product of the public disillusionment with the traditional Unionist parties, delusional views about the EU and, increasingly, the pursuit of populism as the England Independence Party. While it would be easy to dismiss all of this as part of the changing cycle of politics and the temporary loss of confidence in the old parties, evidence suggests that deeper and more significant factors are at work, not only in England but elsewhere in Europe – but not as yet in Scotland, where there is certainly a modest anti-European vote, as witnessed in the recent Euro elections where, by a whisker, UKIP won a seat. At Westminster and in England, neoliberal ideology, a lack of compassion, markets and money before morality and a distasteful form of what could be described as distraction therapy or scapegoating are poisoning politics and contributing to a divided Union in which groups of society are being singled out, abused and demonised for political ends: this action is taking the Union out of the UK where a complex multi ethnic, multi-racial, multi-cultural and multi-nation approach of the post-war period is being deliberately turned into a fractious, divisive, intolerant and insecure Britain where solidarity and social integration are being seriously damaged. But this is not what is happening in Scotland. None of the political parties feel it necessary to create social divisions and political schisms for narrow, part-political ends, and once again the actions of the right in England – not all of England and excluding London – are reinforcing the growing political divide between Scotland and the Union. Some people will argue that we have our own Parliament in Edinburgh to protect us from the excesses of Westminster and Conservative Governments. That is true to a certain extent, but looking forward, the political debate in England may start to look more threatening and alien to Scots uninterested in extremism and turned off by some of the antics of those who wish to tear up the post-war settlement and subject the NHS, pensions, the Social Security system and education to the marketplace. This will move us from a market economy to a market society, which few Scots would want to see. The politics of difference is growing because of the changes in England. This is likely to be another influence in the Independence referendum, as people think about the growing political divide, the apparent indifference of Westminster to what is happening and again contemplate what kind of country you would want to live in: this is where the Nordic or US question becomes important.

The real question is: where are the safeguards to protect nations, communities and vulnerable groups? We have no codified constitution and it is clear that sections of our community feel vulnerable. The nasty side to this distraction therapy, to which we are all being subjected, is the corrosive influence this is having on the ethics, tolerance and cohesion of our society. Welfare claimants, the disabled, immigrants, foreigners, the Islamic faith, trade unionists, the European Union and the European Court of Human Rights are the subject of this deliberate and reckless attack, a smokescreen to divert attention away from our long-term decline as a Union and the massive injustices, deepening inequalities, financial anxieties and personal and family insecurity that currently scar our society. The Union is a very troubled place. Our politicians and political parties seem either oblivious to what is going on, and continue to ignore the signs of social decline, or are part of this obvious assault on groups and institutions that are being held responsible for all the woes of the United Kingdom.

David Cameron and the Conservatives talk about 'Uniquely British' rights when they are universal rights. They want to celebrate the anniversary of the Magna Carta in 2015 but at the same time wish to withdraw from the jurisdiction of the European Court of Human Rights and the European Convention. They seek to demonise and degrade some of the most vulnerable groups in our society but at the same time extol the virtues of big society and a caring capitalism. In whose interest is the UK being run? There are powerful reasons why a codified, accessible written constitution, available in one document, would help open up our politics and our democracy in order to achieve a higher scrutiny of what is being done on our behalf as well as appealing to a higher sense of self and a greater appreciation of our rights and responsibilities.

The Scottish Government has confirmed that in an Independent country there would be a written and codified constitution. Scots, through a YES vote, will show their support for a nation that values the importance of the citizen and is willing to create a document that incorporates how they are to be governed and how their freedoms, liberties and rights will be safeguarded. On the other hand, a NO vote will mean a vote for the continuation of the constitutional chaos at Westminster and the failure over centuries to achieve a written and codified constitution: a situation that is unlikely to change with a YES or NO vote, but is likely to worsen considerably if the in/out referendum on membership of the EU goes ahead in 2017 and withdrawal from the jurisdiction of the ECHR is included in the next Conservative manifesto. There are no curbs on the executive at Westminster and no real evidence to suggest that both Houses of Parliament are able or willing to codify the disparate elements that now make up our so-called constitution. People need to be protected from the excesses of Governments and Parliaments and as the trust and confidence of the public continues to decline, this has become more important and is a legitimate issue for the referendum. If there is a NO vote, this is probably more important for the Union and Scotland's continuing role in it.

For far too long the constitution has been the preserve of the politicians and the privileged. The legacy of our class-based culture, our deference to the establishment and the monarchy, our unquestioning embrace of tradition and our disinterest in a progressive thinking Europe marks us out as a Union of declining expectations, unable to escape the past and unwilling to face up to the challenges of a fast arriving future. A codified constitution would be a step forward in modernising all of the nations of the Union and equip us better to escape the worst excesses of ideology and party politics, putting the sovereignty of the citizen at the heart of our democracy. On subjects such as membership of the EU, the European Court of Human rights, Devolution and Federalism, a codified constitution would help place the rights of the citizen and the interests of the nation above sectional and narrow political interests to ensure a more rational outcome to the challenges that lie ahead.

The New British Constitution (2009) by Vernon Bogdanor is an essential read for anyone interested in constitutional matters. Contrasting the old constitution (largely resting on two classic texts) – *The English Constitution* (1867) by Walter Bagehot and *Introduction to the study of Law of the Constitution* (1889) by Albert Dicey – with the new series of constitutional changes introduced by the Blair Government, Bogdanor sets outs the arguments for and against a codified, written, single and accessible constitution in a single document. Bogdanor argues that the last 20 years have seen radical changes to the way we are governed. The Human Rights Act and devolution have led to the replacement of one constitutional order with another. We are moving towards a new constitution. This is happening, but with little intent or design on the part of our Legislators, as much of it is piecemeal and lacks the ambition to achieve a written or codified constitution. The new or emerging constitution emphasises the separation of powers, both territorially and at the centre of Government. So far so good, but one major problem remains: Westminster, at the heart of the Union, does not recognise the seismic impact that has taken place in regard to theses constitutional changes, partly because that was never the aim, but mainly because the idea of absolute Parliamentary sovereignty allows Britain to retain a ramshackle and largely self-serving uncodified constitution resulting in no power in the land being able to contest or undo the work of Westminster. The grip of history and power in the last 300 years has endured, despite the changing realities. This state of affairs has become a major obstacle to achieving a modern constitution, improving the quality of governance Britain and making sense of the major changes taking place in this country, including the consequences of devolution, which are now 15 years old. There are no constitutional safeguards for devolved governments and assemblies, because there is no constitution. Westminster is the sole arbiter of whether the Scottish Parliament can be abolished. Power devolved is power retained at Westminster. Absolute sovereignty is supreme. And the sovereignty of Parliament plays second fiddle to the sovereignty of the people. As yet these major changes have failed to make any serious or lasting impact on the way British Parliamentarians view their outdated and privileged existence at Westminster. The Independence referendum is a direct challenge to the complacency, orthodoxy, ambivalence and arrogance of the Westminster Parliament and a Union that is in decline.

The growing intensity of the justifiable demands for a different kind of Union reflects the more serious debate in Europe about sub-national government, the issues of nationality and identity and the deepening disillusionment with politics, especially traditional Unionist party politics in this country. There is no escaping the conclusion that this is largely a crisis of Westminster's making where Labour and the Conservatives, post-war, post-'70s and in particular post-devolution, have shared a common indifference to the plight and ambitions of the four Nations of the Union. Westminster is the major driving force behind the collapse of confidence in the Union and it may now be too late for MPs and the institution to adapt and transform. If there is a NO vote in September there may be a brief window of opportunity for Westminster to come to its senses, if not, the decline of the Union will continue and the prospect of creating a rUK or a Greater England will be a reality: the prospects are not encouraging as the post-war period in Westminster is littered with missed opportunities, miscalculations and an insane attachment to a centralised state nation which, up until 1999, would surrender no serious powers or responsibilities to any part of the United Kingdom. Grudging concessions have been the order of the day, but now a written, codified constitution and a Bill of Rights should be at the heart of the national debate after the referendum, whether Scotland is in or out of the Union.

In the spirit of James Carville, Clinton's election strategist, it is the Union, stupid! Constitutional reform is long overdue and is vital if stability, security and solidarity in these islands are to be achieved. Our unwritten constitution has for centuries been lauded, but there is now a clamour for change as the faultlines within the Union are exposed and strains and tensions grow.

The aim has to be to improve the quality of government. The reforms of the past 20 years do not of themselves secure a wider and more popular involvement in politics. The constitutional issues have remained the preserve of politicians, academics, think tanks and key institutions of the establishment. This has helped obscure the decline of the Union and ensured a very limited spotlight on the weaknesses that are so obvious today. In many respects the constitutional crisis has paralleled and in significant ways contributed to a political crisis in Britain where trust in many of our institutions is crumbling, confidence in our politics is fast diminishing, turnout in elections is declining, membership of political parties, especially the three traditional parties, is collapsing and people's expectations of our political system have never been lower. This is a crisis. There may have been a time where the trust of the people was taken for granted and used to buttress the notion of the absolute sovereignty of Parliament. The piecemeal constitutional reforms that have taken place need to be more effectively linked to the social, economic and political forces now at work in every part of the United Kingdom. It is hoped that the a new codified and written constitution will not reflect power stemming from the Queen in Parliament and Westminster sovereignty but instead, as in so many constitutions throughout the world, from the people – where the message from Abraham Lincoln's Gettysburg Address, 'of the people, for the people and by the people', becomes a reality and reinvigorates our democracy.

In *The New British Constitution* Bogdanor notes that, during the '60s, questions emerged about the adequacy of our constitution and institutions against a background of serious economic difficulties. Over recent decades much more importance has been attached to what up to then had been regarded as a subject too technical, abstract and of little relevance to the public. Nothing could have been further from the truth, he argues. We are now seeing the folly of leaving this to Westminster, with their inbuilt bias to a set of justifications as to why their sovereignty should remain sacrosanct while at the same time opposing and sometimes ridiculing voices of dissent that were aware of the damage this was causing. The Independence referendum is the most visible example of what can happen when an institution loses sight of its purpose and pretends in a changing world that all tomorrows just look like yesterday.

The great period of constitutional reform occurred after the election of Tony Blair's Labour Government in 1997. Each of the reforms were significant, but not conceived as part of a root and branch reform of the constitution: a codified or written constitution was never part of this task. Gordon Brown revisited this issue in the first year of his premiership, but nothing happened to the Green Paper he produced. He was keen to talk about a written and codified constitution, but his main focus was how Parliament could exercise more control over the Executive. This was also the time that Gordon Brown was trying to talk up Britishness. The wide-ranging reforms of the Blair era could hardly have been introduced had the British people been as satisfied with their institutions as previously.

One of the central themes of British history during the second half of the 20th century seems to be a striking loss of self-confidence, and this was reflected in a loss of confidence in our institutions and in our constitutional arrangements. Bogdanor lists in *The New British Constitution* the changes since 1997, which he describes as 'marked by an unprecedented and, almost certainly uncompleted series of constitutional changes':

- The Independence of the Bank of England from Government in monetary policy

- Referendums on Devolution to Scotland and Wales

- The Scotland Act, the Government of Wales Act, the Northern Ireland Act and the Greater London Authority referendum

- Completing the list are the Human Rights Act, the House of Lords Act, the Freedom of Information Act, the Political Parties, Elections and Referendum Act 2000 and the Constitutional Reform Act

A new constitution is in the process of being created, but because of its piecemeal nature the extent of change has not been recognised. The USA, where change is obvious and where they have a codified constitution, is in sharp contrast to Britain, where gradual evolution and adaptation have governed change.

Constitutional issues have not been high on most people's list of priorities. This is not surprising, as this has been reserved by the political and governing classes as their sole preserve, aided and abetted where necessary by the establishment.

For example, the constitutional agenda, controlled by Westminster and no one else, allows for:

- Most elections (except for the House of Commons) are by Proportional Representation – so why do we have a First Past the Post system for Westminster?

- Why was the referendum on the Alternative Vote such a disaster?

- Why is the House of Lords in its current form still in existence?

- Why has a bidding war of different devolution packages been created to keep Scotland in the Union when up till the referendum there has been very little interest shown by Westminster?

- Why is Westminster ignoring England except for some marginal and misguided changes around English votes for English laws?

- Why is such an important issue as the EU being used as a political play-thing of the populists and the Conservative right while the progressive parties at Westminster remain reasonably muffled?

- Why does the absolute sovereignty of Westminster continue to dominate our democracy when the constitutional realities of Britain in 2014 have passed it buy and have rendered it irrelevant to anyone other than MPs, successive governments and the institution itself?

- Why don't we have a UK in which shared sovereignty and shared power is the order of the day: power devolved is powered retained?

- Why is it that a Union and Parliament can be constitutionally careless enough to create the conditions in which the UK could leave the EU and Scotland could leave the Union?

These are only some of a huge number of WHY questions that remain unanswered because of a lack of a written, codified, accessible and intelligible constitution.

Scotland, post-devolution and especially in the last seven years, has blown away any pretence that our constitutional setup is fit for purpose and has exposed the faultlines that run through our declining Union. The referendum has brought into sharp focus that the Union of 1707 merely superimposed a structure on different nations and led to the incorporation of Scotland into an English Parliament (which became the British Parliament in 1801 when Ireland was added). There was no attempt at a blend or a mix, there was an accommodation and many historians are surprised that this Union has remained largely intact for such a long period of time.

Since 1997 we have been engaged in a process of constitutional reform. But how can we reform our constitution when we do not have one?

So what is the meaning of a Constitution? Bogdanor sets this out clearly. First, a seletion of the most important rules regulating the government and embodied in a document prepared at a moment in time, e.g. USA or France.

In this sense Britain has no constitution. We have no such document and therefore no framework within which to discuss the rules of Government and the rights of the individual.

Second, we most certainly possess a constitution – we are bound together by rules, and a constitution is nothing more than a collection of the most important rules prescribing the distribution of power between the institutions of government and between the individual and the state. There is no reason why these rules should be written down or brought together in one single document.

Many would say this is anachronistic and it is time the British fell into line and produced a codified constitution, which covers the rules regulating the system of government and the rules regulating the relationship between government and the individual, as well as the collection of rules regulating a country's system of government.

The pros and cons of a codified constitution are worth considering, because the whole idea of a modern and codified constitution has direct links to the issue of citizenship, how we are governed and allows us to make sense of Independence and federalism as ways forward.

Why does Britain not have a codified constitution?

First, lack of interest, but that is hardly surprising.

Second, reasons lie deep in our history, both to our evolution as a society and to the way we understand government.

Third, most codified constitutions had a new beginning: states attain their freedom. The state is constituted, as was the case in Italy and Germany. In Britain there has been no such obvious break in our constitutional development since the 17th century.

Fourth, centralising tendencies at Westminster – the idea of democratic centralism.

As Bogdanor states:

In 1707 the old English Parliament, located in Westminster, remained but the fundamental characteristics remain unchanged and the English felt no need for a new start or a new constitution. The constitution remains uncodified because there hasn't been a constitutional moment. The United Kingdom never began. It is hardly possible to fix a date at which England began a modern State. [There has been] no formal breach in the historical continuity of England since 1689.

It is precisely because there has been no sharp break in our constitutional history that, unlike almost every other democracy, we have felt neither the desire nor the need to enact a constitution.

What then are the reasons for having a codified constitution? It would help to regulate executive power whilst affording some security to rights. It would also hold an important educational and information function. This offers a single recognised source from which citizens can learn about how their State is supposed to operate. It raises the sovereignty of the people issue and, very importantly, defines freedoms.

The UK is more complex than in the past, with a far more diverse population with less trust in politicians, political parties and Parliament, which are seen as the sole arbitrator of constitutional matters. Stability, solidarity and social cohesion are less obvious than in the past. The three pillars of Monarch, House of Commons and House of Lords do not in any way describe the current structure of the British Constitution. Power and authority within the British state is no longer vested in Westminster. Absolute sovereignty is a myth.

The loosening links with the nations of the Union plus our multi-ethnic, multi-cultural society means a very different Britain, where rights and freedoms have to be more effectively and sensitively handled. Indeed, the constitution should be in the ownership of the people, not the peoples' representatives in the British Parliament:

> The disinterest reflects the realities over centuries where the constitution has been uneventful. But in addition to the historical reasons we do not have a codified constitution, there is also another reason.

This is because the only principle at the basis of our system of government has been the sovereignty of Parliament. We have no checks and balances on government and we do not have a Bill of Rights, a document laying out specific rights which the government cannot infringe – such as the separation of powers, federalism and the protection of human rights. These are all principles which serve to limit the power of the government.

Bogdanor concludes:

> It is partly for this reason that what once seemed attractive peculiarities no longer seem quite so attractive. It is partly for this reason that the old constitution has come under strain in recent years. Political developments in post-war Britain have persuaded many that it has outlived its usefulness.

Linda Colley, writing in the *Guardian* in 2011 in reference to the Blair constitutional changes, said:

> ... many of these changes have been rushed through without much effort to inform the public or encourage any serious debate. Little attempt to build consensus mainly because, unlike other countries, Westminster Parliament is the sole creator of the constitution, with no other organisation, institution or entity being able offer a higher level authority or oversight. It is almost as if the redesign of Britain's constitution were just another routine government activity, like updating the country's road or drainage systems.

> Of course that suits those who have a vested interest in minimising change, denying the importance of those measures on the life of citizens, ensuring they don't in any way upset the long serving structures of the State and also failing to recognise the importance of all of this to the way we are governed and how the Union operates... A closed shop for elites, the establishment, the political classes and all those who have a vested interest in the prevailing levers of power and influence in this country. The people of the UK have never had the chance to become interested in what is ostensibly done on their behalf.

Claims that 'ordinary' people are not interested in constitutional matters is plainly ridiculous, she adds, and an implausible defence against the Parliamentary prerogative on constitutional affairs and the reluctance of the establishment to present much of what happens as being of intrinsic interest to the people.

The UK appears increasingly disunited. Current strains within the UK make bold constitutional creativity and wider public knowledge more essential, not less. This calls out for Federalism.

Jonathan Friedland, writing in the *Guardian* 2008 said:

> The weakness of the House of Commons is that the system is wrong. The traditionalists prattle on about the sovereignty of Parliament. But it is fiction. We claim a belief in 'separation of powers', but that is bogus. In Britain the Executive and legislature are fused, the former sitting inside and dominating the latter. The government overshadows parliament utterly. Gordon Brown understands this. A convention much like the one that met in Scotland in the 1990s could draw up a written constitution setting out how we govern ourselves.

Again, and important for the Independence referendum debate, our ramshackle constitution has not only created the issue it is also unable to find solutions to problems because of the politics and ideological obsessions of the Conservative Party, reinforced by the politics of identity and nationality now gathering pace in England.

There is now a case for a larger, all-encompassing constitutional convention to look at the state of the Union and in a reasonable timescale offer a modern and relevant way forward.

Connor Gearty writing in the *Guardian* in 2013:

> The UK has no constitution. It has no constitution written down in one grand document. Rather its laws, conventions, practices, activities and conventions are scattered all over the place.
>
> Why has this happened? Britain never suffered the sort of defeat in war or other upheaval that produced a new constitution, nor has it had to free itself from colonial rule – it was always the coloniser. But most countries now have a written document that captures what a place is about and sets out how power is dispersed. Some of the gaping holes in our thoughts are specifically constitutional: what should we do about the EU? About immigrants? Does the House of Lords make any sense? Who are we anyway? The House of Commons led by any Government is not up to the task of deciding on the big issues of the day. The unwritten constitution is shredded. First, membership of the EU, second by creation of Scottish Parliament, Third by the Human Rights Act. People who passed these laws have denied their transformative status. The old constitution is over. Our democratic will has been shaped to the convenience of multinational corporations, financiers and Europe. The piecemeal breakup of the UK has created a litany of contradictions. Our electoral system cannot reflect public opinion. Our upper house has become less aristocratic but no more democratic. Human migration has shattered assumptions of national identity and shared culture.
>
> It is remarkable that our political classes have not woken up to the fact that change is needed. The process itself could lead to the rebirth of passion and politics, realign our political tribes and conceivably lead to a new sense of British identity and unity.

The Democratic Audit said that there is a great deal of evidence to suggest a written constitution is necessary and would be popular. The reasons are straightforward enough. Who does it serve? Party politicians who hold office. An unchecked executive. An unrepresentative electoral system. A privileged and exclusive elite. The impoverishment of local government. Devolved government, tolerated rather loved. Popular feelings of Parliamentarians are ignored and manifestos are forgotten, raising the question of whether they are now irrelevant with people wanting an informed and inspired narrative instead, and governments, with a few minor exceptions, get their way. The political classes bemoan Britain's apathetic electorate, while the right-wing press seeks to make the electorate angry, fearful, anxious and scared, certainly not encouraging them to vote and take democracy more seriously.

Carwyn Jones, First Minister of Wales, argues that we need:

> ... a convention to debate and build a new constitutional settlement for the UK. In Whitehall devolution has for far too long been viewed as a sideshow, a distraction. Old certainties are being shaken by the Independence referendum. New upper house with representation from the devolved areas. A more federal structure. After a decade of devolution there is an unwillingness to accept that difference exists and it represents a strength, not a weakness.

Devolution posed real constitutional problems. Was this a genuine halfway house between the Unitary state on the one hand and Federalism and Independence on the other? Could devolution really hope to settle the aspiration of the Scots and Welsh, or would it become a slippery slope? Was it compatible with the doctrine of Parliamentary sovereignty?

Labour failed to understand the enormity of devolution and made serious miscalculations for a party that was at best ambivalent about a new way of governing Britain. Unaware of the constitutional nightmare this would advance, they were so preoccupied with the SNP that they failed to realise that what was needed was a political response to deal with the SNP – for that, Labour in Scotland needed to reinvent itself – and not a constitutional one, which Labour was so ill-equipped to deal with. This is a very important point. Consistently the Labour party has failed to appreciate that what was required in Scotland was a political response to the SNP, not necessarily a constitutional one. So what has happened is that we now have a constitutional response, which most people think is inadequate, but we still have no political response. A case of confronting the question with the wrong answer! This is likely to keep happening until there is better understanding by the Unionist parties of what is really happening in Scotland.

Elliot Bulmer, writing in the *Guardian* 2014, talks about the Scottish constitution and shows what the UK is missing:

> With popular sovereignty at its core, Scotland's draft constitution offers a mature, democratic contrast to Downing Street's obsessions.

> 'In Scotland, the people are sovereign.' This is the foundation of the interim constitution that has been published in a draft bill by the Scottish Government. In the event of a YES vote, this would provide the basis for the Scottish state during the first years of Independence, pending the adoption of a permanent constitution some time after 2016.

> A newly Independent state would need a written constitution to define itself, to reassure its citizens, to constrain its politicians, and to be taken seriously around the world.

> At a time when the UK Government is celebrating Magna Carta and trying to enforce 'British values' in schools; when the British establishment seems incapable of reforming either the electoral system or the House of Lords; and when even the moderate gains of the Human Rights Act are under threat – the Scottish Government presents a more mature, principled and democratic constitutional settlement, with the sovereignty of the people at its core.

> The interim constitution offers an Independent Scotland a different future from that available in the UK: one where the people are acknowledged as the source of public power. A provision preventing laws changing the constitution from being enacted – unless endorsed either by a super-majority of parliament or by a referendum – would do much to help this interim constitution live up to these exciting promises.

In *The New British Constitution* Bogdanor argues that constitutions are more than moving the institutional furniture – they are concerned with the grandest and most important issues, such as the conditions of the political order, the relationships between the individual and the state and the methods by which men and women are ruled:

> We are now though in a transition from a system based on Parliamentary sovereignty to one based on the sovereignty of a constitution that is inchoate, indistinct and still largely uncodified. There is much further to go, but we are gradually moving to a constitutional sate not based on Parliamentary sovereignty but based upon popular sovereignty – the sovereignty of the people. We have a changing constitution.

In an Independent Scotland, there will be a written and codified constitution. The Union is likely to remain with the ramshackle version that it has got by on for centuries. This will continue to generate massive uncertainties, and as the absolute sovereignty of the Westminster remains unchanged, in the minds at least of the members of both Houses of Parliament, then there can be no sharing of power, no pooling of sovereignty and no concessions to the sovereignty of the people. This looks like an insane future where, all the political and constitutional problems of the Union are swept under the carpet and the business as usual notice remains firmly stuck on the doors of both chambers of the Westminster Parliament. For the nations of the Union this makes no sense, including England, and this constitutional obstinacy would ensure that minimalist concessions would be the order of the day. Westminster is and will continue to be a block on the modernisation and renewal of Britain's constitution.

CHAPTER FOUR

England, the Elephant in the Room

THERE IS NO DOUBT that the place of England within the United Kingdom is the great unresolved question in the current political and constitutional debate. England remains the elephant in the room. Despite the fact that the people of England are making their views known in variety of ways – the rise of populism politics, the success of UKIP a new and largely English Independence Party, the decline of Britishness, the rise of Englishness, a growing sense of grudge and grievance about the Scottish devolution settlement, a growing disillusionment about Westminster adequately representing their interests and a deepening anti-European sentiment – there is no serious understanding or acceptance of the issues at Westminster and no urgency about the likely impact this could have on the future of the Union and the outcome of the Independence referendum. Scots may feel troubled about these unsettling trends and what kind of unpredictable neighbour England could become. This could impact on the political sentiment surrounding the Independence referendum. Why this is happening can best be explained by the failure of Westminster, over many decades, to recognise that the way we are governed has to be constantly renewed and if for any reason we ignore or neglect the changing needs and aspirations of any of the nations and their perceived role in the Union, we risk undermining social cohesion, solidarity and stability and put at risk any idea of a shared sense of the future. This is the UK today! The Union is on the move but at Westminster our political parties, politicians and the institution itself are stuck in the past and regardless of whether Scotland votes YES or NO, there is a danger that the constitutional integrity of the Union will continue to decline. We ignore at our peril neglecting the England question.

It is typical of the British way that we have viewed the constitutional question through the narrow prism of Scotland's devolution journey instead of accepting from the start that that the future governance of England and its role in the Union require equal consideration. We may regret this miscalculation.

England, Englishness and the Scottish Referendum are inextricably linked and, directly or indirectly, the views, concerns and behaviour of the largest nation in the Union will help shape how Scots vote and also have enormous influence on the post-referendum debate, regardless of the outcome.

This chapter considers the England question and draws on the work of, first, *The UK's Changing Union*, a series of collaborative forums, Wales Governance Centre, Cardiff University and involving Edinburgh University. Second, the work of the Institute for Public Policy Research (IPPR), including *The Dog that finally Barked: England as an Emerging Political Community* and *England and its Two Unions: The Anatomy of a Nation and Its Discontents*. Third, the insights of Linda Colley, Professor of History at Princeton University and author of *Britons: Forging the Nation 1707–1837* and *Acts of Union and Disunion*. Fourth, Michael Kenny, Professor of Politics at Queen Mary, University of London and his work with The Future of the UK and Scotland project and the IPPR.

Unionist parties neglect England

The neglect of England seems all the more remarkable when we consider the excellent work being done by the academic community and think tanks, whose work has been influenced by very extensive survey work, Census findings and the British Social Attitudes Survey.

Michael Kenny poses the question: 'What kind of impact is the Scottish referendum having on public opinion in England? And might the English end up having a role to play in its outcome?' There has been little public debate on these questions, but this partly reflects the narrow parameters defined by the Yes and No Campaigns and the concentration on an in or out result, which hardly invites a broader look at history, a deeper context and a wider understanding of the issues or what a NO vote could actually mean in the absence of a second question on the ballot paper.

A Changing mood

This gathering mood of isolationism, insularity and scepticism, identified by Michael Kenny as underpinning contemporary English attitudes in relation to Europe, was also being reflected in a heightened level of dissatisfaction with the domestic Union. Surveys conducted by the Future of England team in 2011 and 2012 showed the West Lothian Question was unjustifiable, that England was losing out in financial terms due to the higher levels of expenditure in Scotland. Reinforcing these central concerns, Linda Colley in her article 'Linda Colley on Englishness' adds some historical perspective:

> [People are concerned] over the meaning of Englishness, the claims that the Scots are getting too much money from the public purse [and] fear that continental Europe is taking advantage of Britain. You can look at London newspapers in the 1760s and they are making many of these same arguments and accusations. Similarly if you look at the end of the 19th and the beginning of the 20th centuries, there were lots of calls then for England to be granted home rule, as well as Scotland, Wales and Ireland.

Colley also suggests the England and Scotland dimensions are part of a weakening and declining Union, where purpose and cohesion are missing and there is no overarching narrative uniting the nations:

> ... to be an effective state – a State Nation, which I think the UK is, you need not just economic wellbeing but also constitutive stories. The rise of nationalism in Scotland is not just explicable in terms of internal Scottish factors, but it also in part a ramification of a decline in and insufficient attention to British constitutive stories, because a State Nation has to work on several levels. Its leaders need to look after the component stateless nations within their brief, but also sustain some kind of overarching narrative. It seems to me that an overarching narrative at the moment is not really there and politicians have arguably been rather remiss in this respect.

This lies at the heart of the Better Together Campaign, which to all intent and purposes is about rescuing the Union, not rejuvenating it. There is no narrative, and in consequence, there are fewer threads linking the nations of the Union, the idea of Britishness is rapidly declining, especially in England and, like Scotland, there is a diminishing sense of obligation, loyalty and allegiance to the Union.

Englishness on the rise

England is being challenged on a number of political and constitutional fronts, which could have an impact on the Independence referendum and an enduring impact on the stability and credibility of the Union afterwards. First, its relationship with the EU is under severe strain and surveys suggest that public opinion in England is much more anti-Europe than in Scotland. The issue arises of whether an in or out referendum being planned for 2017, conditional on the Conservatives winning the next election, could result in Britain leaving the EU on the back of English votes with Scotland voting to remain. The volatile nature of English politics, the rise of the right, a new UKIP-led populism and the uncertainty about Labour winning power in the General Election of 2015, and indeed whether as a party they sign up to this ill-conceived idea of a referendum, will create uncertainty in the minds of Scots: few Scots in September want to vote NO thinking it might be a YES to leaving the European Union!

The Blair Reforms

Second, while the Blair constitutional reforms were designed to devolve power and acknowledge the right of Wales, Scotland and Northern Ireland to a limited right of self-determination, England was completely ignored then and has been for much of the post-devolution period. Being cynical, many people felt the British Parliament was indeed the English Parliament, with the vast majority of MPs from English seats. There was a feeling that England had no interest in regionalism or any other form of sub-national government or a Parliament.

Who are we?

This is the core of the political danger to Scotland. England is a nation without any consensus or minimal agreement about its future and no answers to the questions: Who are we? Where are we? What do we want? Where are we going? It is a nation fast becoming angry with the present, but no idea about the future. Third, throughout Europe we are seeing the rise of the far right, the conservative right and populism, and, to a lesser extent, the far left in countries such as in Greece. Where there is a political vacuum populism will rise to fill the political space. As far as the traditional UK parties are concerned, the public are disillusioned and disconnected and England and the English feel more than most let down by conventional politics and political parties. UKIP and the Conservative right are fast becoming an outlet for English frustration, self-doubt and, although rarely discussed, the possible long-term realignment of British but mainly English politics.

Threat to the Union and Scotland

The danger for the rest of the UK is obvious. A volatile set of politics and the breaking down of political loyalties and allegiances in England based on socioeconomic class could lead to more coalitions of the right – unless progressive elements within the Lib-Dems join Labour and form a broader social democratic alliance – which could result in a further alienation of Scotland and Wales as England slides from a progressive social democratic agenda. Scotland's nearest neighbour could begin to like the US instead of Germany. This is a scary prospect and could certainly influence Scots in September. These are issues which raise the questions: What kind of Scotland do I want to live in? What kind of Union do I want to live in? Are the two compatible?

Michael Kenny argues in his article 'England, Englishness and the Scottish Referendum' that while the arrival of UKIP has sharpened issues of nationality, identity and Englishness, these sentiments have grown from the mid-'90s and an increased sense of English national consciousness has been 'dramatised and exacerbated' in the post-devolution period. Britishness still exists, but English nationhood has become much more real and sharpens the distinction between England and a wider set of Union institutions and values. The Census in 2011 confirmed a very significant shift in national identity when people in England were asked to select their own preferred national identity for the first time: 70 per cent opted to identify as English compared with 29 per cent British.

Future elections

This shifting pattern of national consciousness could be a factor in the Independence referendum, as well as influencing Scotland's constitutional role in the future, especially in the context of the Westminster and Holyrood elections in 2015 and 2016. Michael Kenny puts the importance of this in two ways:

> First, it is clear that a large number of Conservative MPs are highly attuned to the sensibilities of their English constituents and the threat posed by UKIP's increasingly Anglo-nationalist tunes. Some are clearly prepared to vote against the government on touchstone issues such as the European Union... Tory MPs will not hesitate to express the dissatisfaction felt by

their constituents with the Union and Scotland's perceived advantage within it... Second, should Holyrood receive additional powers following a NO vote, there is every prospect that Conservative MPs will be prepared to revisit the implications of the extraordinarily lopsided nature of the post-devolved Union, which leaves England as the only national territory managed by Whitehall and the UK's Parliament.

This would once again focus the minds of Conservative MPs on the 'West Lothian Question' which then became 'English votes for English laws' and was then the subject of the Mckay Commission, which has now reported and is likely to result in a watered down version being put in place after the 2015 Westminster election.

Labour Thinking

On all of these constitutional issues, and in particular the re-emergence of England and Englishness as powerful influences on both the future of the Union and outcome of the Independence referendum, there has been a deafening silence from the UK Labour Party. Policy papers, pre-manifesto discussions, press releases, leadership and shadow ministerial speeches and general commentary from the party have made little reference to the burning constitutional issues of the day. Observers could be forgiven for thinking that Labour's reluctance to engage is reflective of a party singularly ill at ease when talking about constitutional or devolved matters; worried about the edgy politics of Scotland and Wales in a declining but still incredibly centralised Union; reluctant to talk about sharing power with four the nations where the myth of the absolute sovereignty of Westminster prevents any real progress in that direction; obssessed with localism rather than devolution, serving as it does the party's power base in the big cities and metropolitan areas of England. Or is it because talking about localism is safer and keeps debate within the comfort zone of our early history rather than venturing into areas of national identity and legitimate differences between nations and regions of the Union?

Despite repeated political setbacks in Scotland and the rise of UKIP in England, Labour seems heavy-footed and ill at ease in the post-devolution world. The civic nationalism of the Yes Campaign in Scotland is fusing national identity with wider political aims and this is what makes it such a threat to conventional politics. Whatever the reasons for Labour's reluc-

tance to engage, it is likely to be costly and could have significant conse-
quences for Scotland, England and the constitutional integrity of all of the
Union as we move into a new political landscape. The results of every
General Election in the post-war period should be a wakeup call for
Labour. The Westminster Election in 2010 delivered 41 Labour MPs from
Scotland and in the period from 1959 to the present time the number has
never been less than 40! Of the Labour Parliamentary Party at Westminster in 2010, over 20 per cent were Scottish Labour MPs, despite the fact
that Scotland has only 10 per cent of the population!

EU *Referendum*

The prospect of an EU Referendum in 2017 is the other area where the
mood of England will play an important role in Scotland's constitutional
future. There is now compelling evidence to suggest that Scots are more
comfortable with EU membership than the English, are more likely to
want to retain membership in the event of an in/out referendum and
would view the prospects of a potential exit from the EU on the back of
English votes as a matter of significance. This could influence Scots in
whether they stay within the UK in the Independence referendum and if
there is a NO vote this may be an issue at a later date. This is an important
issue, and one that David Cameron may come to regret.

The idea of a EU referendum being held in 2017 may be popular with
English voters, may keep in check the 100 or so extremists and anti-European MPs in his own party and stem the flow of disillusioned Tory
voters to UKIP, but this piece of ill-conceived and irresponsible opportunism could result in Scots saying YES in September to exit the UK as the
best way of ensuring Scotland remains in the EU. Scots could say NO in
September hoping that the EU referendum will be scrapped, or if not, the
UK votes to remain a member in 2017. If the UK decides to exit and if
Scotland votes to stay in, then the whole issue of leaving the UK will be
reignited, and who knows where that will lead. However this issue is
looked at it will remain as a symbol of reckless political behaviour, putting
at risk Scotland's membership of the United Kingdom and Britain's
membership of the EU. It is hard to imagine what a constitutional nightmare this might be, creating division, uncertainty and accelerating the
further decline of the Union of Great Britain and Northern Ireland. The

European issue could haunt the Unionist parties for the next three years, well beyond the forthcoming referendum.

The Rise of the Right

Recent surveys suggest that there is a strong correlation between Englishness, nationhood and support for parties of the right. The Future of England Survey leads Michael Kenny to conclude that:

> ... the discernible drift towards a stronger sense of attachment to Englishness appears to be draining support from the various forms of multi-national cooperation and involvement which the British state has tended to favour. As such the further development and political appropriation of Englishness may well become a factor in the political and constitutional futures of Scotland and the UK.

A Troubled Country

What is emerging is an unsettled and politically troubled England exhibiting a serious lack of trust in political institutions and traditional political parties. Reinforcing this sense of disconnect is the remarkable lack of urgency, interest or understanding being shown by the Conservative and Labour Parties. Even if you factor in different reasons, excuses and difficulties to explain this collective ambivalence at Westminster, it is impossible to escape the conclusion that we are witnessing the decline of the old parties and the old party system as well as the decline of the Union in an era where conventional politics and antiquated mindsets are not fit for new purposes. England is fast becoming a major threat to the Union, Scotland's continuing role in it and the UK's membership of the European Union.

While all of this is unfolding, the Conservative Government at Westminster is indulging in distraction therapy as England in particular is being asked to ignore the real challenges facing the UK and instead be sidetracked by immigrants, welfare cheats, trade unionists, foreign judges of the European Court of Human Rights and European Union bureaucrats. This 'let them eat political cake' approach – or let us find suitable scapegoats for our current ills – to explaining the long-term decline in Britain's fortunes is both dangerous and divisive.

Recent research has captured the mood of England and the extent to which public attitudes in England are changing in relation to national identity, how England is governed within the UK, devolution, and the European Union. Professor Roger Scully from the Wales Governance Centre at Cardiff University summarised the most important findings of this work – two reports prepared by the IPPR – in his paper *The Seven Pillars of Englishness*, presented to a recent meeting of the UK's Changing Union Forum.

First, Englishness is now the dominant national identity in England.

For England, there has long been the view that most people make little distinction between Englishness and Britishness. The IPPR reports offered a very different picture. Compared with previous studies, they showed much higher levels of English identity. The dominance of English identity was confirmed in the 2011 Census, when for the first time a question was asked about national identity. Englishness was the most widely affirmed identity: English Only at 60 per cent, English and British at eight per cent and British Only at 19 per cent. Another important aspect of the IPPR reports and the Census was the relative uniformity of the findings both geographically and socially across England, except for London, where the Census returns failed to affirm an exclusively English national identity.

Second, there is a substantial unhappiness in England about how it is governed within the UK.

The two surveys underpinning the IPPR reports asked questions about the Governance of England within the UK. The most substantial constitutional preferences in the responses were:

- England should be governed as it is now with laws made by all MPs in the UK Parliament, 21 percent

- England should be governed with laws solely made by English MPs in the UK Parliament, 33 per cent

- England should have its own new English Parliament with law making powers, 18 per cent.

There is a high level of support for an English dimension to constitutional arrangements. 'What appears to be desired is recognition of England as England', was Professor Scully's conclusion, based on the findings of a previous IPPR report, which indicated only eight per cent of English people were interested in the idea of English regionalism with assemblies. There were two further points of interest. First, when the status quo constitutional option was tested against the English Parliament and English MPs at Westminster dealing with English laws, it could only generate 25 per cent support. The second point concerns the salience of constitutional issues, and in particular discontent. When asked to indicate which issues were the most important the following responses were given:

- The UK's relationship with the European Union, 59 per cent

- How England is governed now Scotland has a parliament and Wales an Assembly, 42 per cent

- Scotland's future relationship with the UK, 25 per cent.

The status of England again seems to be the dominant theme.

Third, there is a substantial (and growing) unhappiness in England about devolution. Early research on devolution showed people in England to be indifferent to devolution and its consequences. More recent evidence suggests that has changed and there is a growing perception that Scotland in particular is being unfairly advantaged by current financial arrangements. An absolute majority of all respondents – 52 per cent – in the 2012 survey agreed that: 'Scotland gets more than its fair share of public spending.' Considerable discontent is also being expressed about the current constitutional arrangements. In the 2012 survey, nearly 80 per cent of respondents agreed that 'The Scottish parliament should pay for services in Scotland from its own taxes' and nearly 80 per cent agreed with the statement that 'Scottish MPs should no longer be allowed to vote on English laws.' Again there is the clear message that for devolution and for the status of England, the status quo is not acceptable.

Fourth, English identity is closely linked to constitutional attitudes and discontent. An important finding to emerge from the two IPPR reports is that English identity is not just becoming more important, it is also becoming more politically relevant and increasingly connected to constitutional attitudes. English identity has a strong relationship with attitudes towards the status of England within the EU and towards devolution. Professor Scully concludes that:

> Among those who affirm a British not English or a more British than English national identity, the constitutional status quo is the most preferred option ahead of English votes for English Laws in Westminster; and English Parliament; or independence for England. Among those stating their national identity to be English not British or More English than British, by contrast the status quo is only the fourth most preferred option.

The findings for devolution are very similar. The more English a national identity someone affirms, the more likely they are to agree that Scotland gets more than its fair share of public expenditure, that the Scottish Parliament should pay for services in Scotland from its own taxes, and that Scotland should no longer vote on English laws. These findings are totally at odds with the publicly held views of the two major traditional Unionist parties at Westminster. During the referendum campaign in Scotland, Better Together neither talks about these issues nor seeks to acknowledge their existence. None of the Unionist parties are putting forward a post-referendum devolution package as radical as the people of England appear to want. Indeed, in the anticipation of a NO vote, the bidding war on more tax powers falls way short of English expectations!

Fifth, Englishness is also connected to attitudes to the EU.

The most recent IPPR reports presents some dramatic findings on the extent to which there is a relationship between English identity and related attitudes, such as towards England's place in the UK and towards devolution and the EU. It seems that public views towards Unions, the UK and the EU are much more closely connected than has been realised in the past. 'The same people who are most discontented with the constitutional status quo in England are also those who are most discontented with the UK's relationship with the EU.' The extent of hostility to the EU in England is clear and dramatic. The 2012 survey also found hostility to the EU to be 'an overwhelmingly English phenomenon, not a British one'. Those affirming an English identity were much more likely to show antagonism to the EU, while the main supporters of the EU and the UK's membership of it tended to be among those with a more British identity. This is significant for any future referendum on EU membership. In England, those with British identity would vote to stay in the Union, while those with an exclusively English identity would oppose continued membership by about four to one. English identity linked to constitutional discontent and UKIP (read EIP, English Independence Party) could be the basis on which the UK could leave the EU. Where does this leave Scots now, and in the future if there is a NO vote? Can England be brought round to embrace more positively the EU? Or are we destined for constitutional chaos over the next few years?

Sixth, ethnicity is strongly related to English identity and related attitudes. Black and Minority Ethnic (BME) respondents to the surveys were substantially more likely to affirm an exclusively or mainly British identity than white respondents. They were also less likely than white respondents to support 'English' constitutional options, less likely to see the issue of England as requiring urgent attention, show less hostility to devolution and were also less Euro-sceptic and less likely to support the UK leaving the EU.

Seventh, UKIP is the party of England, not Britain. There is a close relationship between support for UKIP and English – rather than British –identity in England. The surveys show that the majority of UKIP supporters in England identify as exclusively or mainly English. In conclusion, the article states that 'Rather than prompting a resurgence of Britishness, UKIP's rise may be understood as feeding off the confluence of specifically English resentments.'

The Threat of the seven pillars

Overall, the 'Seven Pillars of Englishness' paper provides a concise summary and penetrating analysis of the political and constitutional mood of 'modern' England and its very English identity. This is a nation ill at ease with its place in the world and anxious about its relationship with the EU, the UK and the current operation of devolution and, in particular, Scotland. England is less wrapped up in a positive embrace of a new vision as to where to go, and more caught up in a mood of grudge and grievance and a rapidly deteriorating relationship with the old political parties. In the eyes of the English, Westminster is failing England, and if nothing is done to arrest this profound sense of disappointment and disillusionment then the largest nation in the UK could create further tremors of unrest ,which could result in more populism, more UKIP, a stronger and more isolated London, a Wales demanding more responsibilities and identity, a worsening north-south divide and a UK without Scotland and without EU membership. This clear English identity seems to be emerging as the dominant sense of nationality within most of England. But that rising Englishness is now strongly associated with discontent, and as the article suggests, 'with how England is currently not recognised within the UK; with how devolution apparently favours the other nations of the UK; and with the relationship with England's other union, the EU'. What is worrying is that English identity is very strongly associated with the political right. The left is strangely silent at a time when there is growing risk to the Union. Unless political and constitutional solutions can be found soon or a start made to addressing obvious problems, then a certain level of political and constitutional chaos will prevail. Scotland has a choice. Should it say YES and sidestep much of this UK-inflicted constitutional harm and Westminster paralysis? Does Scotland vote NO in the hope that the Union will come to its senses and embark on reversing the slide of the UK and providing a more sensible role for England in any future settlement or in a new Treaty of the Union as part of a codified and written constitution? Or should we not accept that in or out of the UK, our coexistence with all the nations on these islands will still require a wholesale transformation of the way we and they are governed?

Westminster Still Asleep

The response of Westminster and the traditional political parties over the post-war period or even the post-devolution period to a wide range of constitutional challenges has not been encouraging. These are obviously very difficult issues for political parties schooled in democratic collective centralism, an obsession with the sovereignty of Westminster and a characteristically British dismissal of well-tried subnational governance models in Europe. The fact that the UK, along with New Zealand and Israel, is one of the only three countries in the world that does not have a codified written constitution, speaks volumes as to why we are in emerging chaos. The Union and Westminster have never taken seriously the way the United Kingdom is governed and have shown little interest in constitutional matters: instead we have merely stumbled on and are now paying a heavy price for our disinterest. These sentiments are captured in the final comments of the IPPR report, *The Dog That Finally Barked: England as an Emerging Political Community*:

> It would seem, therefore, that after many years in which prophecies of an English awakening appeared more a case of wishful thinking (or scaremongering), a stirring is finally in evidence. After centuries of being subsumed within the wider state, England is re-emerging as a political community. This is not simply as an unintended consequence of devolution, but it is a development – even a political project that enjoys significant levels of popular support in a country that appears to be increasingly conscious of a distinct national identity that is not simply irreducible to Britain and Britishness. More significantly, perhaps, the strengthening and politicisa-

tion of English identity is taking place in the absence of any formal political mobilisation. Englishness, in other words, has a momentum of its own... However important the Scottish debate is, it must not be allowed to distract attention from a meaningful public conversation about the future of the shape of English Governance. Standing in the way of such a conversation is a British political class which has failed to engage seriously with the changing attitudes.

A very different England

There is no doubt we have a very different England at the centre of the political and constitutional future of the Union. What is clear is that the politics of England are changing and are likely to change further if the rise of UKIP, more extremism in the Conservative Party and the rise of the right continue to take a hold in certain parts of the country. It is a measure of how political and constitutional changes at Westminster have never been seen as part of a strategy for better governance for all of the Union. England has been neglected. So in the absence of any concern about England's role in devolution, the English may be looking to political change rather a practical constitutional way forward. This might in turn encourage the English regions to seek more powers and responsibilities. Nobody is contemplating a Parliament for England at this stage, but some form of federalism, which may be the only way to keep the Union together. In the immediate future, the frustrations and grievances of the English have no positive outlet and as such this could pose a threat to further devolution if there is a NO vote in September. Indeed, polls suggest a degree of ambivalence about Scotland being Independent. The Conservative right and UKIP are not supporters of devolution and are classical centralists of the worst possible kind. Westminster has failed England in the mistaken notion that England and Westminster were interchangeable in the context of describing the United Kingdom. This would make sense in terms of the rise of UKIP and its role as a lightning rod for grudge politics that do not require any policy outcomes. UKIP is a responsibility-free zone. But as Scots vote in the referendum, they should be aware that their southern neighbour has moved from ambivalence on devolution to irritation, then anger and possibly hostility in the years ahead. In addition, England does not figure in the thinking of the major parties in constitutional terms, but only in regard to pursuing a watered down version of the McKay Commission, which has now reported to Westminster on the 'English votes for English Laws' issues. English votes for most things may become common practice. The English story is only beginning.

CHAPTER FIVE

The Question of Europe

THERE IS NO disguising the fact that many Conservative MPs and the UKIP leadership despise the European Union, the European Court of Human Rights and the European Convention. For the populists and the right of the Tory Party, at least on the surface, this is a struggle to protect our national interest and the absolute sovereignty of the Westminster Parliament. But this is far from the truth. What we have is a political façade which masks the true intent and real reasons why the nation is being subjected to a comprehensive and increasingly hysterical attack on some of the most successful international organisations and institutions in European history:

- Delusions about our history and militarism
- A yearning for the days of empire
- Nostalgia about the time when Britain did rule the waves
- Too many wars with the French
- A dislike of continental Europe
- An abhorrence of the environmental, social and employment regulations which protect Britain at times of Tory Governments
- A menacing approach to foreigners and immigrants
- An over-reliance on the special relationship with the US, where President Obama has now many special relationships
- An ongoing commitment to Atlanticism
- A post-war ambivalence to the great European project outlined in Churchill's famous speech in Zurich in 1946, when he wished Europe well but would remain, like Russia and America, a cheerleader on the side lines.

All of this adds up to the Conservative Party and UKIP perpetrating a fraud on the people of the United Kingdom. There are clearly dangers in this for the future of the economy, the environment, industry and social policy of the UK, but there is also a more immediate threat looming in the Independence referendum and what is likely to happen, regardless of the outcome. Scots are now more in tune with the idea of Europe than their English counterparts and the views of the Conservative right and UKIP. Scots voting NO will have at the back of their minds the prospect that staying in the Union of the United Kingdom may mean the end of EU membership in 2017 on the back of England, the Conservative party, UKIP and English votes. What is equally alarming is the right-wing suggestion that we remove ourselves from the jurisdiction of the European Court of Human Rights and the European Convention, which in turn may cast doubt on our membership of the Council of Europe, an organisation that includes every European country except Belarus and Kazakhstan. This chapter outlines the issues involved and highlights the uncertainties posed not only to the immediate referendum vote but also to the credibility, stability and attractiveness of the Union in the future.

European Court of Human Rights

In a 2013 article in *The Guardian*, Jon Henley asks, 'Why is the European court of human rights hated by the UK right?'

> That is why we are here, says the lawyer to the judges behind the bench at the European court

> Conservative MPs have said it is high time for Britain to 'quit the jurisdiction' of a 'supranational quango'. The Justice Secretary, Chris Grayling, is 'reviewing Britain's relationship' with an institution he says has 'reached the point where it has lost democratic acceptability'.

> David Cameron has said the court risks becoming a glorified 'small claims court', buried under a mountain of 'trivial' claims, and suggested Britain could withdraw from the convention to 'keep our country safe'. The Home Secretary, Theresa May, has pledged the Party's next manifesto will promise to scrap the Human Rights Act, which makes the convention enforceable in Britain.

> Former Lord Chief justice, Lord Judges and three other senior British judges have recently backed this stance in high-profile lectures, arguing that by treating the convention as a 'living instrument' the ECHR is 'undermining democracy'. Its judges, rather than Parliament, are now making British law, they allege, and Parliamentary sovereignty should not be ceded to 'a foreign court'. The shadow of the absolute sovereignty of the Westminster

Parliament remains the greatest constraint on progressive modern thinking on the constitution or any other form of political renewal in the United Kingdom.

Parts of the press, especially the right-leaning newspapers, have been more outspoken, arguing against 'meddling, unelected European judges' who are 'wrecking British law' and demanding the Government 'draw a line in the sand to defend British sovereignty' by 'defying Europe … and ignoring the rulings of this foreign court', the article noted.

Out of the Ashes

In a common sense defence of the ECHR, the point Henley is making is that there is no real legal or moral reasons for the UK to contemplate turning its back on one of the successes of post-war Europe. History becomes important at this point, the Council of Europe and the ECHR were set up in post-war Europe to help build a more secure, stable and fair continent where the devastation and destruction of previous wars would not be repeated. This is a very noble sentiment as well as being fundamentally practical in its deliberations and pronouncements. Henley continues by giving examples of what the ECHR has achieved in the past decade:

> The court has required Bulgaria to care properly for people with mental and physical disabilities and Austria to allow same-sex couples to adopt each other's children. It has forced Cyprus to take action against sex trafficking and Moldova to halt state censorship of TV. Its judgments have compelled improvements in Russian prisons, and more effective punishment of domestic violence in Turkey.
>
> In France, laws have been passed to protect domestic servants from forced labour, while illegitimate children now have equal rights to inheritance. Britain has been obliged to take greater care of vulnerable prisoners, regulate the monitoring of employees' communications, protect the anonymity of journalists' sources, bring the age of consent for gay people in line with that for heterosexuals and force local councils to observe proper safeguards in evictions.

Despite the success and the benefits flowing to this country from Strasburg, we are now in danger of being caught up in a new period of isolationism where the Conservative right and the populist leadership in the UK are waging a ridiculous war against 60 years of social progress and the institutions that have delivered this. The Conservative Party is now planning to repeal the Human Rights Act, abandon the jurisdiction of the ECHR, exit the European Convention and risk being thrown out of the Council of Europe. This poses another challenge to Scotland and the future of the Union. Again, we might face the prospect of a Conservative manifesto pursuing isolationism and threatening to confine to the dustbin of history the solid achievement and progressive morals and ethics of great institutions. Our idea of internationalism is shrinking under the Conservatives and UKIP as they pursue ideology and a very basic form of nationalism.

The Issue for the referendum

David Cameron is actively advocating this approach and seems certain to have policies worked out for the next election. For Scots voting in the referendum there will be a choice of where the Union could move after the next General Election in 2015 and what this would mean for Scotland in the event of a NO vote.

The narrow thinking involved in all of this is frightening and only serves to illustrate David Cameron's efforts to damage the long-term interests of the UK, including Scotland, for short-term political gain.

Evidence of David Cameron's opportunism and commitment to these ideas was provided in the recent Cabinet reshuffle, when his senior law officer was sacked because he didn't agree with Conservative thinking on this issue. This is what Dominic Grieve told a Parliamentary committee before he was sacked as Attorney General in the reshuffle:

> It seems to me that one has to think very carefully about what the consequences are in deciding that you can cherry-pick the obligations that you are going to accept... Whilst it may be perfectly possible to disregard them you are creating a degree of anarchy in the international order that you are trying to promote.

In recent weeks the Prime Minister was presented with a plan by a group of Conservative lawyers. It proposes a new law, which would assert that Parliament and not the European Court of Human Rights was the supreme body. BBC political correspondent Nick Robinson weighed in and reported David Cameron will promise to take Britain out of the European Convention on Human Rights. Mr Grieve said he would defend the Convention from the backbenches, saying that it stood alongside Magna Carta and the principle of habeas corpus as a basic defence of individuals' rights. Mr Grieve was widely regarded, alongside the Liberal Democrats, as a 'road-block' to reforming the ECHR. The former attorney general has angered Tory backbenchers by saying that rejecting the treaty would leave Britain 'a pariah state'.

This is serious and powerful politics and raises the stakes for Scots as they prepare to vote in the referendum. We not only have the threat of leaving the European Union, but we now have to deal with the possibility that we will also be leaving some of the most important legal conventions and institutions in Europe. The politics and constitutional thinking of the UK are diverging from what Scotland needs and what most Scottish voters would wish to see.

Membership of the European Union is the other key issue that could influence or even distort the NO vote in the forthcoming referendum. A recent *Scotsman* poll suggested support for Independence would increase in the run-up to the Referendum if Scots feared the UK would exit the EU. This was a powerful reminder that Scottish politics are diverging from England and that the anti-European hysteria being whipped up in England is not shared in Scotland.

> The ICM survey showed a three per cent increase in backing for independence if voters in Scotland thought the UK was 'very likely' to pull out of the EU, with David Cameron pledging an in-out referendum on Europe if he is elected as Prime Minister in the 2015 General Election.

> Support for the NO Campaign also slumped when voters were asked which side they would support, if they thought in September that British withdrawal from the EU was a real prospect in a 'few years' time'.

One poll doesn't represent an overwhelming case for anything, but the *Scotsman* poll does reinforce other academic work which tends to support the overarching view that the prospect of the UK exiting the EU on the back of English votes is not a great encouragement to vote NO. At this stage Labour leader Ed Miliband is opposed to a referendum and only sees the need for one if there was to be a removal of powers from the UK to Europe. This makes sense and hopefully Labour's position may help reassure Scots voters that in the event of a Labour victory in 2015, there will be no referendum in 2017. On this matter the Lib-Dems will be of help.

The *Scotsman*'s findings showed that backing for Independence stood at 37 per cent, with NO at 43 per cent and 20 per cent of voters undecided if Scots thought the UK as a whole would vote to come out of the EU in the in/out referendum Mr Cameron has promised:

> The ICM's findings suggest the issue of Europe could influence the outcome of the referendum, with the poll showing overwhelming opposition in Scotland to EU withdrawal.
>
> Nearly half – or 47 per cent – of the 1,002 adults interviewed said they would vote for the UK to 'stay in' the EU, with just 33 per cent saying they would support British withdrawal. The remainder of those polled were undecided on which way to vote in the EU referendum Mr Cameron has promised.
>
> … The Scottish Government claimed the poll showed many voters feared that a NO vote would put Scotland on the 'fast-track out of Europe'.
>
> Westminster is dancing to a UKIP tune, and this poll shows people are clearly worried that that has put us on the fast-track out of Europe, with all the damaging consequences it would have for jobs and investment.

In a very perceptive postscript, John Curtice said the 'Wisdom of the crowd' may have the answer:

> Scotland will not be surprised if the result is close on 18 September. But most people will be startled if the decision goes in favour of YES… It has been argued that sometimes the 'wisdom of the crowd' can provide a better guide than the polls. And given that one of the features of this referendum is that the polls do not agree on how far NO are ahead, who can be sure that this time it will not be the crowd that gets the forecast right?

This is of course where the important political and constitutional issues impact on the campaign as hearts and minds help voters to decide on how they will vote. It is important to separate the signals from the general noise. Wisdom can be a great thing.

Trying to explain David Cameron's behaviour in Brussels earlier this year, the *Economist*, in a cleverly titled op-ed piece, 'Homage to Caledonia', talked about 'How Scotland's referendum is affecting the politics of Europe':

> David Cameron has won few friends with his demands to renegotiate Britain's relationship with the European Union. But there is one place where he is admired: Catalonia. This is not because he wants a referendum on EU membership, but because he is letting Scotland vote in September on Independence from the United Kingdom. The Catalans plan their own

ballot two months later, although Spain's Prime Minister, Mariano Rajoy, has vowed to stop it. Proof, say Catalan nationalists, of Britain's deep democracy and Spain's lingering authoritarianism.

Romantics see parallels in the fate of Scotland and Catalonia, both small nations merged into larger kingdoms in the early 1700s that now seek to rule themselves. *The Economist*, a supporter of Scotland's continuing membership of the UK, argued that senior leaders in Brussels have taken to issuing increasingly blunt warnings to would-be breakaways. Speaking in Madrid in December, on the day when Catalonia fixed a date for its referendum, Herman Van Rompuy, President of the European Council, said any secessionist region would be treated as a new country, to which the EU's treaties would no longer apply. Such a 'third country' would have to submit an application to re-join.

Commenting on the now notorious visit to London and the ill-advised remarks about Scotland in the EU of José Manuel Barroso, President of the European Commission, *The Economist* reminds us that he said it would be 'extremely difficult, if not impossible' for Scotland to secure the agreement of the 28 other countries to join the EU:

> Mr Barroso claimed he did not want to interfere in the Scottish debate but that is what he did—and he may have gone too far. As the man who runs the commission, he is entitled to set out his views of European law. But he should not judge the likelihood of a successful application, or speak on behalf of Spain, or suggest that peaceful referendums in Western Europe are equivalent to the violent break-up of a Balkan country. After all, the commission's job is to assess accession applications impartially.

The Economist then provided some valuable insights into the wider problems of the EU and suggested that Scotland's possible exit from the UK and a subsequent bid to join the EU could be part of the growing concerns about populism in the EU and the possible exit of Britain from the EU. Much of Barroso's comments were a distraction from the real agenda and reinforces the central point of this chapter – that sensible Europeans are privately dismayed by the behaviour of the Conservative Prime Minister and are more worried about his commitment to an in or out referendum in 2017 than an application from Scotland to join if a YES vote is secured.

While there are worries that, if Scotland votes itself out of the United Kingdom, the more Euro-sceptic remnant of Britain would be more likely to vote itself out of the EU in 2017. This argument applies whether Scotland votes YES or NO. The size of England, representing as it does over 50 million of the near 63 million in the UK, could carry a poll for the UK to exit the EU. What is also worrying is that when you consider the interlocking nature of the political and constitutional issues facing England, especially the rise of the right and the success of UKIP, then the withdrawal of Britain from the EU becomes a nightmare prospect.

Giving a wider perspective and a comprehensive chastising of the EU President, *The Economist* reminds us that the EU treaties allow countries to leave the EU but are silent on what happens if they break up within the club. A split would be unprecedented, even though several EU members were born of earlier secessions. The three Baltic States broke away from the Soviet Union; the Czech Republic and Slovakia came out of the 'velvet divorce' of Czechoslovakia; Slovenia and Croatia emerged from the violent implosion of former Yugoslavia. The rest of the western Balkans is also moving closer to the EU. Serbia has begun membership talks, and even Kosovo is negotiating an association agreement, the first step towards membership.

The membership process

Certainly there is a process to be gone through which is very comprehensive and thorough. The Scottish Government may have overplayed its hand and give the impression that Scotland might not have to go through the formal pre accession, accession and post accession stages, it is clear from EU rules that the formal procedures would not be dropped for Scotland's benefit. But this would still mean that membership would pose no real problems and at the end of the day Scotland, with a YES vote, would be a very attractive candidate seeking to join the EU for very positive reasons at a time when the remainder of the UK – particularly England – was seeking to leave for political reasons. Membership of the EU is important for Scotland and the Union and it remains a big issue in this referendum campaign. *The Economist* is right that it would be unwise for the President of the European Commission or anyone else to insinuate that newly independent states could never join the EU. They ask:

> Would Montenegro and Macedonia really be admitted faster than Scotland and Catalonia, which already apply the EU's rules? Yet it is still more dishonest to pretend that accession would be quick or easy, even in the

best of circumstances. All EU members must agree to open and then conclude membership talks, and to ratify the deal. There are 35 chapters to be negotiated; and these have become harder over the years.

It would probably take longer than the SNP's timescale to join the EU and ratify the accession of Scotland. This is the reality of joining one of the most successful institutions in post-war international development. The real issue that Scots should be concerned about is not the time it takes to join but the fact that if there is a no vote there is no guarantee that Scotland would be part of the EU as the UK may be out in a few years' time.

In conclusion, *The Economist* argues that:

> An amicable break-up, in which all accept and respect the outcome, would surely make for faster Scottish accession. A rump Britain might then be a strong supporter. Spain, despite its qualms, has not said it would stand in Scotland's way. Its refusal to permit a referendum in Catalonia suggests it realises that, in the end, the EU cannot turn down a breakaway region.

This is probably the fairest assessment of Scotland in or out of the UK and future membership of the EU. Opinion polls show that Scotland has a stronger and more positive view about the EU than England. So this should be an important consideration for Scots as the referendum gets closer.

Saying NO, never easy

Saying NO was always going to be a difficult approach to sustain in this referendum campaign. And recent events have only served to deepen fears of a backlash from voters and raises doubts about the Better Together strategy, objectives and political purpose. A total preoccupation with the facts and economics is only half a strategy – what is needed is a reaching out to the heart, emotions and the other big concerns that dominate the lives of Scots. There is no sense of a different future, no vision for the Union of tomorrow, a litany of consequences if Scotland leaves the Union but no idea of the benefits if it stays: one is about the past the other is about the future. The mere existence of the Union for 307 years is in danger of becoming the main argument for its unreformed continuation. This makes little sense and calls out for the NO Campaign to make clear what a NO vote means if Scots reject Independence. But more than the details of any future constitutional settlement, the Unionist parties need to show some sense of commitment, enthusiasm, belief, passion and inspiration about a new and bigger role for Scotland in a modernised and transformed Union. This is what the people want to hear. This was what the second question was all about. This is where a new vision for the Union is long overdue! Many politicians wake up and think it's a new day, but too often, especially at Westminster, they wake up and think it is yesterday. This has to change.

The interventions of Manuel Barosso and George Osborne were timely reminders of over the top political responses to serious issues. These were threatening remarks about a situation that can only be looked at objectively if Scotland exits the Union.

On the European Union, Montenegro, Iceland, the Former Yugoslav Republic of Macedonia, Serbia and Turkey are now candidate countries. Potential candidates are Bosnia, Herzegovina and Kosovo. Barosso's Commission has recommended to the European Council Heads of State that candidate status should be granted to Albania. It is clear that if Scotland becomes Independent then an application to join the EU will go through the pre-accession and accession stage involving the Council of Ministers, the European Commission and the European Parliament in a 12-stage process. Does any Scot really believe that wouldn't happen? Similarly, are we to believe that it would not be in the best interests of the new country of Wales, England and N. Ireland to be part of a Sterling currency union with Scotland? This was Osborne the political street fighter, never the statesman, saying no to a perfectly reasonable request. Clearly a Sterling union is feasible and workable, so was the Chancellor merely bluffing, or was this a threat to withdraw any political goodwill in advance of the referendum result? And yes both countries will cede or share sovereignty for the pursuit of worthwhile objectives! Does anyone think that by sharing sovereignty with 17 other countries in the Euro zone, Germany is a lesser country? The world is changing, but Westminster lives in the past. Germany is a giant in Europe, the UK isn't.

Should we now expect Ban Ki-moon, Secretary General of the United Nations, to visit Scotland and tell us that an Independent Scotland couldn't join the UN as the 194th country?

Will this trip be followed by Anders Fogh Rasmussen, Secretary General of NATO, telling Scots that if they become Independent they can't join as the 29th member? Of course not! Osborne's intervention, sadly supported by Labour and the Lib-Dems, was mean spirited, transparent and potentially damaging to the NO Campaign. To make this Campaign more positive and less threatening, there are certain obvious lessons to be learned.

This is a campaign about the future of Scotland and its role within the Union, and indeed the European Union, but it increasingly appears like a fight with the SNP, Nationalism and Alex Salmond. If nationalism didn't exist we would still need to find a better way to govern Britain, modernise the Union and respond to a nation that seeks to transition to a new and better role within the Union. The hard politics of the economy and Europe have an important role to play and the former Chancellor and President Barroso with experience, expertise and status are able to deal with this. But we also need to appeal to the heart and emotions and be more positive about international issues and the ideas of nationality, identity and difference: the soft politics of this campaign are being neglected. Scotland has a real choice in this referendum. It is up to the other political parties to seriously acknowledge this point and promote the defeat of Independence as a path to a better economic and social future. But for that to happen we need a vision and that seems to be a problem. The EU and the European Court of Human rights speak to the internationalism of Scotland and the idea of justice and freedom. The little Englander mentality being exhibited by the populists and the right of the Conservative Party is distasteful and will only widen the growing divide between the politics of Scotland and the Union, including England.

This type of campaigning we are seeing is to create myths and distortion around policies and issues that people care about. In political campaigns and for tactical reasons, politicians and key players on both sides have to adopt certain postures. But there comes a time when you can't fool the public any longer and while they don't necessarily understand the intricacies of the European Union or how the European Court of Human Rights works, they do have gut feelings and much more nous about these issues than we give them credit for.

The membership issue

Manuel Barroso made a monumental blunder in his intervention in the Independence referendum. Giving his personal opinion, he was clearly at odds with the EU's criteria for membership and the current list of countries seeking to join. Whether attempting to placate an increasingly awkward UK Prime Minister or seeking to reassure the Spanish Prime Minister about Catalonia's ambitions, he was certainly guilty of a clumsy and ill-informed foray into UK politics. Once again the impact of an important issue got lost as electors felt insulted and irritated by another senior political figure lecturing Scotland on what it can't do.

He has was either encouraged in making such inaccurate comments, which seems doubtful, or simply does not understand the context or the nature of the current debate or EU rules.

Based on current European documents prepared by his Commission, 'Enlargement-Extending European values and standards to more Countries' – prepared by the European Commissioner for Enlargement – the 'European Union is open to all democratic countries that wish to join'.

The report continues. Article 49 of the Treaty of European Union states that any European country may apply for membership if it respects the democratic values of the EU and is committed to promoting them. Article 49 reads:

> Any European State which respects the values referred to in Article 2 [may apply to join]... the Union is founded on the values of respect for human dignity, freedom, democracy, equality, the rule of law and respect for human rights' and is committed to promoting them may apply to become a member of the Union.

Currently Montenegro, Iceland, the Former Yugoslav Republic of Macedonia, Serbia and Turkey are candidate countries. And accession negotiations are ongoing with Montenegro and Turkey. Discussions with Serbia started in January of this year. Most of these countries have small populations.

It is clear that if Scotland becomes Independent then an application to join the EU will be straightforward enough, but will have to go through the well-defined pre-accession and accession steps. Alex Salmond's timescale for accession is however ambitious, but subject to the process being adhered to, including satisfying the 32 chapters of the *acquis communitaire* – nearly 1,000 pages of community law – then there should be no serious obstacle to overcome. This covers the practical aspects of joining the EU. Political issues have been raised in relation to Spain and their ongoing constitutional difficulties with Catalonia. Throughout the EU there are other Nation States or nations who will be watching with interest the outcome of the Scottish referendum and its immediate aftermath if a yes vote is secured.

In view of the current list of countries – not the most stable of countries – then membership of the EU should not present any significant difficulties. There woul appear to be no circumstances in which Scotland's application would be declined. Another piece of fiction should be laid to rest.

Looking at the right of the Conservative Party, UKIP and their relationship with Europe, *Rebuilding the Dream* (2012) by Van Jones (a former adviser to President Obama) offers a new perspective. A political concept is something that one thinks, values or believes in, regarding the public or common good. A political action is a step that can be taken to do something about it – either through citizen action or government action or both. This is the political process and without both parts then little progress will be made.

But as George Lakoff notes in his book, *Don't think of an Elephant, Know your Values and Frame the Debate*:

> Liberals have the idea that if you just tell people the facts, people will be rational and reach the right conclusion. The facts will set you free. They won't.

Instead, progressives find themselves constantly frustrated when the real world refuses to conform to this mental construct, often getting results we don't like. Yet we continue behaving in exactly the same way.

Might we have some learning, thinking and growing to do in politics?

Emotions matter in politics. Many progressives pride themselves on being fully rational. So we need to integrate into our model another dimension beyond the rational, the 'Heart Space/Head Space Grid'. Van Jones believes we have four quadrants to play with:

1 Rational and Conceptual head space

2 Emotional and Conceptual heart space

3 Emotional and Actionable outside game

4 Rational and Actionable inside game

Head space, left quadrant head space – this is the home of think tanks, academics and policy wonks – facts and rational arguments, organisations such as the BBC and the *Guardian*.

Heart Space – politics is not just about what goes on in one's head. Politics is also about what happens in one's heart – this is home to the great storytellers. Politics is energised by emotions, feelings of love and rage contempt and compassion and pride and shame. At their most powerful, political ideas touch our soul. They arouse our passions.

Outside game – once people become touched, moved or inspired in the heart space, they will want to take action. Rather than being motivated by factual argument or dispassionate calculation, people are more likely to be inspired to take action based on emotion. The grids lower right: this is the home of activists and volunteers – what moves them is in their heart.

Inside game – this is the home to lobbyists, elected officials and party people. These are the people with the formal authority to make and take decisions. No space for misty-eyed idealism here, this is the land of rational calculation

The political process requires that all four of the quadrants of the grid are activated at different stages.

RATIONAL

HEAD	INSIDE
SPACE	GAME

POLITICAL CONCEPT
POLITICAL ACTION

HEART	OUTSIDE
SPACE	GAME

EMOTIONAL

Van Jones explain this as follows:

> The heart space is the home of narratives that arouse the emotions and touch the soul. Compelling narratives are more important in politics than are facts, policies, or data points. People are rarely moved by facts. We live in a world where people can find facts on their own. Facts are fickle and forgettable. Stories at their best are not. Stories are how humans have passed along values and information for millennia. In politics the side with the best stories almost always win.

> Information is static; stories are dynamic – they help an audience visualise what you do or what you believe. Tell a story and people will be more engaged and receptive to the ideas you are communicating. Stories link one person's heart to another. Values beliefs and norms become intertwined. When this happens your idea can more readily manifest as reality in their minds.

> Narrative is the lens through which humans process the information we encounter, be it cultural, emotional, experiential or political. We make up stories about ourselves our histories our futures and our hopes.

As far as our European narrative is concerned, our effective political stories have four fundamental elements: a villain, a threat, a hero and a vision. When these four parts are clear and compelling, a story has the power to move people to take action. This is the context for a better debate on membership of the EU, which represents a powerful issue for this kind of consideration. The Conservative right and UKIP hate the EU and keep serving up ludicrous and inane arguments condemning Europe and seeking Britain's exit. But in terms of the content of stories, the anti-Europeans have a villain, a threat, a hero and a vision, which is essentially turning the clock back centuries. But where is the alternative story about the EU? There is one, but it is not being presented or argued anywhere, except, unsurprisingly, by the business community. The powerful pro-EU case is there to be made, but is going by default. We have left the stage to the breakup merchants, aided by much of the right-wing press who daily ridicule the achievements of one of Europe's success stories.

We need to occupy the heart and head space and develop a new story.

Pride, patriotism and compassion are powerful emotions and must be closer to the centre stage of politics. Van Jones defines a new way of capturing the weaknesses and strengths of opposing factions or parties, which may be tough, but does describe the two sides of the European debate.

First of all he uses the term 'cheap patriotism' to describe those political leaders who apparently love their country but end up waging war against most of the groups in it and seem too drool over the past while they stir up grudge and grievance politics and often much worse, without offering anything positive in response. He cites the Tea Party in the US as guilty of:

> ... promoting this shrunken, negative and limited version of American values. Left unchallenged this is perhaps the most dangerous ideology in the country right now.

He adds:

> ... the cheap patriots would hand the US over to global corporations to do as they will in the name of the free market. Their version of liberty creates a society in which the market is free and the people are not'

Second, he talks about 'deep patriotism' to describe all those who love their country for all of the right reasons and in the process they don't leave anyone out, including immigrants or people on welfare. No one is left out.

No one is excluded. No one is scapegoated for the benefit of the many. For decades, this end of the political spectrum has tried to monopolise patriotism and pride and have fought against inclusivity, diversity and compassion. There has to be a 'them and us', as this is the way society has to function.

The populist leaders of UKIP and the Conservative right have to be classified as cheap patriots, doing enormous damage to the country and staking out a future that lacks moral purpose and thrives on division. Europe matters and may influence the future of the Union debate before and after the referendum on Independence. We should however be aware that those political parties who wish to isolate Britain will succeed if there is no alternative narrative and a narrow form cheap patriotism remains uncontested.

New EU President

David Cameron's humiliation over the nomination of Jean-Claude Juncker for the Presidency of the European Commission is profoundly embarrassing for the United Kingdom and is deeply damaging to the prospects of the UK remaining in the European Union after his reckless commitment to an in or out referendum planned for 2017. The debacle of his 26–2 drubbing in the European Council could also have a seismic impact on the outcome of the Independence referendum in September. The timing couldn't be worse for the NO Campaign. Another layer of uncertainty has been added, and many Scots will have more doubts about what a NO vote could mean for our 41-year-old membership of the EU. Described by Tory MPs in their post-summit 'a bad day for Europe', nothing could be further from the truth. This was the day when a Union in decline, currently in the hands of zealots and xenophobes, decided to deploy an inept set of tactics not intended to enhance our negotiating position in the event of pushing for reform, but designed to keep all of Cameron's options opened as he focuses on the 2015 General Election and his struggle with UKIP for the soul of the new right and populism in British politics. This is the basis of a nightmare scenario in which growing English nationalism, anti-Europeanism, a dislike of immigrants and foreigners and a series of carefully selected distractions – such as the European Court of Justice, Human Rights and benefit tourists – substitute for progressive, decent and relevant politics. Many of our European colleagues will have been aghast at the breath-taking arrogance of our Prime Minister and the contempt with which many of his MPs and supporters hold one of the most successful post-war organisations and the political, social, economic, security and peace achievements this has delivered for the UK. There is something slightly nauseating about Cameron's behaviour when you consider that in a year, when we commemorate the 100th anniversary of the start of World War One, we are members of a Union that has ensured peace, solidarity and stability within the changing boundaries of the EU for nearly 70 years: remembering the wars that took place in 1870, 1914 and 1939, we should be celebrating the turning of major protagonists into partners and allies who have, since the setting up of the European Coal and Steel community in 1952, been working for the long-term improvement of a continent we all share and care about. Not content with putting at risk our membership of the EU, David Cameron is in danger of forcing many Scots to vote YES if they value that membership. How safe is Scotland in the hands of the Union of Great Britain and Northern Ireland?

Scotland diverging from England

When people in England were asked which party and which political leader 'best stands up for the interests of England', UKIP and Nigel Farage came out on top, at over 20 per cent of the vote. In sharp contrast, only three per cent of Welsh voters identified UKIP as the party that best represents Welsh interests and only one per cent in Scotland as the party that best stands up for Scotland. Despite the poor support for UKIP in Scotland, this party poses a real threat to the interests of Scots, because of our member-ship of the United Kingdom, especially in relation to the EU.

Survey respondents were also asked how they would vote in a referen-dum on EU membership. Only in Scotland was opinion more clearly in favour of continued membership. England was 37 per cent in favour of remain-ing, 40 per cent for leaving and 22 per cent wouldn't vote or don't know. Scotland's intentions were 48 per cent in favour of remaining, 32 per cent for leaving and 20 per cent wouldn't vote or don't know. Of significance, the EU referendum vote by national identity in England shows that those voters who were English only or more English than British voted 26 per cent to remain but a staggering 55 per cent opted to leave! Professor Wyn Jones said,

Such differences highlight the political difference between the nations of Britain. Moreover the strength of UKIP's popular support in England draws on the extent to which the party has become the champion of an increasingly politicised sense of English identity

The Success of the EU

Despite the changes in the post-war period to recast the global order, much of the Conservative Party seems incapable of facing up to the fact that Britain no longer rules the waves, controls an Empire or has any 'special' relationship with the United States.

The right of the Tory Party is consumed with a belief in British exceptionalism, a sense of elitism and arrogance, a mistrust of the rest of the world and an insidious nationalism which is very reminiscent of Republican thinking in the US, where a contempt for the rest of the world sits easily with a neo-con view which rejects partnerships, coalitions and pooling sovereignty.

This is a tragedy. The European Union has been one of the most significant achievements in post-war history and a power for good in both Europe and throughout the world. Since its inception as the European Coal and Steel Community in 1952, the creation of the European Economic Community in 1958 and now a union of 28 countries and 500 million people, there is a great deal to be proud of. Celebrating next year nearly 40 years of EU membership, Britain has made a significant contribution to the widening and deepening of the European project – but it could have done much more. As was the case in 1958, when Germany and France provided the leadership in an EEC of six nations, these two countries still provide the drive and inspiration in today's troubled times.

The development of the EU is still a work in progress. Despite the recent setbacks in the Eurozone and the constraints on further political and economic integration, there is still enormous potential within the EU. And the European Union continues to play an important role in the future of Britain and Scotland: whether Scotland embraces Independence, Devo-Plus or the status quo, Europe will be vital for our future.

Where is the Debate?

Sadly, you would be hard pressed to detect this positive narrative on post-war Europe, as achievements are ignored by much of the right-leaning press, conducted in an absurd and highly critical manner or simply used as a scapegoat for all the ills of a declining Union. All of the traditional political parties have done very little to promote the benefits of the EU and as a result of ambivalence and at times neglect, the UK is edging closer to a possible exit. This would make no sense and would lead to a catastrophic series of consequences for the Union and confirm in the eyes of the world that Great Britain and Northern Ireland had little interest in playing any substantive or significant role in Europe or internationally. The Union would continue its decline and for the first time in the post-war period we would be paying the price of our failure to adjust to new challenges and opportunities. The right wing of the Conservative Party and the populism of UKIP could win at the expense of the national interest. To many people this may seem far-fetched. Sadly, a daily diet of lies, half-truths and fantasy, linked to no serious information or debate, in the context of much of the anti-European sentiment of the right-wing press and played out in a House of Commons suffering from their own delusions, our membership of the EU looks distinctly uncertain. There is another scenario to respond to this madness but, neither the Labour party nor the Liberal Democrats seem interested, confident or committed enough to argue the alternative case. For the Unionist parties, the day of political reckoning may be closer than they think.

Cheap Patriots

This uncertainty about the outcome of the in/out referendum is likely to have a bearing on the Independence referendum in Scotland. This is likely to reflect a more serious sense of internationalism, served up in a less partisan manner and without the distortions of anti-foreigner and anti-immigrant sentiment, which is increasingly the currency of the UKIP/Cameron debate at Westminster and poisoning the debate in England. The cheap patriotism being stirred by populist and right-wing sentiment in British politics is likely to push people into the YES camp.

Currently there is no serious debate on the future of the EU. This is not surprising, as a powerful anti-European conspiracy – including major help from some of our press barons and think tanks – is determined to wreck our relationship with Europe, dismantle progressive legislation that enhances individual rights and workplace protections and seeks our eventual withdrawal from membership.

No-one should be fooled by the recent Tory rebellion in the House of Commons pressing for a referendum on EU membership. Dressed up as protecting British sovereignty and ostensibly about the 'repatriation of powers' from Europe, their efforts are a smokescreen for removing the influence of Europe in an attempt to destroy social, environmental and employment regulations and protections which have benefitted millions of people in Britain. The right wing of the Conservative Party is the most destructive force in British politics and, along with their allies in the press, is poisoning the European debate in this country.

At a time when the purpose of politics is being seriously questioned and public disenchantment with politicians and governments is at an all-time high, the success of the EU should not be overlooked. Remarkable progress has been made since the Treaty of Rome in 1958. The EU has the most successful single market in the world, groundbreaking environmental legislation, the most generous international development aid programme, ambitious social and employment protection and the promotion and protection of human rights.

Even economic and monetary union and the single currency are significant achievements, despite the current difficulties: and despite the claims of the cynics and Europhobes, one of the ways forward is to have more EU integration, not less.

For the real success story of the EU, though, in terms of both ambition and achievement, we have to look further back to the dark days of post-war Europe. Out of the terrible destruction of nations, cities and people, inspired visionaries, determined never to see a repeat of this in Europe, decided to create a new vision, a new narrative that would lead countries in partnership towards a Europe without war.

In 1870, 1914 and 1945, France and Germany were at war and militarism, nationalism and a primitive form of exceptionalism engulfed Europe in a conflagration of epic scale. 'Never again', was the demand of inspiring men like Monnet and Schuman and eventually a start was made in 1952, led by France and Germany. Surely the avoidance of war, within the EEC and now the EU, has been the most striking achievement of the past six decades.

The post-war vision has been security, peace, stability and solidarity in an attempt to rebuild Europe and create lasting prosperity. In that period, the Cold War has ended, the Berlin Wall has fallen, the Soviet Union has collapsed and Germany has been reunified. Eight new countries from Central and Eastern Europe joined the EU and, on the edges of the EU, nationalism, ethnic cleansing and genocide have ended in the Balkans. No doubt there will be setbacks as 'Project Europe' continues to unfold.

An inspiring story

But the story of Europe might inspire a younger generation. Young people are more optimistic and less likely to see their future and that of Europe through the prism of cynicism, narrow nationalism and pessimism. They are also more likely to see Europe and progressive internationalism as an idea and an ideal at the heart of a more peaceful and interdependent world. It was Victor Hugo who coined the phrase 'a patriot for humanity' to contrast being engrossed by one's own nation. Let's hope that tomorrow's world will be less influenced by narrow minds and more influenced by idealism and inspiration.

Britain needs to lead in Europe, not leave it. But more importantly, in the short term many Scots might want to leave the Union of Great Britain and Northern Ireland so they can remain members of the European Union. Rejecting one Union for another seems like a price some Unionist parties are happy to pay. Make no mistake – the European Union continues to play an important role in the future of Britain.

Our ambivalence towards membership, our grudging acceptance of the remarkable achievements since the Treaty of Rome in 1957 and now an alarming level of Euro-scepticism are creating a nightmare scenario with two potential consequences.

We are in danger of sacrificing any prospects of influencing the future political and economic shape of one of the most successful global regional blocks in the post-war period. And at the same time, we will heighten the frustration and doubts of our European counterparts that we are in any way serious about being at the heart of Europe.

This has not been a good year for the EU. The elections to the European Parliament were a disaster for the UK. The 'little Englander' mentality illustrated how much the European debate had been hijacked by a coalition

of extreme anti-European views, Euro-sceptics, racists, narrow nationalists and anti-immigrant sentiment. A powerful coalition of the right-wing
press, UKIP and extreme Tory MPs and MEPs have been running amok with
little resistance being show by the other parties to the trashing of the EU.

Previous treaties, including Maastricht, were much more significant for
British sovereignty but were ratified by Conservative Governments without
a referendum or much regard for the views of the British people. Already,
the British Conservative Party is alienating political allies in Europe. The
Christian Democrats in Germany and Chancellor Merkel in particular, who
seem able to combine, being at the heart of Europe with their own successful
pursuit of Germany's national interest, are embarrassed by David Cameron's posturing. The exit of British Tory MEPs from the European Peoples
Party in 2010 showed Conservative intent, so they have form on this issue.

Surely we need to lead in Europe, not leave it.

Rethinking our role in Europe

In the UK we should reflect on what EU politics could be like in the future
and not dwell on what it has been like in the past. This has to be the new
narrative.

The future of the European Union provides such an opportunity for new
thinking and a chance for Britain once and for all to seriously embrace the
European project, strengthen our position at the heart of the EU and
accept that our future lies within that great organisation.

Labour should be the pro-European party: more engaged and less ambivalent. Britain's future is in the European Union. A more enthusiastic embrace
of the EU should also involve a more realistic assessment of our special
transatlantic relationship with the United States. This does not mean turning
our backs on an alliance that has served us well, but acknowledging that
in the new global order, Britain has to be more realistic about weighing
up what is in our long-term economic and political interests and how best
we can more effectively contribute to the global agenda.

Some commentators and historians argue that, since the loss of Empire
and the emergence of the European Union, Britain is still looking for a role
in the world. It is highly unlikely that Obama's view of the 'special relationship' differs from his predecessors. From Churchill and Roosevelt,
Thatcher and Regan, to Blair and Bush, the alliance has remained strong.

But does it now matter as much? And isn't it the case the case that President Obama has many 'special relationships'?

At the heart of America's world view, only seen in an extreme form under the Bush administration, lies a number of enduring ideas: a reluctance (first advocated by George Washington) to enter into coalitions; the Monroe doctrine, held since the 1890s, which emphasised the importance of America, the Americas and then the rest of the world; an outlook which sees the US constitution and the institutions of Government as vastly superior to anything the rest of the world has to offer; a sense of nationalism and exceptionalism tinged with a cultural conservatism; a mistrust of the rest of the world; and a naivety and ignorance about how the rest of the world operates outside the American mindset.

Faced with this powerful set of ideas, which are unlikely to change in the short term, the European Union should continue to influence US policy but start to strengthen, reform and promote a more confident world view which is less dependent on the US and builds moral authority on a more creative use of 'soft power' and economic strength.

Europe, speaking with one voice on global issues and with the resolve to back words with action, would be a much more credible and effective global player. Recent events, including the Israeli-Palestinian conflict and the Russian-Ukrainian dispute, only serve to reinforce the need for real progress to be made on political integration and foreign policy. The UK Government could play a bigger role in building a credible European voice.

Labour has to reclaim the European political agenda in this country.

Being at the heart of Europe should be about actions, not rhetoric. Our ambivalence, scepticism and at times hostility towards the EU and its institutions are firmly rooted in the political and popular culture of the UK. Ever since Churchill's 'United States of Europe' or 'Tragedy of Europe' speech at the University of Zurich in 1946, a distinctive view of Europe has existed. Churchill, in well-crafted speech, said: 'We must build a kind of United States of Europe'. But he then added in a much more detached way:

> In all this urgent work, France and Germany must take the lead together. Great Britain, the British Commonwealth of Nations, mighty America and, I trust, Soviet Russia, must be the friends and sponsors of the new Europe and must champion its right to live and shine.

Ever since then, a deep seated loathing on the part of many right-wing Conservatives and a failure of Britain to find and fulfil a role in the world have turned Euro-scepticism into something far more destructive and dangerous which threatens our future.

Adding further to the complexity of our relationship with the EU is what might be described as the social protection provided to the British people by the EU when Conservative Government is in power. The Conservatives are incensed with the regulations and directives which offer decent environmental, social, employment and workplace benefits and protection. Part of their thinking about the EU relates to the repatriation of powers to the UK. This is dressed up as winning back the right to legislate for ourselves and not be dictated to by others. This is not the real reason. Much of what emanates from Brussels, both European Parliament and Commission, is progressive legislation which reflects social democracy and the idea of social partnership. These ideas are alien to modern British Conservatism. Winning back powers for the British people is a cruel deception. This is about politics and philosophy.

The fourth and most disturbing level of Conservative paranoia about Europe is the use of the EU to attack immigrants and whip up a barely disguised form of racism, which is then held up as British jobs for British workers or defending the health service or benefits system against the Romanians and Bulgarians. These attacks are both troubling and embarrassing. They are designed to engender a corrosive dislike of fellow Europeans when all the evidence suggests there is little justification for these attacks and, more importantly, the facts indicate that migrants in the main are net contributors to our economy and society. In addition, it was mainly Conservative Prime Ministers such as Margaret Thatcher and John Major who signed up for the Single European Act, the Maastricht Treaty, which created the inspiring vision and strategy of an EU where there would be the free flow of goods, service, finance and people. This was no socialist or Labour plot, much of the thinking was about the free market and completing the single market to let trade flourish in the largest single market in the world. All of this is conveniently forgotten by neoliberals who want free markets but object to the consequences of such policies.

On the face of it and for all the noise surrounding the debate about the EU, there is a degree of consensus about the best policies to promote Britain's national interests in Europe. The leaderships of the three main parties favour reform of European institutions: all want to protect the single market, and all are determined to resist 'ever closer union'. Both Labour and Conservative politicians have expressed an interest in restricting the free movement of labour within the EU.

The essential difference between the parties is not one of tactics. Labour politicians have generally clothed their desire to repatriate powers and resist further integration in the language of commitment and compromise. The Conservatives, by contrast, have attempted to coerce ostensible allies with threats of a British exit from the EU.

The aim of the Prime Minister's European policy was never to protect Britain's best interests within Europe but to appease restive backbenchers. Under his leadership, the Tories withdrew from the European People's Party grouping, abandoning a coalition of the mainstream European centre right for the company of xenophobes and cranks. Tories have characterised eastern European immigrants as benefit tourists. And Mr Cameron has guaranteed that a referendum on Britain's continued membership of the EU would be held in 2017, if not before then.

David Marquand is one of the most respected social democratic academics, a journalist and former MP. In a series of articles for the *Guardian*, he succinctly captures the mood of Conservatives and their enduring dislike of the European Union:

> Cameron's behaviour is just another chapter in a 60-year-old story. Euro-scepticism, ambivalence, a fondness for Empire and an emotional and political attachment to the special relationship with the US have in the post-war period made the channel wider than it is. Not helped by French President Charles DeGaulle saying no to our bid for membership, a lingering mistrust of continental Europe and in particular our old enemy France, an obsession with national sovereignty. The picture is now much more complex as Conservative extremists and the populism of UKIP are bringer a much sharper focus to our membership of the EU as a Union lacking confidence and direction seeks to blame others for our own national shortcomings which in turn is making the UK look mean miserable, intolerant and at time embarrassing.

> But scepticism is being turned into phobia. There is a virulence about today's anti-European rhetoric. It is visceral, not intellectual. There is a deep anxiety being nurtured which, if we are not careful, will not be allayed by mere policy challenges. If Europhobes got their way on the repatriation of powers they would not be appeased, for them this is no longer about reform, it is about rejecting membership. The Brussels they excoriate is a symbol of encroachment, spite and malice. This is all about nationality, spite and a little Englander mentality.

Writing in the *Guardian* in 2011, Marquand said:

Euroscepticism has been constant in British politics since the Attlee Government turned down membership of the European Coal and Steel Community because the Durham miners wouldn't wear it.

Where does this anxiety come from? Whose identity is in question? I used to think it was a post-imperial anxiety, rather like that of Putin's Russia. Now I think it is far more complicated. The Empire disappeared decades ago. Besides, it was British. Europhobia is English. It was English Tory MPs who told Cameron to behave like a bulldog when he got to Brussels and who sizzled with hatred for the Lib Dems after his return.

The crisis in Britain's relationship with mainland Europe has its roots in a peculiarly English identity crisis with no counterpart north of the border or west of the Severn. The Scots and Welsh know who they are.

Above all, the English of the 21st century no longer know who they are. They used to think that 'English' and 'British' were synonymous. Now they know that they are not. But they don't know how Englishness and Britishness relate to each other, and they can't get used to the notion of multiple identities If it isn't, the most likely prospect is of further European political union and the break-up of the UK, with England staying out and Scotland and Wales going in.

We are now in an era of multiple identities, where Britishness is declining and national identity is growing. The Conservative Party is fighting on so many fronts to ensure it doesn't compromise absolute sovereignty or the fundamental nature of Britishness, whatever that means. In doing so it raises the stakes on the European issue and could lead to Scots preferring the EU to the UK. Even if there is a NO vote this issue will remain, and will reignite a controversy around the prospect of the UK leaving the EU on the back of English votes.

CHAPTER SIX

Populism, Extremism and the Rise of the Political Right

THE RISE OF UKIP has sent shockwaves through the political establishment. The traditional political parties, especially the Conservative Party, are at risk as uncertainty grows about the outcome of the next General Election in 2015. Fundamental questions are being asked about the new political landscape in England. Public opinion, on the back of an economic crisis and a deepening disillusionment with Westminster politics, is volatile, social class allegiances and loyalties are breaking down and the 30 per cent decline in the share of the popular vote from the 1950s going to Labour and the Conservatives is likely to continue. This new populism has been accompanied by a rise of the political right, again overwhelmingly in England and at Westminster. The right of the Conservative Party, embracing neo-liberalism, a much more abrasive and intolerant approach to social issues, a desire to reduce the role and size of the state and a different world view, sees UKIP as both an immediate election threat but in the long term as a positive ally in changing the politics of England and hoping for a more permanent realignment of the right. This in turn could have wider political and constitutional implications for the future of the UK, change the direction of social and economic policy, including the post-war consensus on social security and health, and our relationships with the EU and the European Court of Human Rights. Although much of this, if not all of this, would play out in England, the consequences would be experienced throughout the UK, including Scotland. The politics of the Independence referendum campaign can't be immune from what might happen in the future and may be conceived as a threat to Scotland, where the political divide with England is growing. The rise of the right and the arrival of populism should not be underestimated.

Populism and the rise of the right have been a feature of western European countries for some time, where traditional political parties have been in decline, new parties have emerged and, similar to the UK, there has been growing discontent, disillusionment and a loss of faith in the integrity and effectiveness of the political process. Although right wing and populist parties have significant differences, their views often coalesce around Islamaphobic, xenophobic, anti-immigrant/foreigner and virulently anti-Europe issues. This is the dangerous cocktail of prejudice, intolerance and malice that unites UKIP and the Conservative right in England and in particular at Westminster. Most of these non-traditional parties of the right are often delusional about the past, share a completely misguided and distorted view of threats to national sovereignty, and exude a cheap patriotism seemingly derived from hating everything about their country! This is not a political genre you find in Scotland, and while the SNP may be described as populist in approach – transcending issues of class, geography, party affiliation and philosophy – it is far removed from the typical populist parties in Europe. UKIP has Englishness at its core, not Britishness, so national identity is crucial to its politics and aspirations. Mining a deep seam of public discontent with the established political class and primarily aimed at Westminster, UKIP is the English Independence Party. Despite the obvious, this Englishness is not leading to any arguments that want to enthusiastically embrace any new form of Governance or constitutional change for England: instead, it is the grudge and grievance mentality about Scotland and the politics of envy. What is UKIP's policy on devolution? Gerry Hassan, in an article entitled 'The UKIP policy Nigel Farage doesn't want to talk about' said: 'He would return the UK to its pre-devolution settlement in all but name.' North of the border, UKIP has always had a perception, identity and popularity problem. Hassan argues that they are widely seen as an English nationalist party, one whose idea of Britain is narrowly centred on a time when the two terms could be used interchangeably.

> It is a mind-set stuck in a time warp situated between the 1950s and 1970s, between the beginning and end of the Empire, and which yearns for an England which began to completely disappear in the decade of 'The Rise and Fall of Reginald Perrin' and 'The Good Life'. Nevertheless Scottish politics is not immune to people harking back to better yesterdays, and certainly there is a similar popular sentiment but an aura of anti-politics which dismisses all mainstream politics and politicians.

This is an amusing but deadly serious account of a party with nothing to offer except nostalgia, an intense dislike or suspicion of anything that is not British and a 'make it up as you go' list of mad policies. If this is the case, why then are they making such an impact in England? In view of the progress of populism in Europe over the past two decades, have the Unionist parties been asleep on the job? This has to be the classic case of the Unionist parties, by their own weaknesses and lack of leadership, losing the support of English voters, while at the same time vacating the political space and having UKIP filling the vacuum. Scotland has much to fear from England if the rise of UKIP is not checked by the mainstream parties.

Hassan, in an excellent critique of the UKIP phenomenon and its demolition of devolved government, highlights the dangers. The 2011 UKIP manifesto for the Scottish Parliament, 'We, the People', is explicit and unashamed on this point. 'We, the people, shall rule' – its first point – is a declaration that they would 'Retain the Scottish Parliament'. On the next line, 'Replace MSPs with Scottish Westminster MPs'. Strangely, Hassan continues:

> Nigel Farage in his appeal to Scottish voters – 'Power to local people' – fails to mention this policy once. This is abolition of the Scottish Parliament in everything but name; the replacement of a directly elected Scottish Parliament with what is in effect a Scottish Grand Committee. UKIP policy has shifted towards support for an English Parliament, but it is a strange, unreal federalism which proposes the abolition of the directly elected Scottish Parliament and Welsh Assembly.

UKIP is a strange political creature and by most rational considerations should not have the standing in England it currently has. But that in large measure is symptomatic of how critical the crisis of British mainstream politics has become. This in turn is reinforced by the inability of Westminster to move from denial, lethargy and a fear of change.

A fictional party has been created, with such deadly and practical political consequences, not just for England and the Union, but also Scotland. And as Hassan puts it, 'the UKIP answer is to return to a golden age of Westminster supremacy'. This would be an age where there were fewer foreigners and immigrants, no European Union, no devolved government and Westminster had the absolute sovereignty to do anything it wanted to do!

Hassan concludes by saying:

> The emergence and rise of UKIP is a symptom of the deep malaise at the heart of British politics and society, and the failure of mainstream parties

and elites to address the long-term underlying causes or the powerful interests who have produced this state of affairs. People are naturally confused, disappointed and searching for answers, with some looking for them in a mythical Britain which never existed, and cannot be realistically created today. This is an unhelpful reminder to the Conservative, Labour and Lib Dem parties of their shortcomings and the narrow bandwidth of Westminster politics. It isn't surprising that Scottish, along with Welsh, politics should provide such unfertile terrain for UKIP, marching as they are to such a different beat from that of Westminster.

Europe provides a taste of what might lie ahead for the UK and for Scotland if UKIP continues to progress and wins seats at Westminster in 2015. Unlike the rise and fall of the BNP in which they won seats on local councils and the European Parliament, UKIP seem destined to have more long-term success if the present apathy of the traditional parties and the struggle between the right of the Conservative Party and UKIP continues. It is worth noting that all the populist parties in Europe have similarities but also significant differences, some of which could be applied to UKIP, but there is no disguising the fact that UKIP is exceptional in terms of the political context in which it has emerged, the confusing policy platform it pursues and the charismatic personality of Nigel Farage, who has waged a war single handedly against the political establishment.

Michael Kenny and Nick Pearce, writing in the *New Statesman*, 'The End of the Party', said:

> The rise of anti-politics populism in Europe has coincided with the appearance of new charismatic leaders whose appeal rests on their unwillingness to accept the compromises and responsibilities that governing in a representative democracy requires.

Their concerns reflect a growing threat to our politics and the legitimacy of political parties. One response to what is happening is for our party leaders to mimic the populist rhetoric and to contemplate adopting some of their policies. The centre ground is becoming overcrowded as progressives become anxious and seek to replicate what they perceive to be the wishes of the electorate. But there is a pattern to all of this. The rise of anti-politics, deep-rooted anxieties over identity, and the growing discontent at the inequalities and inequities generated by the economic system, argue Kenny and Pearce, lie at the core of much of this anger and frustration. But they also recognise the deepening disillusionment of the public with politicians and political parties: faith and trust in the mainstream of British politics is disintegrating and it makes little sense for the traditional parties to act like populists when much deeper ethical, philosophical considerations and matters of principle are involved.

The electorate may be losing their commitment to representative politics. This is reflected in low turnouts in elections and a general sense of discontent about their lives and what party politics is delivering to them. What should be attracting the interest of our politicians are the historic trends. The breakdown in political alignments associated with class structure, the shift in the economy from manufacturing to a post-industrial one, the impact of communication technologies and a general weariness about the performance of institutions are transforming our relationship with democracy and political participation. In 'End of the Party, Kenny and Pearce note that these social and economic changes have led to a 'more segmented set of audiences for politics' as the idea of a unified public has given way to varied groups that are more fragmented in their cultural backgrounds and values. This process is at work in Scotland where nationality, identities, culture, more fluid loyalties and a shift from old networks to an internet-based population are leading to a different political audience and much more political volatility. Scotland inherited early in the post-devolution years a split personality, which has resulted in completely different voting patterns for the Holyrood and Westminster elections: this difference may not be so marked if a system of Proportional Representation had been in place for the General Election. Concluding on a dark note, Kenny and Pearce reflect upon a growing consensus in the academic and think tank community:

> If we do not address these issues, there is a danger of a further drift towards what some commentators have called a post democracy. This will bring a slide towards the further hollowing out of the democratic process, the terminal decline of mass parties and the disappearance of politicians governing in proactive and far sighted ways.

Changes in society are adding to the increasing alienation of the public. Mass politics may still exist, but there is unlikely to be a renewed interest in party politics without a radical transformation of our approach to representative democracy. We need new forms of participative politics where people have some confidence in leaders and their organisations standing for something, not simply being largely soulless, technocratic, managerial, lacking inspiration and passion and only being around at elections. The renewal of how we organise our politics is long overdue. The idea of manifestos and single parties seeking absolute power makes little sense in a much more pluralistic country, where party loyalties and allegiances are breaking down, membership of political parties is collapsing, young people – although embracing political issues – remain indifferent to political parties and voter turnout is posing the question: do we have a representative democracy? The European models of coalition, alliances, broader interest groups (built around a set of principles and philosophy, and better at reflecting society, its aspirations and needs) are the way forward. This would be possible in Scotland where size and scale make a new politics feasible. Lessons could be more easily transferred from the Nordic countries and other parts of Europe. Party labels can be misleading and we should look for new ways of promoting progressive thinking, action and organisation. Individualism, the internet age and the breakdown of social structures, which provided solidarity and social coherence, and a myriad of other social and economic changes have resulted in declining membership in Trades Unions, voluntary organisations and churches, while the historic links of those organisations with political parties have also been weakened.

Populist parties have been gaining ground – support, votes, seats and influence, the latter often far beyond their size and popularity. They feed of the concerns and fears, especially in the austerity years since the economic and banking crises, of growing numbers of people on a wide range of fronts. They appeal to voters because they encourage anxiety over the political classes and the elites in the establishment who are accused of ignoring the plight of ordinary people; the inability of political parties to resolve some of the most enduring problems and concerns; austerity budgets that are seen to affect the poor the most, bringing calls for greater fairness; promoting national identities and seeking to stir up divisions in society. Sheila Moorcroft in *Politics in Crisis* provides a flavour of some of the parties in Europe:

> These parties and movements take many forms and although their support is fluctuating, their influence continues. Examples abound: the Tea Party Movement in the USA, whose local groups often hold disparate and sometimes conflicting views, has contributed to the stalemate and brinkmanship of recent US debt and tax discussions; Golden Dawn in Greece, which has become almost an extension of the police as well as politics, has 14 per cent of the vote and significant influence; the Five Star Movement in

Italy, which has brought complete political novices into Parliament, eschews the roles of leaders or being on the left or right and would not form a formal alliance to form a government; the Freedom Party in the Netherlands forced an election and radicalised the discussion of the EU budget, before losing many seats; in Hungary the Movement for a Better Hungary is now the third largest party and the True Finns has 39 MPs in the Finnish Parliament; in the UK UKIP has achieved significant success, albeit small in total numbers, in the most recent local elections; even in Germany a new anti-EU party, Alternative für Deutschland, has emerged but not yet faced the polls – although 24 per cent say they can see it doing so. And so it goes on.

We could also add: Jobbik in Hungary; I love Italy In Italy; the National People's Front in Cyprus; People for Real, Open and United Democracy in Bulgaria; the Croatian Party of Rights; Order and Justice in Lithuania; United Poland; Swiss People's Party; and the Northern League in Italy.

These populist and Euro-sceptic parties on the right and far right in Europe are making an impact and UKIP is one of the big success stories in the populist front. At least at this stage of its development, UKIP shows no signs of easing up on the fear it is generating in the mainstream parties.

In an extensive article in January 2014, under the headline, 'Turning Right-Europe's Populist Insurgents', *The Economist* argues that:

> The parties of the nationalist right are changing the European political debate, but that does not guarantee them lasting electoral sense.

Providing a wide range of comments, *The Economist* examines the response of the political establishment to a tide of anti-European populism which draws on anti-immigrant feeling and Islamaphobia. As Catherine Fieschi (director of Counterpoint, a British think tank) argues, to raise the spectre of a return to 1930s fascism is not the right question. Most of these parties have no roots in the far right, so a better question to ask is how far can these parties use popular dissatisfaction to reshape Europe's political debate, and whether they can use that influence to win real power?

What all of these parties have in common is that they are populist and nationalist, that they have strong views on the EU, immigration and national sovereignty. Searching for reasons for success of populist parties, *The Economist* spells out its own analysis:

> The euro-zone crisis, and its aftermath, goes some way to explaining why – but it is far from a complete answer. The populist right is nowhere to

be found in austerity-battered Spain and Portugal. But it thrives in well off Norway, Finland and Austria. Between 2005 and 2013, according to calculations by Cas Mudde, at the University of Georgia, there are almost as many examples of electoral loss for parties of the far and populist right (in Belgium, Italy and Slovakia, among others) as there are of gain (in Austria, Britain, France, Hungary, the Netherlands).

But if euro-zone economics are not a full explanation, the crisis has been crucial to setting the scene for the potent new pairing of old nationalist rhetoric with contemporary Euro-scepticism. Across Europe, disillusionment with the EU is at an all-time high: in 2007 52 per cent of the public said it had a positive image of the EU; by 2013 the share had collapsed to 30 per cent. The new identity politics is a way of linking the problems of Europe and those of immigration. It also taps into concerns about the way globalisation, defended by the mainstream political consensus, undermines countries' ability to defend their jobs, traditions and borders.

The best example of how the new nationalism can pull the political debate in its direction by getting others to ape it is offered by UKIP. It has ten seats in the European Parliament (one of them Nigel Farage's) but none in Westminster; it secured just three per cent of votes in the 2010 general election. Yet, as Heather Grabbe of the Open Society think tank in Brussels points out, good poll numbers and impressive showings in by-elections have been enough to give its views potency, strengthening the hands of hard-line Euro-sceptics in the Conservative Party. As a result, David Cameron has promised a referendum on British membership of the EU. He also sounds an increasingly hard-line note on immigration from the EU, and on the need to clamp down on 'welfare tourism'. The Labour Party, relaxed in the past about open borders, now promises to be tougher, too.

This success, Grabbe adds, is largely Nigel Farage's:

> His canny deployment of saloon-bar blokeishness as common sense is the most potent tool of a party which lacks any strength in-depth and is prone to chaotic squabbling behind the scenes. His importance is typical of the populist parties' heavy reliance on one-man brands.

UKIP stands out because not only is it winning votes, it is reframing the arguments and ideas of both Labour and the Conservative Parties, raising Euroscepticism and toughening approaches to immigrants. This apparent fusion of populism and a kind of English nationalism, filtered through the prism of UKIP, an increasingly hostile press and more extreme conservatism is now in danger of influencing the thinking of the Labour Party. This is unwelcome at a time when Scots need reassurance about their future and not more uncertainty about the drift of England towards a negative national identity crisis.

Meanwhile overall membership of political parties is declining fast and to a larger extent in the UK than in any other country in the EU. As noted previously, faith in institutions such as the EU or national governments is also declining sharply, and anti-EU sentiment is rising. Based on information from the Eurobarometer – a survey conducted across all member states of the EU on a regular basis – trust in the EU (the average across the 28 nations) has fallen from 50 per cent in 2004 to 33 per cent in 2012; trust in national parliaments and governments has fallen from 38 per cent and 34 per cent respectively to 28 per cent and 27 per cent. Negative views of the EU have risen from a low of 15 per cent in 2006 to 29 per cent in 2012, with positive views falling from 50 per cent to 30 per cent over the same period.

Many of the mainstream political parties are seen as part of the problem, unable to find or suggest solutions. But associated with these new parties are more nationalism, more populism and less willingness to compromise to find solutions. Sheila Moorcroft concludes:

> Will people draw back – as the Dutch did in the face of radical views – or are we seeing the emergence of new radicalism and direct politics? Is the stalemate of US politics going to become more widespread, leaving millions feeling let down, ignored and forgotten by remote political elites? If democracy is in crisis in the West, how can we hope to promote it effectively to the rest of the world?

The mood of people throughout Europe is getting darker, mainstream parties in many countries are becoming more disconnected from their electorates and the institutions of Government are fast losing the trust and confidence of citizens. Into this vacuum have stepped populist parties, and in a world of uncertainty there is no idea of how this revolution in our democracy and politics will work out. For Scotland this is an anxious time, not only in terms of the ideas and policies UKIP stands for, but also in relation to the complete failure of the two major parties to confront what is happening. Equally worryingly is the prospect of Labour shifting their policy perspective on immigration, border controls and possibly the idea of a referendum on EU membership. The state of Union politics is best explained by the rise of UKIP in England and the rise of the SNP in Scotland. The political mould is being broken, traditional Unionist parties are struggling to find traction in this new political landscape and there is a growing lack of trust in the old politics which urgently needs to be addressed.

Anti-EU sentiment is growing, raising the spectre of xenophobia, intolerance, racism, anti-minorities and anti-Islamic sentiment. The continuing decline of mainstream parties and politics only serves to drive more people into protest, divorcing them from party loyalties and encouraging the acceptance and conversion to extremes. It is often the failure of moderate politics that leads people to extremes.

Politics and democracy are complex, but there is now overwhelming evidence that our politics is in decline, democracy is at risk and our political classes are either in denial, ignoring the signals or accepting the inevitability of what is happening and deciding to let things slide.

The undoubted beneficiary of this change in Scotland has been the SNP. Skilled in building a one-issue campaign and attracting a broad cross section of public support from their competence in Government, they have been able to move the same strategy to a multi-policy environment and take a wider group of people with them. They are a party for all political seasons consolidating as they have travelled since 2007. All of this has been reinforced by the decline of the Unionist parties and the general disillusionment of the public with old and traditional parties. So populism, constitutionalism, appealing to all shades of political opinion, framing a new form of civic nationalism, neither left nor right but appealing to all when required, charismatic leadership and a vision for the future, have been a successful mix. The last seven years have seen a formidable assault on the idea of business as usual. National politics in Scotland has changed forever.

There is of course a paradox at the heart of Scottish politics. The SNP has managed to escape the problems being experienced by the Unionist parties, continued to win elections, remain in power for seven years at Holyrood, navigate the legislation for the first ever referendum, change completely the face of Scottish politics and benefit from the problems facing Unionism and turn them into a success story for the SNP. The rise of the SNP and the decline of Labour in Scotland in the post-devolution years has been dramatic, relentless and in many ways, hardly surprising. Labour has made a series of political and constitutional miscalculations which have extracted a high price and may have set the Party back 20 years. The Party in its current denial, its inability to deal effectively with Scotland's role in the Union and its failure to create a progressive left of centre policy platform or to revive social democracy have left it vulnerable as two elections and a tough referendum loom large. Labour is in need of a total overhaul, without which its future cannot be guaranteed.

The SNP's success revolves around the fact that they appeal to the widest spectrum of voters – some right, some left, some populist, some centrist, some nationalist, and some radical, and for many just because they are not the other Unionist parties. In addition, they represent Scottishness, patriotism and pride in country. Salmond has managed to put together a remarkable coalition of voters. It may not survive, but for now the performance of the other parties is making their task very easy.

They also remain a protest party. And they still serve faithfully their nationalist base. How has this been allowed to happen?

A very British political Crisis

When Boris Johnson and Nigel Farage are described as 'anti-establishment' figures, then politics in Britain is clearly some way between farce and fantasy. A reality check on this kind of political nonsense is required! The idea that the beer drinking, rich, eccentric, city financier leader of UKIP will help take his followers – and chunks of the Tory Party – to a right-wing land flowing with milk and honey is outrageously funny and certainly worth a new series of *Spitting Images*. What is tragic and serious though is the state of the body politic in Britain, the deplorable nature of what masquerades as political debate in this country and the crisis of relevance facing Labour and the Liberal Democrats as grudge, fear, resentment and division gain traction as the mainstay of our politics. UKIP – more appropriately the English Independent Party – is a symptom of this political malaise and not the solution. All the polling suggests that UKIP is seen as the best bet for England and that of itself should spell out some of the dangers for a Conservative Party that still believes in the unity of the Union. This crisis of British politics has created the space for UKIP to succeed. Pandering to their excesses will only demean our politics further.

So where is the voice of reason and moderation? What is the opposition saying to this potential new right-wing coalition of Tories and UKIP? How do we get politics in Britain back to a level of sanity and substance? What is the progressive centre left response to the madness that is gripping this country? These are important questions that need urgent answers.

Setting aside the bias of much of the media and the self-serving nature of some of the newspaper owners, why are we allowing Farage and his right-wing associates to rubbish the European Union and the European Convention on Human Rights? Our membership of the EU is vital for the future of Britain, as it has been since we joined. But the positive case is never put forward and for the last 40 years we have allowed the debate to be hijacked by those on the right of British politics. For them, their assault on the EU is expressed in sweeping, general and prejudiced concerns without ever detailing what it is they are really concerned about. What kind of political process allows this drivel to masquerade as common sense? Much of the political right hates the EU. They cannot thole the idea of trusting others to be involved in the governance of Britain. They are so consumed by exceptionalism and reject the idea that we need, in an interdependent world, to work with our European colleagues. They overvalue the strength of the transatlantic relationship at a time when US foreign policy is more flexible and where Obama is seeking new 'special relationships'. They cannot live with the free market in goods, services, finance and people that was negotiated by Thatcher and implemented by Major when they signed the Maastricht Treaty – the biggest single surrender of British sovereignty. Their objections to immigrants – especially the concerns about Bulgaria and Romania – are stirring up much hatred and unnecessary fears and the real concerns of the public are being exploited for the wider goals of right-wing politics. But of particular concern is the fact that right-wing politicians dislike the social, financial, environmental and employment legislation and regulation which emanates from the EU and which makes this country much more civilised and a more decent place to live in. Social democracy in action makes many on the right feel ill at ease, but they don't have the courage to spell out their real political distaste for measures that help 'hard working British families'.

So instead of this revelatory debate we are treated to a phoney war on the EU, which comprises on the one hand of an onslaught from the right based on distortion, fiction and downright lies. On the other we have a so-called progressive left that just doesn't engage and put forward the real case for Europe. The trouble is that this phoney war could have real consequences. A decision to leave the EU, largely based on the views of England, could destroy the fragile solidarity of Britain, boost the case for Independence for Scotland and damage our economic prospects.

Labour and the Liberal Democrats, as the key players in a positive and progressive realignment of British politics, should now take on the Tories and their allies and put the alternative case to the public. Time is running out. So far no positive case is being made for the benefits of EU membership. The framing of the debate, the language of withdrawal and the hijacking of the agenda will inevitably result in next year's European Elections being used by the Tories and UKIP as an early referendum that requires no legislation from Westminster.

Edmund Burke believed that 'political reason is a computing principle' and a matter of 'adding, subtracting, multiplying and dividing', with the emphasis on continual adjustment and recalibration of the existing order. Burke also warned against the destabilising perils of extremist policies of any kind. British Conservatives are ignoring all of this. They see cause as more important than values or principle, pre-determined outcomes more attractive than consensus, reason or civilised debate and where ideology always trumps pragmatism and progressiveness. There is an alternative. Labour needs to inspire, enthuse, educate and provide politics with purpose, relevance and soul. The last few years have exposed a deepening crisis in politics. The alarm bells are ringing loudly, but is anyone listening?

The Tories, the Tea Party and UKIP

A visit to the United States of America is never dull. This is a country that is consumed by a total lack of belief in its law makers in Washington and the insane, dysfunctional and partisan failure of Capitol Hill to settle the long-term issues of raising the debt ceiling and keeping Government open and properly funded. Visiting Tulsa, Oklahoma (a seriously republican state that has never voted for a Democratic President since 1945), there is a palpable sense of anger at what is happening to their country. But remarkably, even 1,500 miles from Washington, partisan politics of the worst kind is evident as people scramble to discern who is to blame and what could be done to run the business of the country in a sane and grown up fashion. There are many people though who argue that this is just a natural consequence of the US Constitution, the founding fathers' idea of checks and balances and a healthy display of ideology and values being argued in the nation's capital. Whatever the explanation being offered, the US has serious debt, finance and fiscal problems that need a solution. Unfortunately the national interest is currently a bystander as the US legislature fights to the death on a partisan agenda.

The struggle between the two main parties is of course not the real story. The Tea Party is the architect of this crisis, with a degree of intent and malice unparalleled in modern US politics. Driven by constitutionalism, a hatred of Washington style politics, an obsession with cutting budgets regardless of the social consequences, an unqualified embrace of the market, tax cuts for the rich and a flair for the fanatical, the mainstream of the Republican party simply cannot cope with Tea Party aggression and conviction and are now panicking about the loss of moderates in the forthcoming primaries for this year's Congressional elections. The Tea Party is causing enormous damage to the Republican Party, humiliating the US abroad and promoting a near evangelical fervour of intolerance, hatred and division. For now the crisis has been resolved, but this is merely a ceasefire and the respite is likely to be temporary.

It is hard to avoid seeing some parallels in the UK, where the right is on the march in England. The Conservative Party has at least 100 MPs who are extreme by the standards of the traditional Labour and Conservative Parties and where UKIP is creating a Tea Party type headache for David Cameron. They threaten to target Tory seats where the incumbent MPs refuse to toe the insane UKIP line on leaving the EU and closing the door to immigration.

So the overall strategy is clear.

The battlegrounds are to be Europe, budget cuts, immigration, welfare, the poor and vulnerable and the European Court of Human Rights – and maybe even the idea of protecting human rights.

The approach used is lies, half-truths, distortion, sensationalism and deceit, all of which are reinforced by a very compliant right-wing press who often put the politics of their owners above the interests of the people and the country. The strategy of the right for the General Election in 2015 is now in place. We at least have to thank them for their total transparency!

Drilling deeper, there is a far more intriguing seam of right-wing thinking which the opposition parties and the public need to understand and expose. Fareed Zakaria, CNN host and editor of *Time Magazine*, talks about 'Conservatism's dark side'. In a recent article, 'Conservatism needs to lighten up,' Zakaria, says:

> Extreme rhetoric is just a way to keep the troops fired up. But conservatism's language of decay, despair and decline have created a powerful group of Americans who believe fervently in this dark narrative.

They are misty-eyed in their devotion to a distant myth and memory, yet passionate in their dislike of the messy, multi-racial, quasi-capitalist democracy that has been around for half a century. At some point, they will come to recognise that you cannot love America in theory and hate it in fact.

For America read Britain, and you see the threat posed by the right. In the UK the Conservative leadership is comfortable with austerity and recent comments from George Osborne suggest that it will continue for some time. This view reflects some dark age economics: no vision of good times ahead, the notion that it is 'all Labour's fault' and the Conservatives are without blame, a diet of false history leading to the myths and memories of bygone eras, of how shocking the collapse of family and society has been and the notion that the Government is only there to make the market function better. It is important to remind ourselves that the great enduring, popular and progressive institutions of this country, including the NHS, were created by Labour, not the Conservatives. Labour needs an inspired narrative. We don't need to live in a permanent state of pessimism and anxiety, this is just the Conservative way.

What ever happened to Decent Conservatives?

The Conservatives may be a spent force in Scottish politics, but the antics and activities of the Cameron-led Government south of the border pose a real threat to our politics and our democracy. The last few months of 2014 have been unprecedented in British politics. Humiliation for the Conservatives, and hell for the country, sums up a level of incompetence, ideology and indifference rarely seen in recent times. But why should we be surprised by these new levels of reckless and at times barely concealed abuses of parliamentary and political behaviour? Equally important, what moral compass is now driving the Lib-Dems as they continue to provide the day to day cover for a full-scale Conservative onslaught on the British welfare state? And are we so gullible that we can any longer fail to see British onservatism retreat from its own traditions and instead look more and more like the Republican Party in the US, now embracing 'movement conservatism' and identity politics, which combines a hatred of the State with an unconditional embrace of the free market and an appeal to the worst instincts of ordinary people?

Under the 'we are all in it together' banner, most of the nation signed up for the deficit, debt and cuts agenda, believing this to be right in the face of an unprecedented banking, financial and economic crisis. But austerity Britain was never supposed to be the cover under which the Conservatives would start a quiet revolution to dismantle and ultimately destroy decades of significant social, political and economic progress. This is a Party that couldn't win a Parliamentary majority, now implementing policies that were never included in a manifesto and bulldozing through Parliament with the passive compliance of Clegg and company: whatever happened to the party of Asquith, Palmerston, Lloyd George and Paddy Ashdown?

This should be a wake up call to all of us who value politics, democracy and the ideas of fairness and justice at the heart of our political system.

In the US there is a debate taking place within the Republican Party which revolves around mainstream conservatism and movement conservatism. The latter has become profoundly and defiantly un-conservative – in its arguments and ideas, in its tactics and strategies, and above all in its vision. Obsessed with its hatred of the State, the power of Government for collective good and linked to the importance of the free market, movement conservatives seem to be at war with the whole idea of modern America. This is ideologically driven and the complete antithesis of the originator of modern conservatism, Edmund Burke. Burke warned against the destabilising perils of extremist policies of any kind. British Conservatives are now the movement conservatives, where cause is more important than values or principle, where pre-determined outcomes are more attractive than consensus, reason or civilised debate and where ideology always trumps pragmatism and progressiveness. Similarly to the Republicans, they are trying, through identity politics, to turn people into victims of the State and Government: this is classic Tea Party politics.

Cameron and Osborne's neoconservatism has been for a long time hidden from view. This has been helped by the public's acceptance of the fact that austerity was the name of the game and we all had to buy in to it in the national interest. This charade has been exposed and laid bare. The Conservatives are past masters at framing issues where they get the language that fits their worldview and are then able to promote ideas. And when you control the language, you control the message, and much of the media does the rest.

Scots will be content that devolution protects us from most of the excesses of this form of radical conservatism, but they will also worry about the long-term implications of Westminster being controlled by such an alien outfit. This could have implications for how people vote in the forthcoming referendum on Independence.

Jason Farago in the *Guardian* in 2012 said the economic crisis in Europe has fuelled right-wing populism. But it lacks its American counterpart's free-market fundamentalism. In the US, we still think of the extreme right as anti-government, but these right populists often thrive in countries with strong welfare states, from Finland to Austria.

If that all sounds a bit unnatural to American ears, that's only because the right in the US is so thoroughly entrenched within the logic of corporatism that we cannot even conceive of another kind of right wing, says Jason Farago:

> They are 'Pinos', populists in name only: sooner or later, they always end up endorsing radical anti-tax proposals that favour the rich and sometimes actively penalise the poor.

The Rise of the Right

The Rise of the right in the Union (and overwhelmingly in England) is unsettling for progressives, but hardly surprising when you consider the large number of Conservative MPs – nearly 100 – who form the extreme end of the Conservative Party at Westminster, the transfer of US experience to Tory Party thinking and policy, and the compelling need to confront and then trump UKIP on some of its more toxic policies.

To understand the DNA of populism and the rise of the right, it is important to look at three imports from the US that influence the politics, psychology and strategy of campaigns. First, there is the idea of narrative and the framing of issues using relevant language. Second the idea of 'Cultural Wars'. Third, the idea of wedge issues, which help to divide and confuse political groups perceived to be reasonably homogenous, predictable in their voting intentions based on social class and who normally represent a stream of political loyalties and party allegiances. Helping to break down the DNA of voting groups is a key part of understanding how people vote against their economic interests, combine national identity with multiple identities and put personal or family values before concerns about community or society.

Don't Think of an Elephant! Know Your Values and Frame the Debate (2004) by George Lakoff explains how the radical right has been able to

convince average Americans to repeatedly vote against their own economic interests. His aim is to understand how the conservative right thinks,
what their moral values really are, and how to articulate the progressive
moral vision to reframe and reclaim political discourse. Lakoff's work is
relevant to what is happening in the UK and spells out the need to have a
narrative (which Labour often finds difficult) and to transform the language
of politics. Framing becomes key: this means getting language that fits
your worldview. Progressive parties like the Labour Party have often been
under the illusion that if only people understood the facts, that would be
the key to gaining support, but that invariably doesn't work because
people make decisions about politics based on their value systems and the
language and frames that invoke these values. The Independence referendum is a case in point, where overloading the campaign with masses of
facts and statistics may not have the desired effect. Similarly, the success
of UKIP does explain that insane economics and contradictory policies
may not matter, as the frames UKIP invoke address peoples values and
identity issues. Lakoff argues that progressives believe in three myths:

> First, truth will set us free. If we tell people the facts, since people are
> basically rational beings, they will all reach the right conclusions. Second,
> it is irrational to go against your self-interest and therefor a normal person
> who is rational reasons on the basis of self-interest. Third, that political
> campaigns are marketing campaigns, leading to the conclusion that
> polling should determine what issues a candidate should run on.

In the UK we can see the Conservative Party and UKIP deploying a number
of strategies which concentrate on values and identity issues – immigrants,
criminals, scroungers, Europe – framing them in such a way that people
vote for their values and not their economic self-interest. The Conservatives and UKIP see electoral advantage in framing the message in their own
language, constructing the wedge issues into groups that might normally
be more unified in voting patterns and political loyalties, waging the
cultural war to enthuse people into voting their values and making it
difficult for the progressives to respond because they have been politically
and tactically marginalised.

Borrowing from the US and Australia, the cultural war strategy has a
set of key elements at its core, including division and disunity. First, in
very simplistic terms, there is economic disunity, the two-tier economy,
with the undeserving poor remaining poor and the deserving rich being

lauded to do better. This leads to the absurd situation where the largest part of the non-pension social security budget is used to prop up low pay rather than change the economic system or legislate for a living wage and at the same time cut taxes for the rich as they need this kind of incentive to do better. In between is the 'excluded middle' who are caught in this twilight zone and are now more conscious than ever that they may be losing out in the battle for economic security. But the right and the populist need the votes of the poor and certain sections of the middle class to achieve this and require them to vote against their economic self-interest. So the scene is set for work to be done to dismantle economic self-interest and promote the social and personal values of those groups. People vote their values and identities more than their economic self-interest, so this becomes the political battleground for the right.

Second, social disunity becomes the objective through the idea of the cultural war and the political wedge. The assault on immigrants, welfare claimants (including some with disabilities), foreigners, trade unionists and the Islamic faith is an example of this. Powerful, evocative, divisive and identity-building at the same time, this creates new strands of voting intention where economic self-interest gives way to values. This, if the USA is anything to go by, is attractive to those who feel they have nothing to lose in economic terms and may in the past have had little interest in voting.

Third, political disunity emerges as mainstream Conservatives, Labour and the Lib-Dems lose out to the right and UKIP. Party allegiances and loyalties are breaking down, the certainty of voting patterns based on economic self-interest and social class are collapsing and the atomisation of society, helped by the internet age, is leading to social involvement at community level diminishing and membership of traditional churches, trades unions and social organisations – all contributing to a very different population and electors.

Finally, there is constitutional disunity. Membership of the EU, which is a metaphor for immigrants, foreigners and much else, is now being heavily contested by UKIP and the right. National identity is being undermined by our membership, our culture is in danger of being swamped by Bulgarians and Romanians taking advantage of the free movement of people and there is the reality of Britain being dictated to by France and Germany, and so the myths, fantasies, half-truths and lies go on and on! But this is creating a powerful focus for the right and UKIP, again getting people to think values, identity and culture in a negative and potentially destructive way.

Devolved government is another divisive issue for the populists, as in their eyes it takes power from Westminster and undermines control from the centre. But it is becoming a wedge issue because it allows the public in England to be stirred up by notions of Scotland getting a disproportionate amount of public finances, too many free services and Scottish MPs being able to vote on English matters at Westminster. This is grudge and grievance politics and illustrates a populist strategy that is consistently negative.

Disunity is the key to understanding the populists and the right of UK politics. Economic, social, political and constitutional issues are all being used to redraw the political map of the Union and alter the debate. This is essentially a battle being fought in England, but with enormous consequences for the whole of the UK and in particular at this critical moment, Scotland. The size and scale of England within the Union is overwhelming. Unless the threat from populism and the conservative right is understood and confronted, the Union's decline will continue and the fallout could be dramatic. The Independence referendum puts the Union on trial. While it may pass the political and constitutional test with the support of Scots this time, it may fail sometime in the future.

In the political battles that lie ahead, why does Labour want to keep moving on to the mythical common ground of UK politics? The Conservatives are never asked to go there. It seems entirely inappropriate for Labour, on the basis of where UKIP is, to be considering shifting ground on major issues such as Europe, immigration, the free movement of people and the European Convention on Human Rights on the basis of expediency and not values, principle and philosophy. The political right in the UK stands for what is described in the US as cheap patriotism. Standing for something is the key and while progressives want to be popular and keep on the side of the public, they must develop a strong alternative narrative. This should be founded on philosophy and principles, be constructed on the values of fairness, justice, equality and the common good, be framed in ways that capture the needs and aspirations of people, be written in language which is relevant, modern and persuasive and is offering security and solidarity and a life of opportunity for the many, not the few.

In *The Death of Conservatism*, Sam Tanenhaus argues that:

> The right has always been split between two factions, the consensus driven realists who believe in the virtue of government and its power to adjust

to changing conditions and movement conservatives – the conservative right – who distrust governments and society and often find themselves at war with America itself.

His comment could accommodate the current schism in the Conservative Party and the role of the right as movement conservatives. A paradox lies at the heart of the modern right: in its arguments, ideas, tactics and strategies and above all else in its vision it has become profoundly unconservative.

Tanenhaus asks:

> Why has movement conservatism pursued so destructive a course? Why has it depended so long on a politics of enmity of polarising divisiveness rather than common concerns? Why does the contemporary right define itself less by what it yearns to conserve than by what it longs to destroy?

These questions should be addressed to the conservative right in Britain. They pretend to be patriots loving their country, seeking in the process to defend our national interest and act in the vanguard of what being British means. Nothing could be further from the truth! There is a place for real conservatives in Britain, but surely one that conserves, not destroys. In his book *Rebuild the Dream*, Van Jones, former special adviser to the Obama White House, distinguishes between 'cheap patriotism' and 'deep patriotism'. Cheap patriotism fits the conservative right, who seek to destroy rather than conserve. They pretend to love the idea of country but talk and act as if they were at war with it and dislike most groups in it. They pretend to embrace difference and diversity, but are unsure of recognising that we live in a union of four nations and spend much of their rhetoric attacking any of the groups that contribute to a multi-ethnic, multi-racial and multi-cultural Union. They pretend to be concerned about inequality but believe in an unfettered capitalism, with rising levels of poverty and a growing gap between rich and poor. They pretend to support the interests of all of the people but would be happy with a society where the market is free but the people are not. The list is endless. Progressives have to waken up to the fact that the UK is under attack from the right and the populists and that much of what is happening comes from Westminster and England. The Independence referendum gives Scotland the chance to escape this madness and build a different kind of Scotland – a vision which would sharply contrast with what may emerge in England over the next decade. This is just one of the dilemmas facing Scottish voters.

The contrast with deep patriotism couldn't be starker. The only problem with this is whether the UK or Britain can be the repository of passion, pride or patriotism or will this fall to the four nations of the Union to embrace. This approach is clever because it puts the opposition on the back foot and as certain sections of the press mobilise in favour of the assault on these groups, there is no finely developed alternative narrative and as a consequence a complicated, nuanced and hard to deliver response makes little impact. Finally, and far more disconcerting, the opposition party, obsessed with polls and headlines, starts to move towards the UKIP or Conservative positions on some of these wedge issues. This is Labour's problem. Labour needs to expose what is happening in England and take the long view of current political developments. Crucially, all progressives must accept that populism and the rise of the right are not short-term blips on the screen that monitors the health of UK politics. Two forces – the decline of the Labour and Conservative Parties and the rise of the right and populism – are inextricably linked to each other and both are changing the nature of politics, shaping the social and economic agenda and framing the values, principles and philosophy behind the public discourse. For progressives, the outcomes often look crude and unthinking but for the populists and the right they reflect a sophisticated, smart and scientific approach achieving their political goals. Progressives, especially Labour and the Lib-Dems, need to wake up! If any evidence was needed to illustrate the problems facing the politics of England we need look no further than the rise of the SNP in Scotland and the way it has moved from a party on the margins to the mainstream of Scottish politics; from a single issue to a broad platform of attractive policies; shifted from a narrow nationalism to a more inclusive civic nationalism; ensured a change from cranky leadership to charismatic; has transformed the one time dream of an Independent Scotland into a possible reality in a referendum agreed by the Prime Minister of the UK; and have moved effortlessly from a feeble opposition to become a strong majority Government of Scotland – and all of this has happened in the space of seven years! In the context of Scottish politics, this is a political earthquake or revolution. Political leaders of the Westminster parties should reflect on why this happened in Scotland and the possibility of it happening in England.

So we have four contexts to consider when looking at the rise of the right and populism. First the US, where the Tea Party has had a significant impact on Government and will continue to have a disruptive impact on the workings of Congress. This poses serious consequences for the Republican

Party, especially in candidate selection in the forthcoming House and Senate elections. This provides a timely reminder that a combination of public disillusionment with the mainstream, an excess of constitutionalism, hatred of government and the role of the state, being able to promote cultural wars, an abundance of cheap patriotism, having an endless supply of charismatic ideologues, confused and contradictory policies, and having certain sections of big business on your side, may be the main drivers of the new politics.

Secondly, we have the lessons of Europe, where populism and the new right have been able to flourish in conditions of fear and uncertainty. The old political parties, having lost much of their philosophical and ethical moorings, losing the trust and confidence of the public and unable to deal effectively with globalisation, are increasingly being seen as having little relevance to the lives of citizens, especially those who are poor or disadvantaged.

Third, there is the neoliberal right at Westminster challenging the social democratic politics and old fashioned right of centre politics of the post-war period. Under the cloak of austerity, the foundations of a new and more aggressive form of conservative thinking are being slowly put into place, in health, education, social security and in the economy. The EU is being demonised and scapegoated for all the ills of the UK. David Cameron is urging reform and then a Referendum in 2017, but the extreme right of the Conservative Party is urging removal from the EU in 2017 or earlier if some of the Euro-haters have their way. Devolved government is at best a distraction for the Conservatives and while Scotland leaving the Union would be a humiliation, for them it might be better than giving up the absolute sovereignty of Westminster. Slowly but surely, our Union and each of the four nations which make it up are being prepared for a long-term political journey whose destination might be unknown, but whose direction is obvious, unattractive and divisive.

Fourth, there is UKIP. The success of this maverick party, sustained by a charismatic leader, a rag bag of policies, a public deeply disillusioned with the old Unionist parties performance, a hatred of the EU, a toxic campaign against immigrants, foreigners and benefit claimants, a contempt for the political establishment, an obsession with national sovereignty and a confused view of devolution, which on bad days and dependent on who is commenting could be interpreted as abolition. But these contradictions and inconsistencies are of little interest to their voters. Like the Tea Party, this is about the weaknesses of the mainstream parties, identity politics and a sentimental and emotional attachment to the past, whatever it was. Farage, in a remarkable way, has created a narrative that is both compelling and beguiling, but essentially fraudulent. This is a manifesto for change based on grudge and grievance, the negative politics of discontent, which is persuasive but empty. This is a party whose leader is a complete fiction and the antitheses of the downtrodden working man wrestling with the everyday problems of working people. But despite all of this he is the most popular party leader in Britain, one of the most successful in Europe and is not only changing the political landscape of Britain and England, he is forcing the Conservative Party to stiffen their resolve on the European Union and is enthusing the right of David Cameron's Party to look to some kind of relationship with UKIP after the 2015 election. If that wasn't bad enough, Farage may be having some policy impact on the Labour Party as it hesitates and reflects on immigration, border controls, reform of the EU and a tougher stand on benefit claimants.

So why is this happening? Why are the political offerings of the other parties so unappealing to a growing cross section of public opinion? Why have the Unionist parties allowed this to happen? This is not rocket science. Labour and the Conservatives should have seen this coming, but didn't. We are now staring at a possible future where Scotland exits the United Kingdom, the Conservatives and UKIP form some alliance of the right after the next General Election and the UK exits the European Union in 2017. This is not a sound basis for Scots to vote NO in the Independence referendum, nor is it reassuring about the politics of England after the referendum. For Scots, the prospects of a Labour Government at Westminster will certainly influence how they might vote on Independence. As the political storm clouds gather over the Union, we should never underestimate how unpopular the Westminster-based Conservative Party is in Scotland and the threats, real or imagined, that are now facing Scots as the politics of England and Scotland further divide. Scotland is a different country and it makes no sense to be in denial.

To understand how populism may develop in the UK, the Spinelli Group, in their report produced in 2013, 'The Rise of Populism and Extremist Parties in Europe', set out why populism was attractive in Europe. They asked if this require a more radical Europe and in the immediate future is Europe powerless? Using reports and research findings, seven observations were seen as critical to a broader understanding of the phenomenon of populism:

- First, the growing electoral success of extremist parties in Europe and their rise from the margins to being part of the political scene.

- Second, the major European parties are losing votes and the report describes increasingly low turnout as a real European disease. The public are losing confidence in the political discourse and ask if the traditional parties have the ability to adapt and respond.

- Third, the report questions whether there is left-wing populism.

- Fourth, the report looks at the role of the economic and social crisis in the rise of populism. While accepting the consequences of the economic crisis and the criticisms of EU governance, the report concludes this is not enough to explain the rise in the populist movement.

- Fifth: are national identity, statements of belonging and European political identification important issues? Since 1992, populism sees the European political project as an integrationist and perilous enterprise for the nation which will be crushed by a federal structure that has no soul. So the EU has a very low political identification power, which hardly gives rise to collective identity.

- Sixth looks at the Democratic shortcomings of the EU. The European Institutions are widely castigated by populist parties who consider them to be distant, technocratic and undemocratic.

- Seventh, the traditional moderate parties are losing out in the populist discourse. There is an alarming radicalisation of public opinion to which the traditionally moderate parties are trying to respond.

While the report is mainly about populism within the EU, it does reflect what is happening in the UK, especially in England, and certainly places UKIP in the mainstream of the anti-European debate. What is clear is that the traditional parties of the EU are finding it difficult to retain traction in a political landscape that is rapidly transforming, experiencing rapid declines in turnout as people turn away from traditional ways of democratic participation and being squeezed by the debate on supranationalism v intergovernmentalism, the present state of affairs or the challenge ahead for most Eurosceptics, the battle between federalism and boosting the nation states.

A recent article in the *Observer* looks at the Tories as the real Marxists and agrees that some political forensic science is needed to understand how they work, think and function in our politics. Political profiling and some DNA approaches may help explain what Conservatism is today. For a significant minority of Tory MPs ideology, extremism, and, in a curious way, anti-British sentiment is now the agenda. What does the right stand for in British politics? No such thing as the middle ground – a fiction – how is it defined? People have multiple identities and have complex views, specific or general notions about things and certainly rarely carry or committed to a whole agenda of one party views about their own future or that of their country. Voting values are becoming a powerful force alongside economic interests as a reason for voting and preference.

Nationality is increasingly important and a powerful force in devolution. The politics of Scotland, Wales and Northern Ireland can no longer be ignored. Heading to America – a nation that does not pretend to be egalitarian or socialist or collective or concerned about fairness in what it does – but it does have powerful ideas based on its constitution and it has no class system similar to Britain. It is a massively unequal society, as is Britain and Scotland. Why shouldn't we be like Scandinavia or Germany or other parts of Europe? We are global and European but we have arguments from the right about merely being British, isolated and disconnected from a world and a Europe that needs to be more integrated, united and equal. At every turn right-wing politics is in danger of isolating Britain. An offer of the past, from the past, by the past –there is an astonishingly open goal, but we can't seem to see the opportunities presented to us.

The level of political or public literacy is woeful and this is dangerous. We need an informed electorate and a party that understands change; a party that has a philosophy that intelligently and effectively exposes the Right in British politics; a party that has a vision for the world we live in and a serious view on how we can be a positive part of change; a party that understands and respects its citizens. We need a party that values the future more than the past; a party that reaches out and is less concerned with archaic machinery and cultures of party politics. We need a party that sees the moral limits and excesses of markets; a party that can thread together and advocate the benefits of the State, Government and the private sector. Above all else, a party that both understands and promotes the common good where an enabling, empowering and equal society is built around the idea of the equal worth of every child, young person and adult in our country. Tackling inequality must be our major objective.

With this in mind, the DNA of the Right is pretty objectionable: xenophobic, authoritarian, Europhobe, anti-foreigner, anti-immigrant, pro a society divided on class and income, nostalgic and sentimental about the Britain of the past and oblivious to the real needs of the public.

Scotland is by no means a perfect political environment, but so far some of the excesses of the Union, especially England, have not being experienced. This could change in the future, but for now there is a pressing need to renew our politics and whether the boost for that comes from continuing membership of the UK or Independence is not clear. Regardless, what is happening in England will begin to impact. If conservatism is unpopular in Scotland, it is hard to imagine what more populism and the rise of the political right will do for Scots.

CHAPTER SEVEN

Britishness and National Identity

BRITISHNESS IS COMPLEX, confusing and constantly changing. But one thing is clear: there is much less of it around than there was 50 years ago. Argued over by historians, politicians and academics and now pollsters, Britishness is playing its part in shaping the political and constitutional future of the United Kingdom and will have an impact on the Independence referendum. More recently, Britishness has been discussed in relation to the national identities of Scotland, England and Wales. What is not in doubt, based on a general or generic description of Britishness, is that in the three nations of the Union the number of people affirming Britishness has declined dramatically and as a result the national identities of Scottishness, Englishness and Welshness have risen, and in the case of England has increased markedly in the post-devolution years. What is also significant is that the number of people affirming both Britishness and, for example, Englishness, has also declined. There are clearly major shifts in national identity taking place. But what is not clear is the impact this will have on the current debate taking place on the future of Scotland, the political and constitutional structure of the Union beyond the referendum or the integrity and shape of our democracy.

Three Prime Ministers

This chapter looks at some of the concepts and ideas surrounding Britishness, considers how this is influencing the debate and then, trying to capture the politics of this powerful idea, highlights the very different contributions of three Prime Ministers – Tony Blair, Gordon Brown and David Cameron – who over the past 15 years have been very keen to embrace Britishness (not always for the same reasons), to define what it means and spell out its importance for the UK, the four nations and each citizen.

Treaty of Union

Since the Treaty of Union in 1707, there have been many high points for Britishness as Britain became a more established fact in the fortunes of

Scotland, England and Wales. Many historians agree however that the post-war period has been important in making the Union less attractive, the idea of Britishness less relevant and the idea of individual national identities more important. Looking forward, these historical, political and constitutional trends seem likely to continue and this raises the question of what kind of response we can anticipate from the United Kingdom and Westminster to these increasingly significant changes in the mood of the four nations, their needs and ambitions and in particular the overwhelming sense of grievance and discontent being expressed in polls and attitude surveys by England.

Definitions of Britishness

The concept of national identity has been an enduring subject of debate for centuries and historians and social scientists have considered at length what it means. Some have argued for a cultural definition. Some have argued that the concept of nationality is essentially a socially engineered construct. In this regard the importance of social phenomenon, such as class, has been emphasised. Some have defined national identity as one of a number of multiple identities which in turn are influenced by race, gender, ethnicity, religion and globalisation. Some believe that national identity could be experienced differently based on the social characteristics of the individual. Many accounts of national identity are a combination of some or all of these issues. A library note on Britishness from the House of Lords in 2008 provides an excellent summary on the concept:

> National identity is the result of the interaction of the ethnic past and the forces of modernity. This approach has allowed social scientists to identify different types of national identity – civic and ethnic. Civic national identity refers to residence, shared political values, common civic institutions and shared language, whereas ethnic national identity is seen as being related to ancestry and emersion in national customs and traditions.

The concept of Britishness has been the source of some recent debate amongst historians. Some commentators have noted that the study of Britishness as a distinct national identity is complicated by the fact that many accounts tend to conflate Britishness with Englishness, and often treat English events and trends as though they were synonymous with British developments.

Has English history become British history?

Importantly, some commentators have argued that no formal attempt was made to make Britishness a primary cultural identity, which allowed a number of interpretations of what being British meant to develop. Instead, they point to the various social and economic processes of industrialisation and the distinct role of Parliament in the acceptance of Britishness.

Some typical examples of Britishness as a current national identity are expressed by John Major, the former Prime Minister, through various images of long shadows on county cricket grounds, warm beer, invincible green suburbs, dog lovers and, as George Orwell said, 'old maids bicycling to Holy Communion through the morning mist'. In 2005, the *Daily Telegraph* published what it called the 10 core values of British identity, which underpinned its campaign for Britishness. These values were:

- The rule of law. Our society is based on the idea that we all abide by the same rules, whatever our wealth or status. No one is above the law – not even the Government.

- The sovereignty of the Crown in Parliament. The Lords, the Commons and the monarch constitute the supreme authority in the land. There is no appeal to any higher jurisdiction, spiritual or temporal.

- The pluralist state. Equality before the law implies that no one should be treated differently on the basis of belonging to a particular group. Conversely, all parties, sects, faiths and ideologies must tolerate the existence of their rivals.

- Personal freedom. There should be a presumption, always and everywhere, against state coercion. We should tolerate eccentricity in others, almost to the point of lunacy, provided no one else is harmed.

- Private property. Freedom must include the freedom to buy and sell without fear of confiscation, to transfer ownership, to sign contracts and have them enforced. Britain was quicker than most countries to recognise this and became, in consequence, one of the happiest and most prosperous nations on Earth.

- Institutions. British freedom and British character are immanent in British institutions. These are not (mostly) statutory bodies, but spring from the way free individuals regulate each other's conduct, and provide for their needs, without recourse to coercion.

- The family. Civic society depends on values being passed from generation to generation. Stable families are the essential ingredient of a stable society.

- History. British children inherit a political culture, a set of specific legal rights and obligations, and a stupendous series of national achievements. They should be taught about these things.

- The English-speaking world. The atrocities of September 11, 2001, were not simply an attack on a foreign nation; they were an attack on the Anglosphere –on all of us who believe in freedom, justice and the rule of law.

- The British character. Shaped by and in turn shaping our national institutions is our character as a people: stubborn, stoical, and indignant at injustice. 'The Saxon,' wrote Kipling, 'never means anything seriously till he talks about justice and right.'

A Confusing Subject

Setting aside the right-leaning nature of the *Telegraph*, this presents an important insight in to the London/England mindset and the use of the word, 'Anglosphere' explains a great deal about the issue of Britishness. Any discussion of Britishness will by its very nature be complex and often highly personal or political.

The public debate has also focussed on the merits of multi-culture, multi-nation, multi-ethnic and multi-religion, often in relation to national identity, and this just adds to the complexity of what Britishness means in the Britain of the 21st century.

The Idea of Multiple identities

In a Demos pamphlet, Vince Cable, the Liberal Democrat Shadow Chancellor, contended that multiculturalism was often a poor description of what exists and a poor guide to how the politics of identity can and should evolve. He thought that it underestimated the complexity of ethnic groups. Furthermore, while 'multiculturalism' may have played a positive role in encouraging respect for other faiths and traditions it had the:

> ... negative effects of stereotyping, of encouraging exaggerated deference to unrepresentative 'community leaders' and creating in the political world the dangerous – and erroneous – idea that Britain's ethnic minorities are 'vote banks' rather than aggregations of individuals.

He called for the abandonment of multiculturalism and the creation of a tolerant British national identity based on the concept of 'multiple identities', whether national, ethnic, geographic or religious, and combined with a strong commitment to the rights of the individual and law and order.

The Break-up of Britain

Part of the debate surrounding Britishness was the perception by some that it was in retreat. Tom Nairn, who had predicted the breakup of the UK in the late 1970s, argued in 2007 that the 'passion of "Britishness" has lost all weight and gravitas'. He suggested that processes of globalisation and Scottish nationalism, especially in the wake of devolution, made the breakup of the Union very likely. Linda Colley argued that Britishness was threatened by the decline of Protestantism, the absence of war and the end of Empire, which had removed the ability for Britain's to define themselves with the 'other'.

Andrew Marr suggested that Britain was suffering from its inability to evolve 'into a popular modern democratic society', which had led to the unpopularity of British political culture and its institutions and which led some to seek political expression elsewhere.

Peter Hitchens argued that the decline of Britishness was largely due to politically engineered reasons. He thought that these included the questioning of traditional values and institutions, such as the Church of England.

Gordon Brown, the then Chancellor of the Exchequer, set out his views on history, ideas and British national identity:

> I would want to stress a belief in tolerance and liberty, a sense of civic duty, a sense of fair play, a sense of being open to the world. The real challenge over the next few years is to see how our institutions can better reflect these values. That may mean quite profound changes in how our constitution is organised, how civic rights work – especially at a local level, where big changes need to be made – and an anti-protectionist approach to the wider world. And we've got to think about the symbols of integration for the future – this is not just about a national day, or how to treat the festival of remembrance, it is about greater emphasis on the shared values that unite us. Our values have influenced our institutions and traditions in a particular way – partly because we have been a multinational society over centuries. And one proposition that I am keen to support is the idea of an institute of British studies, or something similar, that looks in depth

– and in a non-partisan way – at how the ideas that shape our history should shape our institutions in the future and what effect that might have on policy.

Another period of Denial

In the years immediately after Tony Blair's Government introduced a raft of constitutional changes, there was a semblance of a debate in which the political classes seemed willing to engage in the issue of Britishness, national identity and on the wider and more general question of the constitution. But in the last decade interest seems to have waned. Westminster seemed to have lost interest, with that whole agenda in retreat. The rise of the SNP, quite remarkably, failed to generate much interest despite their spectacular victories in 2007 and 2011. It was only in the last two years, when David Cameron acknowledged he had a major problem on his hands that the debate on the constitution exploded onto the political scene. Once again, it was a reaction to a perceived threat, rather than there being any enthusiasm or interest in the wider issues, of which Scotland was only part. Sadly, the most important point had been missed. This was not so much a question about Scotland, but how the UK and Westminster through neglect and indifference have allowed the constitutional, political and democratic agenda to unravel and are now largely responsible for the crisis they are dealing with. Political unionism, Westminster ambivalence, a comfortable complacency and probably much more have combined to put the future of the Union at risk. During the passage of the Scotland Bill in 1998, the vast majority of MPs hoped this issue would not resurface for a very long time. This is Westminster's worst nightmare. So if Scotland exits or remains, does Westminster really believe that all that is required is a few more powers and tax concessions to be dispensed to Scotland and Wales? This seems to be the mindset at Westminster, in which Scotland is seen as the only problem, and the Union should not be the focus of any further attention! Scotland's referendum may have ended this period of indifference.

Blair, Brown and Cameron

In order to contrast and compare how three Prime Ministers – Tony Blair, Gordon Brown and David Cameron – have sought to embrace the idea of

Britishness, extracts from their speeches over the past 15 years are presented, which in themselves are of interest, but more importantly, they also capture their own personal views, their level of understanding of a really complex issue and to what extent there was an appreciation of where Britain or the Union was heading.

Gordon Brown has, without a doubt, a sharp intellect and a well-developed understanding of politics and constitutional issues. Of the three PMs his comments have context, a deeper understanding of the issues and a better sense of history. On achieving office in 2007, he produced a Green Paper and it seemed progress might be made on giving more powers to Parliament to oversee the work of the Executive. There was also discussion about the need for a codified constitution to bring some order to the rag bag of statutes, conventions, laws and procedures that currently make up our so-called unwritten constitution. Unfortunately very little progress, if any, was achieved and this new-found interest in the politics and constitution came to an end when David Cameron became Prime Minister.

On becoming Prime Minister, Gordon Brown – as a Scot in a Westminster where there was growing anti-Scottish sentiment – had to defend Britishness and make the case for a new Britain. Some extracts from his time as Chancellor are also included.

In the 2004 British Council Annual Lecture, Brown set out the key elements of his views on Britishness: commitments to "'iberty for all, responsibility by all and fairness to all'. He believed that the establishment of such shared values could foster:

> A new British patriotism that would move beyond ethnicity, race and institutions, and which would allow people to share... a common view of challenges and what needs to be done, forge a unified and shared sense of purpose about the long-term sacrifices they are prepared to make and the priorities they think important for national success.

He hoped that this Britishness would allow 'a rich agenda for change' based around:

> ... new constitutional settlement, an explicit definition of citizenship, a renewal of civic society, a rebuilding of our local government and a better balance between diversity and integration.

Proud to be British

A multinational state with England, Scotland, Wales and now Northern Ireland, we are a country united not so much by race or ethnicity but by shared values that have shaped shared institutions. But when people are also asked what they admire about Britain, more usually says it is our values: British tolerance, the British belief in liberty and the British sense of fair play. And there is a golden thread which runs through British history – that runs from that long ago day in Runnymede in 1215 when arbitrary power was fully challenged with the Magna Carta, on to the first Bill of Rights in 1689 when Britain became the first country where Parliament asserted power over the King, to the democratic reform acts – throughout the individual standing firm against tyranny and then an even more generous, expansive view of liberty: the idea of all government accountable to the people, evolving into the exciting idea of empowering citizens to control their own lives.

Just as it was in the name of liberty that in the 1800s Britain led the world in abolishing the slave trade – something we celebrated in 2007 – so too, in the 1940s Britain stood firm against fascism, which is why I would oppose those who say we should do less to teach that period of our history in our schools.

The Britain of fairness to every individual we see expressed most of all in Britain's unique national health service, health care free of charge to all who need it, founded not on ability to pay but on need – at the core of British history, the very British ideas of 'active citizenship', 'good neighbour', civic pride and the public realm.

Secessionist Forces

In 2008, Gordon Brown wrote an article in which he warned against 'secessionist' forces. He disagreed that people had to choose between different territorial identities. He sought to stress the tangible advantages of the Union, but also the benefits of shared understanding and values: there is no Scotland-only, Wales-only, England-only solution to transnational challenges that range from terrorism to foot and mouth disease, and from avian flu to security and climate change. So for these islands an environmental Union, a security Union and a Union for defence is to the benefit of all. But what matters even more are the common values we share across the United Kingdom: values we have developed together over the years that are rooted in liberty, in fairness and tolerance, in enterprise, in civic initiative and internationalism. These values live in the popularity of our common institutions.

In a speech in Glasgow 2014, Brown calls for constitutional reforms tying Scottish prosperity to UK:

> Constitutional reforms should be made to create a 'Union for social justice' in which the UK can pool and share resources for the benefit of all, according to former prime minister Gordon Brown.
>
> Brown said Scotland would be strengthened by his proposed constitutional changes while remaining within the Union. The MP wants the Scottish Parliament to be made irreversible, with 'maximum devolution of powers in training, transport, health, the Crown Estates Commission and the running of elections'.
>
> He has proposed UK legislation to state the shared purpose of the union, 'namely the pooling and sharing of resources for social justice'.
>
> I am of the view that the party that first created a powerful Scottish parliament is best placed to strengthen devolution and to create a stronger Scottish parliament in a stronger UK. – *The Guardian*

Gordon Brown's speeches talk about history and, while embracing a range of values common to all the PMs in this chapter, there is more authority and commitment to the idea of a Union of social justice. This provides for much of his constitutional thinking to be linked to concepts, not territories, and to collective centralism, redistribution of resources and retaining the Westminster dominance and the absolute sovereignty of Parliament that goes with it. There is an element of caution and care in his comments which are reflected in the speeches of both Blair and Cameron. To a great extent, his words highlight the problems that Britishness and national identity pose to parliamentarians schooled in the Westminster way, suspicious of anything that might cut across history and the authority of the Palace of Westminster.

Tony Blair's Britain speech, 2000:

> My argument today is this. Britain is stronger together, than separated apart. True Britishness lies in our values, not unchanging institutions. The Constitutional changes we have made and a new attitude of engagement with

Europe are not a threat to British identity but on the contrary are the means of strengthening it for today's world.

We have to recognise the huge changes we are living through and the challenges they present to this country. But also the opportunities for renewal that they offer.

Standing up for our country means standing up for what we believe in. It means standing up for our values and having the strength to realise them in the modern world. It means standing up for the core British values of fair play, creativity, tolerance and an outward-looking approach to the world. It does not mean an unthinking resistance to change. It does not mean railing against the outside world.

Our national identity is not some remote and abstract issue.

In this new world, it has become increasingly fashionable to predict the death of the nation-state. A world in which capital crosses national frontiers at the push of a key, where air travel has made the outside world personally familiar to millions, where television has brought it into the homes of millions more, a world where supra-national organisations like the EU and WTO play an increasingly important role is a world where questions are inevitably going to arise about the continuing significance of national identity.

What makes Britain and Britishness important, valid and as necessary today as ever is a powerful combination of shared values and mutual self-interest? We are stronger together, economically and politically with the nations of the UK able to maximise their collective will and authority. In defence, foreign policy, economic weight, we are better off and stronger together.

It is when our values fail to be reflected in the institutions that govern us that Britain and British identity is under threat. When we came to office, the Party of no change – the Conservatives – were left without any seats in Scotland or Wales. Forces for change were left with no alternative but status quo or separatism. Devolution at long last offered a sensible modernisation of the partnership in the UK. Let Scotland and Wales do what they do best locally. Let the UK do what it is right to do together.

The Conservative Party, in the Tory policy document on five guarantees for Britain, proposes 'English votes for English laws'. While rejecting a proposal to set up a wholly separate English parliament and now today re-affirming that they support devolution, they propose to exclude the Scots, Welsh and Irish from any discussion of laws defined as 'English'. The rest of Britain's MPs would, in effect, become second class citizens in the UK

Parliament – voting on some issues but not on all of them – and the make-up of the executive would have to reflect the possibility of defeat on English issues even if a majority was available for British issues.

On Europe, standing up for Britain does not mean being anti-Europe. It is not pro-British to be anti-Europe. The EU is part of the modern world. Britain is part of the EU. Standing up for Britain means fighting for British values, getting the best for Britain, whether it is economic reform, moving Europe closer to the USA or protecting the British rebate.

I believe few would disagree with the qualities that go towards that British identity: qualities of creativity built on tolerance, openness and adaptability, work and self-improvement, strong communities and families and fair play, rights and responsibilities and an outward looking approach to the world that all flow from our unique island geography and history.

If these values are what makes us British, rather than unchanging institutions, the devolution is a necessary part of keeping Britain together: more regional decentralisation in England makes sense.

On the contrary, it is quintessentially British, it is one of our distinguishing characteristics as a people, that we have always been willing to adapt our institutions to changing circumstances. In the 19th century, in response to tumultuous economic and social change, we reformed the suffrage not once, but three times.

And, of course, there are those, like the SNP, who argue that this would be positively desirable and that the Union has had its day and the sooner it is unravelled, the better.

This nation has been formed by a particularly rich complex of experiences: successive waves of invasion and immigration and trading partnerships, a potent mix of cultures and traditions which have flowed together to make us what we are today.

Blood alone does not define our national identity. How can we separate out the Celtic, the Roman, the Saxon, the Norman, the Huguenot, the Jewish, the Asian and the Caribbean and all the other nations that have come and settled here? Why should we want to? It is precisely this rich mix that has made all of us what we are today.

Both current critiques of our constitutional reforms, I believe, are rooted in a fundamental misunderstanding of the relationship between a democratic people and the institutions they consent to have rule over them. New institutions do not necessarily create new feelings. They can just give long held feelings new – and often better – expression.

This government's progressive programme of constitutional reform is now moving us from a centralised Britain, where power flowed top-down, to a devolved and plural state. A new Britain is emerging with a revitalised conception of citizenship, as the House of Lords finally is reformed to remove the democratic anomaly of the hereditary peers, as the European Convention of Human Rights is incorporated into British law and as we bring in, for the first time, rights to Freedom of Information.

The Blair speech contains few references to the constitutional changes he made being part of a wider and more coherent vision for the future. Instead they seem to stand out as complete in themselves and necessary to keep the Union together. There is no broad sweep of history and every conceivable characteristic associated to British identity is deployed without conveying a real sense of what the values, vision and outcomes are likely to be. This was more of the 'Cool Britannia' approach to constitutional change than opening up a new chapter in modernising Britain's still ramshackle constitution. There is little political or constitutional depth to the speech and although written nearly 15 years ago, it neither spells out the lasting benefits of the reforms that Blair introduced or gives any indication that the reforms were part of any radical transformative strategy that would address the deep constitutional, political and democratic weaknesses of the Union.

David Cameron, speaking in Edinburgh in 2007 on the importance of the Union, expressed his concern at the union's fragility and the 'ugly stain of separatism seeping through the union flag'. He thought the best way to counter this was through the creation of a clear identity:

But in the search for identity, here in Great Britain we have the best possible start. Not just English, not just Scottish, not just Welsh. But British. That is because being British is one of the most successful examples of inclusive civic nationalism in the world. We are a shining example of what a multi-ethnic, multi-faith and multi-national society can be. And the challenge now is to renew that sense of belonging by creating a positive vision of a British society that really stands for something and makes people want to be part of it. A society in which we are held together by a strong sense of shared history and common values and institutions we cherish. Britishness is also about institutions, attachment to our monarchy, admiration for our armed forces, understanding of our history, recognising that our liberty is rooted in the rule of law and respect for parliament.

David Cameron speaking in June 2014:

> This week there has been a big debate about British values following the Trojan Horse controversy in some Birmingham schools – about what these values are, and the role they should play in education. I'm clear about what these values are – and I'm equally clear that they should be promoted in every school and to every child in our country.
>
> The values I'm talking about – a belief in freedom, tolerance of others, accepting personal and social responsibility, respecting and upholding the rule of law – are the things we should try to live by every day. David Cameron wants British values taught in every school.
>
> To me they're as British as the Union flag, as football, as fish and chips. Of course, people will say that these values are vital to other people in other countries. And, of course, they're right.
>
> But what sets Britain apart are the traditions and history that anchors them and allows them to continue to flourish and develop. Our freedom doesn't come from thin air. It is rooted in our Parliamentary democracy and free press.
>
> Our sense of responsibility and the rule of law is attached to our courts and independent judiciary. Our belief in tolerance was won through struggle and is linked to the various churches and faith groups that have come to call Britain home.
>
> These are the institutions that help to enforce our values, keep them in check and make sure they apply to everyone equally.
>
> And taken together, I believe this combination – our values and our respect for the history that helped deliver them and the institutions that uphold them – forms the bedrock of Britishness.
>
> Of course, we should teach history with warts and all. But we should be proud of what Britain has done to defend freedom and develop these institutions – Parliamentary democracy, a free press, the rule of law – that are so essential for people all over the world.
>
> But there are two other reasons why we should promote these values.
>
> The first is economic. I strongly believe our values form the foundation of our prosperity.
>
> The Western model of combining vibrant democracy with free enterprise has delivered great progress and prosperity, but it faces a challenge from more authoritarian models of economic development, like in Russia.

Now is the time to demonstrate confidence.

The simple yet profound fact that, in our system, governments can be defeated in a court of law, politicians can be voted out of power, and newspapers can publish what they choose: these things aren't weaknesses, they are fundamental strengths.

The second is social. Our values have a vital role to play in uniting us.

They should help to ensure Britain not only brings together people from different countries, cultures and ethnicities, but also ensures that, together, we build a common home.

So I believe we need to be far more muscular in promoting British values and the institutions that uphold them.

What does that mean in practice? We have already taken some big steps.

We are making sure new immigrants can speak English, because it will be more difficult for them to understand these values, and the history of our institutions, if they can't speak our language.

We are bringing proper narrative history back to the curriculum, so our children really learn our island's story – and where our freedoms and things like our Parliament and constitutional monarchy came from.

In sealing the Magna Carta on 15 June 1215, King John had to accept that his subjects were citizens for the first time, giving them rights, protections and security.

Next year it will be the 800th anniversary of Magna Carta. Indeed, it was on this very day, 799 years ago, that the Great Charter was sealed at Runnymede in Surrey.

It's a great document in our history – what my favourite book, *Our Island Story*, describes as the 'foundation of all our laws and liberties'.

The remaining copies of that charter may have faded, but its principles shine as brightly as ever, and they paved the way for the democracy, the equality, the respect and the laws that make Britain.

So I want to use this upcoming 800th anniversary as an opportunity for every child to learn about the Magna Carta, for towns to commemorate it, for events to celebrate it.

David Cameron's contribution to the political and constitutional challenges facing this country could be described as limited and superficial to the extent that Britishness is embraced without criticism: freedoms and rights, although existing in other developed countries, are essentially British, and anything from fish and chips to the Magna Carta are to be celebrated as being part of our rich history. The Conservative Party has never been overly concerned about the deeper significance of the constitution and the politics of change. For them, life will always revolve around Westminster, where the absolute sovereignty of that Parliament ensures that very little need be done in response to either uncomfortable political demands or troublesome neighbours. But it is this overwhelming complacency that is difficult to understand. The idea of four nations is not a concept or idea or a reality at Westminster and successive Prime Ministers are always looking for solutions to problems without Westminster being in any way responsible for what has happened or being conceived as part of the solution.

The 'ugly stain of Separatism'

The idea of Britishness, national identity and the Union are sensitive and emotional issues, but so are the emerging issues of Scottishness, Englishness and Welshness, which should form the basis of a modern Union but are still being given less attention by Unionist political parties and the present Government. Inclusive civic nationalism is not old style Balkan Nationalism. Identity is not Independence. And patriotism and pride are no longer the exclusive preserve of Britishness. This referendum is about Scotland, not the SNP. The contributions from our Prime Ministers illustrate the danger of assuming that Britishness has as much relevance as they think it has, that the national identity of the four nations of the Union should be secondary in importance or that suppressing the legitimate aspirations of Scotland, England, Wales and Northern Ireland will in the long term save Britishness when the likely effect is to destroy the current structure of the Union and end up in the mess everyone is avowedly trying to avoid.

The Union has reached a crossroads and bold and inspirational leadership is needed both to understand the challenges and more importantly do something to start a debate that seriously looks at all the options for far reaching change. Scotland is likely to stay in the Union this time round, but without a change of heart at Westminster and a real intent being shown by the Conservative and Labour parties after the referendum, another day of destiny will happen. David Cameron's reference to the 'ugly stain of separatism' demonstrates the difficulties of this referendum campaign. Politics

is everything and currently party politics is the conduit for our concerns
and aspirations. But when an issue such as Independence cuts across political boundaries of class, religion, race, ethnicity and many other aspects
of our varied cultural life, political parties carry on as if it was still a party
political battle rather than settling the future of a nation and a Nation State.
At a time when public disillusionment with traditional Unionist politics
is so widespread, this highly partisan and tribal approach doesn't seem to
be the best way forward! Unlike 1997, when there was a substantial degree
of consensus about a way forward, subsequently endorsed in a referendum,
Scotland in 2014 is bitterly divided, partly because of the short-term tactics
of the Unionist parties to exclude a second question. YES or NO leaves no
room for consensus, so it remains to be seen whether or not a NO vote will
produce a response from Westminster that will look credible to a substantial number of people who will vote YES. Equally fascinating and probably
more important for England and Wales, will Westminster after a YES vote
merely sulk for a while, or will the MPs now recognise that the unhappiness and discontent in Scotland could manifest itself in other parts of the
Union if no action is taken. Westminster may be the road to ruin for the UK.

Tony Blair is a natural centralist and never embraced the spirit of the
devolution changes, but he delivered on the John Smith Commitment to
deal with the settled will of the Scottish people and complete the unfinished business. Only the extraordinary ability of Donald Dewar and the
single mindedness and leadership of Tony Blair ensured the White Paper
on Scottish devolution was not watered down by other members of the
Cabinet. What is quite remarkable is the fact that Tony Blair delivered the
most comprehensive set of constitutional changes Britain had seen in a
generation. But he didn't see this as part of a real shake up of Britain and
allowed his measures to look piecemeal and without an overall vision. In
the momentum created after the Labour victory in 1997, Blair could have
started a debate on the need for a written codified constitution for Britain.
This would have been radical, but it didn't happen.

Gordon Brown understood history, politics and the constitution and
again provided huge support in the delivery of the Scottish Parliament. As
a Scot, he knew more than most that the road to home rule, starting nearly
a century ago, was tough, uncompromising and had created divisions within
the Labour Party that still exist today. But, as a democratic centralist,
Brown had always been wary and suspicious of Nationalism and the SNP.
Leaning heavily on the fundamental ideas of post-war settlement – health,

pensions and welfare – the benefits of scale that the Union can provide for the redistribution of income and wealth and the concept of the Union as protector and guarantor, the former Prime Minister remains committed to staying in the Union. There is no doubt that without his popularity, indelible Scottishness and political gravitas, the Better Together Campaign would be struggling.

David Cameron is also a centralist and very much part of the 'Anglozone' talked about by the *Telegraph*. Conservatives do not have a good record on devolved government, with the exception of Edward Heath's promise of an assembly for Scotland made in a speech to the Perth conference in the early '70s. There has never been a solid corpus of philosophical or intellectual thinking on any form of Government outside Westminster. Confusing Englishness and Britishness and having little real understanding of national identity allows the Prime Minister to talk about fish and chips and the Magna Carta as examples of Britishness or national identity, without batting an eyelid. One great strength of the Edmund Burke type conservatism was its reluctance to flirt with populism and to be faithful to the idea of conserving and building sensibly forward. The Conservative right is not constrained by such political nuances, but instead may seek to align itself with the 'England Independence Party' of Nigel Farage. England, the conservative right and the EIP are not only ambivalent to Devolution or the European Union, but are actively hostile to any ideas that cut across or removes the absolute sovereignty of Westminster. Keeping his political options open for the General Election in 2015, David Cameron may not be in a good place if the Conservatives win the election with the support of the populists and then find that more devolution does not justify a top ten slot of useful legislative things to do.

CHAPTER EIGHT

Inequality Poisoning the Well of British Society

Inequality – A Crisis at the Heart of our Politics

GEORGE OSBORNE AND David Cameron continue to perpetrate the cruellest myth in UK politics: 'we are all in it together'. Each Autumn Statement and Budget provide a shocking reminder of how far the Conservative Party has abandoned the post-war consensus about the social security state, how they have embraced the idea of the richest groups in British society being indulged in an unfair and generous tax regime and how the lives of the poor and disadvantaged are being diminished and demonised in an aggressive display of right-wing ideology rarely seen in this country, even in the Thatcher years.

Inequality is likely to play an important role in the Independence referendum as Scots weigh up whether Independence or staying with the Union will be the best bet for tackling the lack of fairness, poverty, lack of mobility and inequality in Scotland. These issues are inextricably linked and are cumulatively causing great damage to every nation in the Union. Inequality is poisoning Scottish society and it is likely to worsen as the Conservative Party continue to use austerity as a cover for the commercialisation of more public services and cut backs in government and marginalise the poorest and reward the richest.

We talk incessantly about GDP or Gross National Income if it was the most important measure of a nation's progress. Rarely do we reflect on what a limited measure it is and often discuss it to the exclusion of other measures that would give a more rounded assessment of our wellbeing. At the University of Kansas in 1968, US Presidential candidate Robert Kennedy expressed his views on how this measure falls short and described GDP as measuring everything except that which is worthwhile. As our GDP figures are announced in the UK, these wise words should be a constant reminder of what we don't measure:

Even if we act to erase material poverty, there is another greater task, it is to confront the poverty of satisfaction – purpose and dignity – that afflicts us all. For too long, we seemed to have surrendered personal excellence and community values in the mere accumulation of material things. Our Gross National Product, now, is over $800 billion dollars a year, but that Gross National Product – if we judge the United States of America by that – that Gross National Product counts air pollution and cigarette advertising, and ambulances to clear our highways of carnage. It counts special locks for our doors and the jails for the people who break them. It counts the destruction of the redwood and the loss of our natural wonder in chaotic sprawl. It counts napalm and counts nuclear warheads and armoured cars for the police to fight the riots in our cities. It counts Whitman's rifle and Speck's knife, and the television programs which glorify violence in order to sell toys to our children. Yet the gross national product does not allow for the health of our children, the quality of their education or the joy of their play. It does not include the beauty of our poetry or the strength of our marriages, the intelligence of our public debate or the integrity of our public officials. It measures neither our wit nor our courage, neither our wisdom nor our learning, neither our compassion nor our devotion to our country, it measures everything in short, except that which makes life worthwhile. And it can tell us everything about America except why we are proud that we are Americans.

If this is true here at home, so it is true elsewhere in world.

It is true elsewhere in the world and certainly in the UK, where Chancellors, economists and MPs embrace, and if the GDP figures are positive, often worship at length the publication of the quarterly statistics. Robert Kennedy's point was valid in 1968 and remains to this day: it acts as a reminder of how the economics of any society are viewed not as a means, but as an end.

Britain is fast becoming a bitterly divided country where any sense of fairness, justice, equality and virtue are being sacrificed on the altar of narrow neoliberalism. Using austerity as a cloak, the Conservative Party is embarking on an audacious assault on any lingering notion of the common good, national solidarity or ethically based politics. What is sad and dispiriting about this is that it is being delivered by a Coalition propped up by Lib-Dem MPs. Our fragile economy and the prospect of more years of austerity has to be viewed against a background of declining social mobility, rising inequality, increasing levels of material deprivation and poverty, an unfair tax system and high, but reducing, levels of unemployment, especially among young people. But towering high above most other social and economic issues is income and wealth inequality, which by their very nature have profound consequences for the life chances and opportunities of individuals, families and the four nations of the Union.

Poverty and inequality are also important issues for Scotland as the Independence referendum approaches. Would an Independent Scotland be able to tackle inequality and be able to follow the more progressive policies of the Nordic countries where the gap between rich and poor is much narrower? Is there an alternative vision based on justice and the ethics of the common good and narrative of change more in tune with the 21st century. Or is it better to stay with a UK where the very foundations of the post-war social security system are at risk? Does it make sense to remain with an unfair taxation system which, despite some further concession being offered to both Wales and Scotland, is unfair and unlikely to change under the Conservatives? How much longer do we have to tolerate our low wage economy being made more acceptable by transfers from the social security system, before we start to face up to markets without morality and a capitalism that requires taxpayers' money to blunt the edge of its excesses? Or faced with the depressing realities of the present Coalition Government, is there a possibility of a Labour Government being elected in 2015 that would address the massive and growing levels of income and wealth inequalities in the UK? These are philosophical questions about how we want to live in the 21st century. These are ethical questions about the organisation of our economy and the quality of our society. These are all ultimately political questions about our political parties and their resolve to change the condition of millions of people in the UK, including Scotland, who live on the margins and who in increasing numbers are not voting and increasingly ask, why should they? So the politics of inequality will figure in this referendum and play a part on how people vote. Regardless of the outcome of the vote, inequality will remain an unfolding tragedy and a challenge to all nations of the UK. The Union is wealthy and it's the politics that now have to matter. Many Conservatives see the misery they are inflicting not as unintended consequences, but as necessary outcomes to a political strategy that is seeking to change the economic and social outlook of the UK by reducing the size of the state, reducing permanently public expenditure, creating a market society (not just a market economy) and seeking to portray people on benefits, the unemployed and sometimes those with disabilities as skivers, scroungers and seeing them as lesser citizens who have to be demonised excluded. This is profoundly insulting to nearly 80,000 young Scots who are out of work and who are desperately looking for a job. Former Tory Chancellor Norman Lamont once described this as 'a price well worth paying'. We need to look at philosophy for some inspiration as to how we can become a more equal society.

In his new book *The Soul of Politics*, Jim Wallis, a new wave Christian intellectual, talks about the relationship between politics and morality being absolutely vital for the future of society. Wallis asks the question:

> Is it possible to evoke in people a genuine desire to transcend our more selfish interests and respond to a larger vision that gives us a sense of purpose, direction, meaning and even community?

Though speaking about the US, his comments could equally apply to Britain and Scotland, where the increase in economic inequality since the 1980s has no counterpart in the advanced world. The inequality gap is widening. There are serious doubts about our commitment as a society to justice, fairness and equality, the fundamental issues at the heart of our politics. Since ancient times – when philosophers such as Plato, Aristotle and Socrates sought to understand society, exploring ideas of governance and politics and giving meaning to the lives of individuals – political debate has rightly been preoccupied with the values, ethics, virtues and principles which should drive any form of progressive politics. This debate is disappearing. Traditional Unionist parties are in danger of competing with each other on who can be tougher on benefit claimants and marginalising those in greatest need in society, lacking compassion and inspiration.

We should be aware of the ideological mindset shared by neoliberal Conservatives in this country and right-wing Republicans in the US. They see poverty as the product of the feckless and the undeserving. They like the idea of smaller government to dismantle welfare dependency. Both want lower taxes, regardless of the consequences for others. They see the poor outside the mainstream and as a burden on society. They believe the market should dictate health and education outcomes. And they see unemployment as an economic variable like inflation or interest rates. Let's remind ourselves that while the USA has great virtues, it also has obscene levels of poverty, a widening gap between the rich and poor and embarrassing levels of inequality. Most people in Scotland and the Union don't want to end up like this, but many Conservative MPS and Ministers do.

The relationship between our politics, our ethics and our public life remain at the heart of this inequality story. Towering above everything else is the idea of fairness in the context of justice and opportunity for all regardless of economic or social status. Fairness and equality have slipped down the political agenda. Despite the weak reassurances of the Government at Westminster, Britain remains deeply divided, where any sense of solidarity and a sense of common purpose are disappearing.

The nature of injustice, inequality and poverty has changed from the era of Beveridge and his five giants of Disease, Idleness, Ignorance, Squalor and Want. No matter how the statistics stack up, there is still an overwhelming sense that the idea of 'one nation' politics has little resonance in Scotland or Britain. Kenneth Galbraith, in seeking to understand why poverty and prosperity lived side by side in the US, was convinced that the power of a 'contented majority' was at work: the notion that poverty was a problem for the poor and not anyone else was clearly on his mind. Scotland provides a powerful reminder of how those who do not feel part of society can be seen not only being materially disadvantaged but politically disenfranchised: in the 2011 Holyrood elections in five of the poorest areas of Glasgow, nearly 70 per cent of eligible voters didn't vote.

So why does inequality, social and material poverty perpetuate itself? Daniel Dorling in his book *Injustice: Why Social Inequality Persists* argues that injustices are now being recreated, renewed and supported by five new sets of beliefs. These beliefs have old origins, but have taken new faces. In this context five beliefs give new life to upholding injustices: elitism is efficient; exclusion is necessary; prejudice is natural; greed is good; and despair is inevitable. A growing part of the Conservative Party is a cheerleader for this type of thinking. Those who uphold these beliefs find it hard to see possibilities beyond the current situation and are not only allowing injustice and inequality to continue but to get worse. The current power structure of the modern Union, reflecting an imbalanced economy, the north-south divide and the disproportionate impact of London, and influenced by party politics and reinforced by large sections of the press ensures the real issues of poverty, inequality and fairness are viewed negatively and cynically: the myth of affordability is raised and tackling inequality, based on that criteria, is something which will always be out of reach! The wealth of our nations is not in doubt, but how we spend and redistribute that wealth is a political issue and not in the first instance an economic one.

This is a debate about justice, fairness and equality of opportunity and how these philosophical issues play out in the way we conduct our national affairs. The idea of the common good is wired into the public's DNA, but we now seem at a loss as a society and as a Labour Party to be able to articulate the better side of our humanity and impose this virtue on the excesses of free market thinking.

Instead, we seem captivated by the power of money, obsessed with opinion polls and far too easily ambivalent to the Coalition Government's attacks on pensioners, the unemployed and benefit claimants, and their embrace of feather bedding the rich. Labour – in both Scotland and Britain – has to come off the fence and fight the Government over benefit cuts, demand a progressive tax system and lay the foundations defend the Welfare State.

Throughout history, the philosophical debate has been about important principles. Our society, though, has got it dangerously wrong. Without a rethink of the enormous excesses and staggering differences of income and wealth in Britain, we will undermine solidarity, destroy trust and mutual respect, undermine the motivation of the many and continue to undervalue certain important aspects of our economic and social wellbeing. More importantly, if we are not careful we could sow the seeds of political and social trouble as trust in Government and institutions collapses and Britain becomes more bitter and divided.

There has to be a better way of doing our politics and a more enriching way of living our lives.

We have growing income inequality and declining social mobility. The gap between rich and poor in Britain is well above the OECD average and far greater than Sweden, Denmark, France, Germany and Holland, and income inequality in the UK is now as high as any previous time in the last 30 years. Through the prism of modernity, compassion and fairness, the Conservative right and UKIP are now a dangerous and divisive distraction. The progressives in Britain have a real opportunity to reinstate decency, fairness and justice at the heart of our political debate and seriously confront the fact that Britain, including Scotland, is a very unequal society. We need, more than anything, to escape from the poverty of our own thinking.

The referendum debate is addressing the real issues at the heart of the choice Scotland has to make in 2014. Social justice, economic inequality and social mobility are issues which are vital to the success of Scotland and the building of a fairer, more enlightened and stable society. Former

Labour Minister Alan Milburn, Chair of the Commission looking at social mobility, has frequently commented on the progress we are making on social mobility and how it continues to underline the chronic inequality of opportunity we have throughout Britain. For far too long these issues have been cast to the margins of our debates and indeed under the Conservative-led Coalition, the poor and disadvantaged have become more marginalised, demonised and the focus of right-wing press coverage and ill-informed political rhetoric. We are now back to the Victorian era where the 'deserving' and 'undeserving' labels are being implied and sometimes used to further divide society and create a them and us underpinning to what is already becoming a fractured and ill-tempered United Kingdom. Scotland and England are two of the worst countries in Western Europe for glaring and growing inequalities. And all the evidence confirms that unequal societies have far more social problems. Does an unchanged Union offer any hope that these enduring problems will ever be seriously addressed? Are the prospects any better with Independence? There are serious doubts about our commitment to justice, fairness and equality, as fundamental issues at the heart of our politics and our democracy.

The referendum campaign gives us the opportunity to talk about the kind of Scotland we want to live in; the vision we want to see for our country and its relationship with the rest of the UK; the fact that too many people are not making it and are being left behind; and whether the choices on the ballot paper reflect sufficiently the ideas of the common good, common purpose and common trust needed to transform both Scotland and the Union in the tough years that lie ahead. This should be the debate. No one now disputes the fact that Scotland can be a successful Independent country. The debate has moved on to the substance of whether issues like equality the Union or Independence or indeed some other alternative is the best way forward for Scotland. Rather than just exchanging partisan blows about whether we will have any influence on the MPC of the Bank of England or whether Scotland will see its credit ratings slump after Independence or will Scotland be able to join a Sterling currency union in the event of Independence, we need to decide if an Independent Scotland will have the political will and the national resolve to follow the Nordic example and become a less unequal society. Progressive parties like Labour, the Lib-Dems, the Greens and the SNP are well placed to set out a new platform for tackling inequality and poverty. The people of Scotland should require this as a priority regardless of the constitutional status of Scotland after the referendum. More fundamentally, do we wish to take a lead from the Union and England as a way forward where growing inequalities, increasing intolerance, market driven consumerism the commercialisation of education and health are underway or dominate or do we want to aspire to the quality of life, the solidarity and civilised ways of life and the world class public services of the Scandinavian countries and some other parts of Northern European States? The debate on the political and constitutional future of our country has to be more relevant!

The lack of vision in our politics is depressing. What kind of future can we dream about? Where are the inspirational ideas that can transform our country and our prospects? There must be more to political life than the current Unionist parties are providing. We are not providing any vision for our young people. They need an imagination, idealism and hope for the future. Most of us have seen our exclusively British characteristics: unsustainable materialism, a relentless assault on our senses through advertising and a society where superficiality, greed and rampant consumerism are in danger of destroying any sense of solidarity or concern for each other. Margaret Thatcher's comment that 'there is no such thing as society' is all too easily being realised in a world where our politicians lack optimism and confidence. We are moving from a market economy to a market society. Our politics and our democracy were established to control the excesses of capitalism, but money and the markets still dominate. Vast numbers of people are losing out because progressive political parties are no longer fired by the inspiration and vision of the founding fathers who brought such passion to our politics in the pre and immediate post-war period.

Why are our politicians so afraid of the 'vision thing'? Political parties and party leaders in Britain and Scotland in the past decade – the SNP have led and innovated – have never been particularly comfortable with the bigger picture of inspiration and vision. This referendum is about the future of our Nation, not Nationalism, is about identity, not independence and about progressive policies, not populism: this is about a vision for a just, fairer, more equal and progressive Scotland

Borrowing on the experience of US Presidents, there is a history of capturing the mood of an era or inspiring the transformation of a society or embracing the idealism required to face new challenges and opportunities. Of course some of the inspiring rhetoric has to give way to the more pressing needs of office.

Some of these have become iconic and inspirational and have been associated with great moments in US history. Barack Obama's powerful 'Yes we can' inspired Americans to believe in change and embrace and confront challenges and problems.

The 'new covenant' of Bill Clinton outlined in his 1992 Democratic National Convention speech talked about a new pact between citizens and government. We can go back to Theodore Roosevelt and his 'Square Deal' and Harry S. Truman and the 'Fair Deal'. Franklin D. Roosevelt, inspirational war and peacetime President, initiated the enduring and very popular 'New Deal'. And in one of the greatest and shortest – 246 words – speeches of all time, Abraham Lincoln's Gettysburg Address embraced the powerful notions of hope and democracy when he said, 'government of the people, by the people, for the people, shall not perish from this earth'.

One of the most under-rated Presidents, Lyndon B. Johnson created in 1964 the notion of the 'Great Society' to describe his aspirations for his civil rights. President John F. Kennedy, facing a period of transition in the '60s, used the idea of 'The New Frontier'. In his acceptance speech in 1960 Kennedy said:

> We stand on the edge of a New Frontier – the frontier of hopes and dreams, a frontier of unknown opportunities and beliefs in peril. Beyond that frontier are uncharted areas of science and space, unsolved problems of peace and war, unconquered problems of ignorance and prejudice, unanswered problems of poverty and surplus.

At a time when Scotland is about to take the biggest decision in its history, the SNP is offering a vision, however incomplete, but where is the vision for the Union?

Modern conservatism has abandoned any pretence of concern for the poor and disadvantaged and instead sees inequality as merely an inevitable and apparently acceptable consequence of the economic strategy the Government is pursuing. Pity we don't have a modern day Charles Dickens to comment on this pathetic poverty of hope for all of our nation at a time when right-wing politics are in the ascendency, 'responsible recovery' clearly means for the few, not the many, and where Britain is becoming more bitterly divided than ever on social, economic and financial grounds. People forget austerity is a political strategy, not only designed to tackle debt and deficits but to slash public spending, downsize the state, promote the market and commercialisation, weaken the great pillars of social progress such as the Welfare State, pensions and the NHS, and destroy the post-war consensus of society where justice and fairness matter. Tackling poverty and all forms of inequality is a political choice we can make or we can do as the Tories are doing and ignore the issue by blaming the poor and hiding behind the cloak of austerity.

The inequalities of wealth in Britain are shocking, the gap between rich and poor is widening and, as we have known for many years, we are one of the most unequal societies in Western Europe. Sadly none of this is new, but what is different under the Tories is the accelerating rate of poverty and disadvantage and the number of people who are being drawn into this depressing Tory world of Wonga, soup kitchens, food banks, low pay and charity. We should be aware of the ideological mindset shared by neoliberal Conservatives in this country and right-wing Republicans in the US. They see poverty as the product of the feckless and the undeserving. They like the idea of smaller government to dismantle welfare. Both want lower taxes regardless of the consequences for others. They want tax cuts for the rich. They see the poor outside the mainstream and as a burden on society. There is no commitment to redistribution or equality. They believe the market should dictate health and education outcomes. And they see unemployment as an economic variable like inflation or interest rates. Let's remind ourselves that while the USA has great virtues, it also has obscene levels of poverty and a widening gap between the rich and poor. We don't want to end up like this, but many Conservatives do! This is political ideology not the public interest. We need to resist the Americanisation of our society.

Recent surveys of household wealth in Britain reveal embarrassing inequalities: wealth is measured in private pensions, property, financial and physical:

First, the least wealthy 50 per cent of all households owned just nine per cent of all wealth, but the top 20 per cent owned 62 per cent of the wealth and the top ten per cent owned nearly 44 per cent.

Second, the average household wealth of the bottom ten per cent is £13,000, the top 10 per cent is £967,000! And the wealthiest ten per cent is £2.8 million!

Third, the wealthiest 10 per cent of households owned more than 40 per cent of overall wealth and were 850 times wealthier than the least wealthy ten per cent of households.

Fourth, the share of the wealthiest households by region/nation shows the South East the highest with 15.5 per cent and Scotland the lowest with 6.9 per cent. There is of course a profound north-south divide in the distribution of household wealth. There is no reason to doubt that in 2013 the comparative differences will be as bad, if not worse.

Phillip Inman, writing in the *Guardian* in 2014, said:

> Britain's richest one per cent own as much as the poorest 55 per cent of population. Britain's richest one per cent have accumulated as much wealth as the poorest 55 per cent of the population put together, according to the latest official analysis of who owns the nation's £9.5bn of property, pensions and financial assets.
>
> In figures that also lay bare the extent of inequality across the north-south divide, the Office for National Statistics said household wealth in the south-east had been rising five times as fast as across the whole country.
>
> The average wealth of households in the southeast had surged to £309,000 at the end of 2012, up 30 per cent since the first wealth report published by the ONS covering 2006–8 while the average rise in England was only six per cent.
>
> But wealth in the north-east had fallen, the only region where it did so, to an average of just under £143,000. In Scotland the figure was £165,500.

Rachael Orr, Oxfam's head of poverty in the UK, said the figures were a 'shocking chapter in a tale of two Britains'.

The charity recently reported that five billionaire families controlled the same wealth as 20 per cent of the population. 'It is further evidence of increasing inequality at a time when five rich families have the same wealth as 12 million people,' she said.

Larry Elliott, in the *Guardian* in 2014 wrote that 'Britain's five richest families worth more than poorest 20 per cent' reveals scale of inequality in new Oxfam report.

In the Tale of Two Britains Report, Oxfam said the poorest 20 per cent in the UK had wealth totalling £28.1bn an average of £2,230 each. The latest rich list from *Forbes* magazine showed that the five top UK entries – the family of the Duke of Westminster, David and Simon Reuben, the Hinduja brothers, the Cadogan family, and Sports Direct retail boss Mike Ashley – between them had property, savings and other assets worth £28.2bn.

> It's deeply worrying that these extreme levels of wealth inequality exist in Britain today, where just a handful of people have more money than millions struggling to survive on the breadline.

The UK study follows an Oxfam report earlier this year, which found that the wealth of 85 global billionaires is equivalent to that of half the world's population – or 3.5 billion people.

Oxfam said that for the first time, more working households were in poverty than non-working ones, and predicted that the number of children living below the poverty line could increase by 800,000 by 2020. It said cuts to social security and public services were meshing with falling real incomes and a rising cost of living to create a 'deeply damaging situation' in which millions were struggling to get by. Oxfam's director of campaigns and policy, Ben Phillips, said:

> Britain is becoming a deeply divided nation, with a wealthy elite who are seeing their incomes spiral up, while millions of families are struggling to make ends meet... It's deeply worrying that these extreme levels of wealth inequality exist in Britain today, where just a handful of people have more money than millions struggling to survive on the breadline.
>
> Increasing inequality is a sign of economic failure rather than success. It's far from inevitable – a result of political choices that can be reversed. It's time for our leaders to stand up and be counted on this issue.

Tom Gordon writing in the *Herald* said:

> The richest ten per cent of households in Scotland have 900 times the accumulated wealth of the poorest ten per cent, according to a new Scottish Government analysis showing the scale of the country's wealth gap.

The study also found that 30 per cent of Scotland's children live in households which between them own less than two per cent of the nation's private worth.

These figures suggest that almost one third of children were not getting the start in life they deserved. The most recent figures show total household wealth in Scotland was £811 billion, of which almost half – £402bn – was attributable to private pensions. Property accounted for £230bn (28 per cent), financial wealth such as savings, stocks and shares covered £90bn, and physical wealth such as cars and jewellery £89bn (both accounting for 11 per cent).

Published by the Scottish Government, the analysis used data collected by the UK Office for National Statistics for its Wealth and Asset surveys conducted between 2006 and 2010 – the most up-to-date information available.

It confirms the old saying that money goes to money, with those who have a large slice of one form of wealth having other kinds too, while the poorest have little wealth of any sort, making it hugely difficult for them to accumulate some.

Some 2,000 Scottish households were surveyed in detail about their assets. The wealthiest 30 per cent of households had 76 per cent of all private wealth in Scotland: 84 per cent of pension wealth, 81 per cent of financial wealth, 70 per cent of property wealth, and 54 per cent of physical wealth.

The report concludes:

The wealth gap at the extremes of the wealth distribution is substantial ... the wealthiest 10 per cent had 900 times the wealth of the least wealthy 10 per cent.

The report also found that household income was slightly more evenly distributed than wealth, and that there was 'little difference in the level of wealth inequality in Scotland compared with Great Britain as a whole'.

In his book *The Soul of Politics*, Jim Wallis talks about the relationship between politics and morality being absolutely vital for the future of society. Wallis asks the question: 'Is it possible to evoke in people a genuine desire to transcend our more selfish interests and respond to a larger vision that gives us a sense of purpose, direction, meaning and even community?' He adds:

Too many people are not making it and are being left behind. Neither the injustices built into our social system nor the irresponsibility this generates is tolerable any longer. Controlling the poor is not the only alternative to abandoning them.

Though speaking about the US, his comments could equally apply to Britain.

The relationship between our politics, our ethics and our public life remain at the heart of this inequality story and of course the Independence referendum. Towering above everything else is the idea of fairness in the context of justice and opportunity for all regardless of economic or social status. Fairness and equality have slipped down the political agenda.

So why does inequality perpetuate itself? Why are we not angry about the injustices of modern Britain? Writing in the *Observer*, Will Hutton said:

George Osborne's plan is to cut government spending to a point where it would be proportionately no larger than in 1948. The work of three generations building the sinews of a state is to be summarily withdrawn.

The Tories are marginalising and wasting people and creating two nations.

Despite the serious commitment of successive Labour Governments to tackling inequality and the indifference of the Conservatives, the inequality gap is growing. This debate seems sadly lacking in Britain, where we continue to be preoccupied with the economic and financial crisis and retreat into our own self-interest and revisit the poor and excluded with the 'undeserving' label of the Victorian era. The Conservatives are in the forefront of demonising the poorest sections of society for reasons of economic necessity, political ideology and the ethics of the undeserving: we should easily see through the idea of compassionate conservatism and their cynical reframing of the language of ideas. The relationship between our politics, our ethics and our public life remain at the heart of this inequality story. Towering above everything else is the idea of fairness in the context of justice and opportunity for all regardless of economic or social status. Although few people say they agree with injustice, we do live in an unjust world. In the world's richest countries injustice is caused less and less by having too few resources to share around fairly but by arguments and beliefs that help maintain it. The debates about 'absolutes' are now couched in relative terms, so invariably the debate rages on about definitions, levels of opportunity and obstacles.

So this is not just a debate about the redistribution of wealth or levels of taxation or dependency on the state or deserving or undeserving labels or demonising an underclass. This is a debate about justice, fairness and equality of opportunity and how these philosophical issues play out in the way we conduct our national affairs. This is why the issue has such significance and resonance for a modern society such as ours.

The idea of the common good and common purpose are wired into the public's DNA, but we now seem at a loss as a society and a political class to be able to articulate the better side of our humanity and impose this virtue on the excesses of free market thinking.

Instead, we are captivated by the power of money.

The founder of John Lewis in a BBC broadcast in 1957 said:

> Capitalism has done enormous good and suits human nature far too well to be given up as long as human nature remains the same. But the perversion has given us too unstable a society. Differences of reward must be large enough to induce people to do their best but the present differences are too great. If we do not find some way of correcting that perversion of capitalism our society will break down.

People accept that effort deserves reward and usually they discriminate between different types of effort. Throughout history, the philosophical debate has been about important principles. Our society, though, has got it dangerously wrong. Without a rethink of the enormous excesses and staggering differences of income and wealth in Britain, we will undermine solidarity, destroy trust and mutual respect, undermine the motivation of the many and continue to undervalue certain important aspects of our economic and social wellbeing.

There has to be a better way of doing our politics and a more enriching way of living our lives. We need a political philosophy which accepts that the worth of the ends we pursue, the meaning of the lives we lead, and the quality of the common life we share are inextricably linked to fairness, justice and equality

A just society can't be achieved simply by maximising utility or by securing freedom of choice.

Michael Sandel, Professor of Philosophy at Harvard University in his book *Justice: What's the Right Thing to Do?* says:

> Justice is not only about the right way to distribute things. It is also about the right way to value things. Justice involves more than the size and distribution of the gross national product... it is about higher moral purposes.

Child poverty and the massive inequalities this creates have no place in our modern world. In economic and financial terms Britain and Scotland are wealthy countries, but in terms of politics and political philosophy we are poor. What is the right thing to do? Will inequality decline in an Independent Scotland where we start to look like a Nordic country or can the Union turn its back on the rising inequality of the past 30 years and take a bigger interest?

Books abound spelling out the extent of inequality and in particular in the US and the UK, including Scotland. *Capital in the 21st Century* by Thomas Piketty, the most recent bestseller, *Chavs: The Demonization of the Working Class* by Owen Jones, *The Price of Inequality* by Joseph Stiglitz and *The Spirit Level* by Wilkinson and Picket of are only a few of the books documenting the rise in inequality. In a remarkably researched book, Richard Wilkinson and Kate Pickett argue convincingly that inequality is the root cause of many of society's ills. A mass of evidence is put forward to demonstrate that levels of violent crime, mental illness, drug addiction, illiteracy, teenage pregnancies and obesity that are almost always higher in more unequal societies and that even the affluent are adversely affected by inequality.

The UK is near the top of the income gap league, with twice as much inequality as Scandinavia and Japan and consequently experiences more social problems. The book is an important contribution in urging politicians to see social problems as having social solutions. Wilkinson and Pickett argue that widespread inequality helps increase a huge range of social ills, with the result that everyone suffers – even the most well off. Inequality in their view isn't just bad for the poor, it's also bad for the rich.

In a paper 'Inequality in Scotland', prepared by David Bell and David Eiser about the implications of inequality for the Referendum debate, the authors pose the following questions:

> What is the level of income inequality in Scotland? How does income inequality in Scotland compare to the rest of the UK, and to other OECD countries? How has income inequality in Scotland changed over time? What has caused inequality to change, and how effective is the tax and benefit system at mitigating inequality? This paper seeks to answer these questions, and draw messages for the Scottish Independence debate.

This is a summary of the findings:

By international standards, the inequality of gross earned income (measured before the effects of taxes and benefits) in Scotland is relatively high. Inequality is much higher in Scotland than in the Nordic countries.

Since the mid-1990s there has been relatively little increase in inequality in Scotland across most of the distribution.

However, inequality at the extreme ends of the distribution has increased in the last decade. The incomes of the top 1–2 per cent of earners have increased compared to the average. At the same time, those in the bottom 5–10 per cent of the earnings distribution have fallen further behind the average.

Much of the increase in inequality has been driven by increased variability in working time. This is particularly the case in lower-paying occupations, where there has been a significant increase in part-time working. Although this has increased inequality, the welfare implications are unclear because some workers may prefer shorter hours.

The Scottish labour market became increasingly polarised between 2001 and 2010. This means there while the share of higher paying and lower paying jobs increased, the share of middle-wage jobs fell, contributing to inequality growth.

There has been virtually no increase in net income inequality in Scotland (after taxes and benefits are taken into account) since 1997. Increased government transfers, particularly to families with children and the elderly, have offset the small increases in earned income inequality that occurred.

Background

Scotland is an unequal society and those in favour of constitutional change argue that increases in inequality have been driven by UK government policy; that reduced inequality is desirable; and that only under Independence will it be possible to introduce policies that will narrow the gap between the rich and poor. An example of this argument is the 'Common Weal' vision for economic and social development in Scotland, which would involve more radical changes to the welfare and taxation systems than seem likely under Westminster governance.

Wealth is news. The *Sunday Times* Rich List tells us the top 1,000 have doubled their wealth in five years, the UK has more billionaires per head of population than any other country and that London is the world capital of the super rich.

According to the Office For National Statistics, the number of millionaires has risen by 50 per cent in four years despite the financial crisis. Nine per cent of households have assets worth more than £1 million. Should we be celebrating? It *is* good news that more British people are more prosperous and that the richest people in the world regard Britain as a safe haven and politically stable.

The bad news is that growing inequality is approaching pre-First World War levels. The richest 10 per cent in Britain own 44 per cent of total national wealth, five times more than the poorest 50 per cent of the population, who collectively own nine per cent. The figures for share of national income are even more startling. The share going to those on the lower half of earnings has fallen by 25 per cent since the 1970s (OECD) whilst the slice going to the top one per cent has increased by 50 per cent. The most recent figures from HM Revenue and Customs confirm that the return of economic growth in the last year has overwhelmingly benefited the top one per cent of earners.

This matters because the more unequal societies are, the more dysfunctional, unhealthy and violent. Looking ahead, there are danger signals: persistently high youth unemployment, the threat to middle-class jobs by digitisation, unaffordable housing, the increasing cost of energy, transport and higher education, limited legal aid, declining trust in authority (who trusts the police?) and public disengagement from democratic politics. If the 30 year trend towards greater inequality continues and the middle classes lose more wealth, power and influence to a plutocracy, the fundamentals of democratic society will be compromised. There will be little room for mutual interest, mutual respect, contract and consensus in a world where the super-rich are in control.

The crucial factor that should concern us all is that the young are likely to be less prosperous than their parents whilst a tiny minority grows fantastically rich. That could undermine commitment to civil society and would be bad news for everyone.

Earlier in 2014, the International Red Cross, based in Geneva, has been in the headlines with a new report from the Federation of Red Cross and Red Crescent Societies saying:

> Whilst other continents successfully reduce poverty, Europe adds to it. The long term consequences of this crisis have yet to surface

The report then warns of the potential impact of austerity policies in terms of deepening poverty, mass unemployment, social division, exclusion and growing inequality. This highly respected international aid agency also warns of the potential social consequences where young people fail to find some purpose in their lives, more people drift into poverty, illegal migration generates more xenophobia and there are growing risks of political unrest and division. This is certainly Conservative Britain in 2014: a country fast becoming bitterly divided and dispirited where any sense of fairness, justice and equality are being sacrificed on the altar of narrow and backward policies.

This Government is an embarrassment. But there is more to come. The Red Cross said they would start to collect and distribute food aid in Britain for the first time since the Second World War. We appreciate the fact that charities do good work all the year round helping people in need, but under the Conservatives we are trawling new depths of misery, hardship and children are going hungry in our country. We are one of the richest countries in the world but now we are increasingly a beacon for poverty and growing inequality. The Red Cross works in disaster zones around the world and is widely respected for the humanitarian commitments it brings to a troubled world. But now part of their effort will involve going to supermarkets across Britain to find food for the needy.

This seems like a dramatic escalation of the soup kitchen, food bank and Wonga world of Osborne and Cameron. Imagine, as the ultimate in national humiliation, what could happen in the run up to Christmas. At a time when thoughts are on giving and goodwill to all, your TV screen has an advert inviting you to make a donation to help the needy, not in Sub-Saharan Africa, India or Pakistan, but to feed the poor of Britain. This may be a step too far, but we are surely reaching a shocking and deeply embarrassing point in the social and economic history of this country when the plight of the poor is being made much worse as the Conservative Government targets the poorest and most vulnerable for more misery and hardship. More worrying is the notion that our moral indifference and acquiescence is growing and as a society – including our politics – we lack the passion, the anger and the ethical values to do something about it.

The Conservative Government is unlikely to be moved by the plight of the poor, but progressive political parties should be moved to confront this threat to national cohesion and solidarity. We can no longer ignore the growing divisions in our country and the scary comments of Lord Freud, Government Minister, who believes people who use food banks 'just want a free meal', or former Education Secretary Michael Gove, who said the users of food banks 'were often [used by] those who could not manage their finances properly. It is the lack of money and respect to blame, not the individual.

Poverty and children starving in modern Britain is not just about austerity and mean spirited conservatism: it is about what is right and wrong in society, how the national wealth is distributed and what kind of country we want to be. These are philosophical questions which seem sadly lacking in our political debate to the point where the Churches, including the Archbishop of Canterbury and Pope Francis, the aid agencies such as the Red Cross and enlightened single issue groups and individuals in society are generating debate and action, while political parties seem muted, unsure and afraid to talk about the big issues in our country while the mayhem and madness of modern conservatism wreaks havoc on a great swathe of our fellow citizens.

Are we to believe that we have become immune to the suffering of others?

Or have we bought into the farcical idea that we are 'all in this together', or because of austerity we can do nothing to close the widening inequality gap between rich and poor? That we cannot confront the excesses of the market, which is sacrosanct for the current Government, or that we have no moral views about the role of fairness and justice in our society? Much of our country is frustrated because of the lack of leadership on these important issues. Many people are simply asking why this social, economic and moral decline is taking place.

'The poor you will always have with you', says the Book of Mathew, Chapter 26. George Osborne has taken this to heart and endorsed the concept, but the Bible doesn't say anything about enthusiastically expanding the numbers!

Human capital-the wealth of a nation

Tackling inequality starts with addressing the real wealth of our nation, human capital – our most precious renewable resource. Scotland has a chance to make choices. More investment in this area is one of them. Aristotle said: 'All who have meditated on the art of governing mankind have been convinced that the fate of Empires depends on the education of youth.' This inspirational quote, linked to the ideas contained within Adam Smith's treatise *The Wealth of Nations*, leads us to the conclusion that the wealth of our nation, Scotland, is human capital.

Education, learning and the development of the human mind are the driving forces behind any concept of a modern, successful and fair Scotland in a highly competitive global world. Our long-term future as a nation depends on how serious we are about embracing this idea, increasing our investment in the development of human capital and acknowledging the common sense belief 'that a mind is a terrible thing to waste'.

Throughout recent history, key drivers of economic development and social progress have embraced land-labour-capital-skills, each in turn acting as the resource base, but now knowledge is the key in this new information age which in turn demands the utmost development of human capital. Scotland is a rich country. We have old energy in the shape of oil and gas, new and quite remarkable renewable energy resources, spectacular natural assets and a history influenced by the Enlightenment, productive industries and of course the early development of education. But now, and towering above any of these, has to be our commitment to the new wealth of our nation, human capital. Scotland can only become a progressive nation in the 21st century if we start once again to realise the importance of people and what they have to offer: not just for an elite but for every child, young person and adult in our country.

The development of our human capital is inextricably linked to tackling poverty, inequality and the lack of social mobility in Scotland. It is time we reaffirmed our commitment to education and learning and their vital importance to the future of our country. We can no longer argue that Scottish education is one of the best in the world, if indeed that was ever the case.

What we should be doing is generating a more informed, intense and urgent debate about education in Scotland and its role in a modern and rapidly changing economic, social and political landscape. This requires a rethink of the current levels of investment and to give education and learning parity of esteem with healthcare in our deliberation of spending levels and political priorities.

Jean-Francois Richard, former President of the World Bank Europe, is the author of *High Noon: 20 Global Problems, 20 Years to solve them*. This book captured the enduring importance of education by arguing its benefits: the key to building a sense of global citizenship; central to the construction of democratic societies; one of the most powerful instruments for tackling poverty and inequality; vital for dealing with the new world economy and the knowledge society; making nations and communities more tolerant and cohesive; and the key to personal development and fulfilment.

The greatest reward from education, however, is the idea of lifelong learning, which can equip children not only to acquire knowledge in their early years but to create the capacity, enthusiasm and desire to keep learning throughout their lives. Who knows what the challenges and opportunities will be in the next 50 years if we consider the extraordinary changes that have taken place in the last 50!

Today, Scotland needs to invest more in all aspects of education and learning, not less. Education is not just another public service. It is the most important ingredient in the mix of essentials that will determine the future of Scotland and the achievement of every individual. This is also a matter which requires a political consensus.

There are areas of education such as nursery and primary where real improvements have been made and we can argue, with pride, that we compare favourably with other countries. Yet in other areas, like comprehensive schooling, universities and colleges, a more ambitious and ongoing debate is needed. The Government's recently announced reforms to college and higher education are a very positive step in the right direction, but more needs to be done.

Debates have often been narrow in their focus. More importantly, we have failed to address the institutional issues and the constraints they impose on achieving real and substantial change. Scotland is not good at dealing with Institutions. Mindsets and cultures are difficult to change and present formidable obstacles to reform. Scotland is too often the victim of history and legacy, and we seem unable or unwilling to pursue new and radical ideas that will allow us to break free from the past. Again there are real signs that the present Scottish Government is willing to step up the pace of change.

We are fortunate in having talented children and young people and teachers and lecturers who are skilled and motivated. This, however, will not deliver for Scotland unless there is institutional change, leadership that is willing to embrace new ideas and some greater urgency and honesty being shown about the challenges we face. None of this is easy. But questions still need to be asked.

In *The Culture of Contentment*, J. K. Galbraith asserts that as affluence advances the political class, other organisations and collective bodies weaken. Their collective resolve to tackle difficult issues and intractable problems, despite being part of the political rhetoric, is diminished.

Learning and education are the keys to promoting social mobility, tackling the deep inequality that exists in Scotland and building a fulfilling social and economic future for millions of Scots. The gap between ambition and achievement has to be closed.

The dilemma is real and the challenge is obvious. Human capital is the key to unlocking Scotland's potential.

If the debate on the political and constitutional future of our country is to be meaningful, these are the issues we should be talking about. So will inequality be better tackled in an Independent Scotland or an unreformed Union?

CHAPTER NINE

Labour and Federalism

CAN LABOUR WIN the next General Election in 2015? And if successful, will they eventually come up with a more radical and progressive plan for the future of Scotland and the Union? Seems an appropriate question to ask when you consider how important that might be to Scots voting in the referendum and pondering what a NO vote will mean. Scots have lost interest in sending Conservative MPs to Westminster since they were wiped out in 1997 and now have only one MP. For part of the post-devolution years, Scotland has had a split political personality: voting Labour for Westminster and the SNP for Holyrood.

Labour is ahead in the UK polls and has every chance of being the largest party at Westminster, and because of the distribution of electors and seats may have an overall majority. But England is politically troubled. As shown in other chapters of the present book, populism and the rise of the Tory right on a raft of policy issues could make the outcome of the election more problematic for Labour.

So if Labour is elected, what would their policy platform be and to what extent would they be committed to changing the political and constitutional structure of the UK in addition to moving on more powers for the Scottish Parliament? Already we have seen the Labour Party in Scotland produce the most disappointing set of proposals for more devolution of all the parties. The Lib-Dem solution, federalism, was by far the best package. Labour's Commission proposals were compromised by Westminster after signals suggested a much more radical package would be on offer from Labour. The ongoing battle between UK Labour and Scottish Labour requires attention because if the Scottish Party has to constantly look over its shoulder to Westminster then it will always be shackled and be at a competitive political disadvantage with the SNP.

Labour is now part of the bidding war with the Conservatives and the Lib-Dems to try to persuade NO voters that there will be constitutional change after the vote.

UK Labour should now accept that tinkering on the margins of the constitution will not be enough. There is every indication that a large number of people want a different country but may be deterred this time from voting

YES because of fears and worries about the transitional issues and the big step Independence would be. Labour in the UK would be well-advised to see a NO vote as the platform from which to launch a new, bold initiative rather than seeing it as an opportunity for Westminster business as usual and a minimalist response. This campaign has shown that the political and constitutional battle for Scotland and the Union will continue apace.

Labour, both in Scotland and the UK, needs to look at a different future and ensure a debate that will create a new Constitutional Convention and a settlement for the four nations of the Union through the prism of federalism, removing the idea of the absolute sovereignty from Westminster in order to share power, not devolve it. Britishness and the Union are declining rapidly. We also need a codified constitution to make sense of the ramshackle setup we currently operate in the UK. Labour has an enormous opportunity to learn lessons and salvage new ideas from what is widely recognised as a lacklustre and uninspiring debate.

Unless the future of the Union can be secured and reconfigured then there is every possibility Scotland will choose to exit sometime in the future, assuming the Union can survive the vote this year. But the signs are not encouraging. Labour's thinking on devolved matters and constitutional issues has not progressed. Looking to England as the main priority, there has been a great deal said about localism and strengthening the power of the major metropolitan areas but with the exception of the Commission established in Scotland, major political and constitutional issues have not been given much prominence.

There is an axis of interest to be cultivated with the Lib-Dems who are the only genuine Federalist Party. Federalism makes sense because it is not Scotland that is out of step with modernity and progress, it is the Union that is collapsing and is in urgent need of some serious surgery. England is changing and the politics of Scotland and England are diverging.

Labour needs to establish a credible Constitutional Convention with the Lib-Dems and other progressive parties to look at the political and constitutional structures of the Union and report and legislate within the parliamentary cycle of the next five years. Without some demonstration of real interest and intent on the part of the Labour party, Scotland will eventually leave. Federalism is the only way forward.

For far too long the Labour party has struggled to deal with the SNP. This is understandable. The SNP is a political problem, but unfortunately Labour has offered a constitutional solution. What is needed is a strategy that combines a political response to the SNP and a constitutional response for Scotland and the Union. Whether or not the SNP existed we would still have to improve the quality of how the Union is governed and argue about what structures would be appropriate. The main focus has to be the Union.

History is always a useful window through which we can view some interesting aspects of a debate we think of as a recent creation. Labour's road to home rule has been difficult and to a considerable extent is now being reflected in the kind of limited debate that we are seeing within the Labour Party. The Tory *Ayrshire Post* reported in 1888:

> Among the candidates brought forward for the expected vacancy in Mid-Lanark, through the retirement of Mr Stephen Mason, is Mr J. Keir Hardie, Cumnock. A correspondent interested in the election asks us whether there is any truth in the rumour that Mr Hardie was a Unionist in 1886. The rumour is an absurd one. Mr Hardie has been a consistent and pronounced Home Ruler since the beginning of the controversy. Whatever faults he may have, sitting on the hedge is not one of them. Right or wrong, you know what he means.

> On the question of Home Rule Keir Hardie said, 'I will support the Irish Party in winning justice for Ireland, and in the event of a difference between them and the Liberal Party, would vote with the Irish'; and to this he added, 'I am also strongly in favour of Home Rule for Scotland, being convinced that until we have a Parliament of our own, we cannot obtain the many and great reforms on which I believe the people of Scotland have set their hearts.'

Keir Hardie's comments are worth noting. From the early years of the Labour Party, the issue of home rule and constitutional change has been on Labour's agenda. Certainly, interest has ebbed and flowed and in recent times has reflected the fortunes of the SNP. But a glance at Hansard from the House of Commons shows that in the last years of the 19th century and the first decade of the 20th century there were some remarkable debates in the House of Commons. In 1913 a Home Rule Bill was passed on second reading and while the Bill had no chance of becoming legislation, the start of the Great War ended any possibility of further discussion. What was inspiring about these debates was the fact that all the current debates had been rehearsed a century earlier!

This is about taking the lead again in an area of public and constitutional policy where for over 100 years, from Keir Hardie to the Scotland

Act of 1998, Labour has had radical ideas. While the interest and enthusiasm of Labour has diminished somewhat over this period, there is corpus of intent, commitment and serious thinking that once again has to surface and defeat the claims of the doubters and constitutional non-believers who could inflict serious harm on the Party, convince people that Labour is once again facing both ways and allow the uninterrupted success of seven years of SNP Government to continue. There will be a high price to pay if the next six months is all about dissent and a failure to listen to Scots who don't want Independence but instead want their aspirations for a more powerful Parliament to be realised.

Crucially, the public will not tolerate any form of opportunism on the part of Labour if it appears that this is merely being done to blunt the edge of Nationalism as a short-term strategy to get beyond the referendum and not about a real commitment to a set of proposals, which will be given a high priority in the manifesto of the next Labour Government. Labour's credibility on this issue has slumped and that is why this question of Scotland's Government is not a distraction from other serious political issues, as some would have us believe. Constitutional change is key to the renewal of a declining Union and Scotland's future and not just an issue for Scotland. Denial is not a policy option. Unity of purpose and argument is crucial because there is a deepening disillusionment about Westminster politics. MPs and political parties should realise that the decline of the Union over the past 40 years is making an impact, not just in Scotland, but throughout the UK. Scots want Labour to talk about the future of Scotland and not about the future of the SNP, but for that we need Scottish Labour speaking with one voice.

The recent publication of the findings from Labour's devolution commission was designed to answer the question of what a NO vote will mean in terms of new powers for the Scottish Parliament. There was also the hope that Labour would acknowledge that the Union itself has to be transformed and provide a more sensible context in which the four nations of the Union could flourish and pursue – at different speeds and at different times – their own form of political self-determination. Public and press reaction suggests that Labour's efforts have not been reassuring or inspiring and for many have fallen well short of what was anticipated, especially after a much more upbeat interim report. This is reflected in a penetrating analysis by John Curtice, writing in *Scotland on Sunday*:

The NO side is beginning to look like a campaign in trouble... The lessons
for the NO side are clear. Frightening voters with messages of economic
doom and gloom is not working.

As someone who works with facts, not fiction, Curtice goes on to say that
Labour's vision of the UK as a 'sharing Union' is evidently not one that
comes readily to most voter's minds. There are also signs that the idea of
sticking with the Union because we can redistribute resources from the rich
South East to a poorer Scotland completely misreads the public mood and
has moved to a point where people are now more insulted than irritated.
The Curtice analysis also reveals the general disillusionment with politics
and specifically the lack of trust when it reveals the most worrying fact
that few people believe that a NO vote will result in more powers for the
Scottish Parliament:

> No less than 68 per cent of Scots agree that, in the event of a NO vote,
> the Scottish Parliament should become primarily responsible for taxation
> and welfare. But just 39 per cent think Holyrood will actually be given
> powers and responsibilities should Scotland vote NO.

More challenging is the point:

> Even among those who want more powers, only just over two in five (42
> per cent) believe the promises of more powers will be delivered. It is here
> perhaps that the Unionists' credibility gap is most striking.

Setting aside whether the numbers are accurate or not, the questions of trust
and confidence lie at the core of this referendum campaign and are directly
linked to the key questions of what do people anticipate if they vote NO
and what in reality are they likely to get.

The electors are way ahead of the politicians. Dramatic changes are
taking place in Scotland and political parties have to catch up!

Against the wider sweep of constitutional history and reaching deeper
for a better understanding of the future, we need to start talking about federalism. The Liberal Democrats have a worked out vision for the future that
is coherent, reasoned and workable. Federalism is the answer to the multi-
faceted problem of the Union of Great Britain and Northern Ireland. We
too often forget history and the fact that the Union is four nations brought
together before and after 1707. Building on the Steel Commission's 'Moving
to Federalism', Sir Menzies Campbell in 2012 published a paper on Home
Rule for Scotland within a Federal United Kingdom. This report talks about

continuing partnership and the need for the UK to reflect the aspirations of the people of the four nations within a modern democracy. The tone is upbeat, the style is simple and the arguments are based on common sense and seek self-determination for each part of the UK and federalism as a way of expressing different identities within one system where cooperation, for common purpose and the common good, is the driving force. Launching the report, Menzies Campbell said:

> We have set out in detail in our report how to proceed on the road to Federalism. We shall not be content with assuring a good outcome for Scotland – we regard it as the first step for the UK towards a modern constitutional future. Others may in sincerity want no more than to redefine Scotland's relationship within these islands, but our ambition is necessarily greater.

Labour needs to understand the importance of the phrase 'but our ambition is necessarily greater' and see the need for a more radical, comprehensive and inspired transformation of the Union. This is the reason why Labour's approach is too often seen as minimalist, incomplete and, more damagingly, grudging! Being left is not enough. Labour needs a progressive constitutional agenda which starts to engage in the battle of ideas, not be held back by comfortable sentiment or a desire to cling on to an old political era that has passed or to ignore a set of new political realities and challenges, nor to be in denial of how much the world has changed: this is Scotland today. We should be talking about the 'F' word, federalism, both as a workable option for the future of the UK as well as an alternative to Independence. Scotland has a real choice in this referendum. It is up to the other political parties, especially Labour, to acknowledge this point and promote federalism as a path to a better constitutional, political, economic and social future for Scotland and the Union.

CHAPTER TEN

Rethinking our politics

BY ALL ACCOUNTS the film *Lincoln* was an outstanding success. Starring Daniel Day Lewis and directed by Steven Spielberg, the film captured the transformational period in American history when the House of Representatives passed the Bill abolishing slavery, followed by the ending of the Civil War and, a few months later in 1865, the assassination of President Abraham Lincoln. Setting aside the wonderful cinematography, the engaging narrative, the costumes, sets and the humour and storytelling of the film, there were also some powerful political messages for politics in the Union, including Scotland, and certainly for this referendum campaign, which has lacked inspiration. Lincoln remains one of the most popular and important presidents in American history. Gripped by a sense of outrage about slavery and the injustice and inhumanity it stood for, Lincoln provided the leadership, vision, moral courage and tactical political nous to rid America of this threat to its ideals of freedom, liberty and justice. It would take another 100 years before President Lyndon Johnson was able to pass the civil rights laws necessary to finally remove the shackles from African Americans and allow Lincoln's dream to be realised.

It is always useful to be reminded of what should drive politics and the search for not only a better society, but for a constantly improving and more meaningful life for all individuals. Politics today are often soulless, contrived, managerial and uninspiring – lacking any sense of conviction, justice, fairness or equality. Lincoln's Gettysburg Address referred to 'of the people, for the people and by the people'. Our democracy today is not well served by this noble ambition of Lincoln. Instead, there is little inspiration or leadership around, especially at a time when there are so many big issues to be tackled, including whether Scotland should remain in the United Kingdom.

Regardless of the outcome of the referendum, there is a need to rethink our politics in Scotland and start to build a different kind of nation, less hidebound by the past and more enthusiastically embracing the future. But our new politics don't need to wait until Scotland is Independent, or part of a status quo plus Union, or part of some transformed and federalist structure. We need to start now. Politicians and the political parties, especially Labour and the Conservatives, are facing a growing discontent and disillusionment with their performance, so, in or out of the Union, political change has to happen. For progressives in Scotland, the referendum debate has been frustrating and overshadowed by the lack of a second question on the ballot paper, the partisan battle between the SNP and Labour and the lack of depth in relation to what kind of Scotland we want to live in. For Labour, the attitude of their support is crucial. After the referendum vote on the 18 September, there are two vital elections in the 2015 Westminster and 2016 Holyrood elections. Labour, as one of the key parts of what should be a progressive left of centre platform in Scotland, should be leading the debate on a new politics, but this is not happening. People are unsure about what Labour stands for in 2014. They feel that the campaign alliance with the Conservative Party is confusing and are at a loss to understand why the Better Together Campaign looks as though it was made in Westminster, with very little input from the Scottish leadership of the party. There are a number of reasons why Scottish Labour is in this position, but none of them make a great deal of sense. This led to a strange political contest where the YES campaign talks about Independence, the NO campaign talks about the Union, but because a more progressive option for Scotland is being denied to the electors, no one is really making the political case for a different Scotland, in a transformed Union. Labour has missed a great opportunity to make a positive political case for Scotland which would survive either a YES or NO vote. Scotland the nation, the country, the concept, the idea, deserves to be talked about, not just in terms of this narrow debate, but as something significant and substantial in its own right.

We need to make a start at putting together the outlines, a democratic and progressive case, for the kind of country Scotland could become.

This requires us to look anew at some of the big issues of our time and be unapologetic for shifting our focus on to the foundations needed to support a new approach to politics in Scotland. Our Unionist politics are broken and this has to be the context for our rethink. This will enable progressive politics to stake a claim for more legitimacy than it currently has in a country that has seen the SNP rise as Labour declined. For seven years the SNP has dominated Scottish politics. Change can only happen if Labour decides to step out of the past and create a modern, progressive and left of centre platform that includes other political parties and recognises that old style party politics is finished. The realignment of politics and political parties is long overdue: the Lib-Dems, the Greens and Labour are in position alongside the SNP to create a progressive alliance for a real difference in Scotland. The vision or idea of an Independent Scotland will not disappear even with a NO vote, the decline of the United Kingdom will continue and the politics of England will become a more significant factor in the immediate years ahead.

What could the politics of Scotland look like, and more importantly, how can Labour reinvent itself in the post-devolution era if it is a NO vote and maybe in the post-Union period if the YES vote wins? For Labour, there are a number of crucial steps to be taken.

Philosophy, Ethics and Values

The party has to have a much sharper and distinct definition of what it stands for and be able to articulate to a more sceptical and questioning public and who are disillusioned with what passes as party political debate, public discourse and political literacy. This is all about philosophy, ethics and values. The mythical centre ground of politics is congested and confusing. There is a need for a new political enlightenment that seeks to rekindle a real sense of purpose and importance to politics and a transformation of what politicians and political parties do in the name of the people they serve. There are remarkable examples down through the centuries of inspired ideas and philosophical thinking that could form the cornerstone of a more modern and, at the same time, deeper approach to our democracy.

The history of political philosophy, from Aristotle to Amartya Sen and from Socrates to Sandel, provides a remarkable insight into man's search for meaning and understanding of our world, with huge concepts and ideas being debated and seeking to deal with the very basis of our society and civilisation. Ethical principles and the core issue of morality have been the focus. This debate, which has continued for over two millennia, now seems largely absent from our politics, leaving an enormous vacuum around the purpose of politics and its role in modern society. What useful purpose, if any, do our politics seek to achieve? Surely it is time for a rethink? We need inspiration to lift the debate. We need, once again, to show that politics matters and that despite the discredited nature of our current politics, it doesn't need to be like this! Scotland needs to move in a new direction and philosophy is a good place to start.

One of these examples of inspiration is well documented. Between 1337

and 1339, a picture was painted by an Italian painter, Ambrogio Lorenzetti, and today it covers three walls of the Sala dei Nove in the Palazzo
Pubblico of Siena in Italy. It is called the Allegory of Good and Bad Government and what Lorenzetti's fresco does, first of all, is depict the nature of
good and bad government by means of figures who represent the qualities
that rulers should and should not have, and then show the effects of the
two kinds of government on the lives of ordinary people. So, in the case
of good government, we see the dignified ruler dressed in rich robes and
sitting on his throne, surrounded by figures representing the virtues of good
government: peace, courage, fortitude, strength, prudence, magnanimity,
justice, wisdom, temperance and the theological values of faith, hope and
charity. Beneath him stand a line of citizens encircled by a long rope the ends
of which are tied to the ruler's wrist, symbolising the harmonious binding
together of ruler and his people. As we turn to the right, we see Lorenzetti's
portrayal of the effects of good government, first in the city and then in
the countryside. The city is ordered and wealthy. The fresco's message is
spelt out in a banner held aloft by a winged figure representing security:

> Without fear every man may travel freely and each may till and sow, so long
> as this commune still maintains this lady sovereign, for she has stripped
> the wicked of all power.

The fresco on the other side, representing evil or bad government, is less well
preserved, but its message is equally plain: a demonic ruler surrounded by
the vices of avarice, pride, vain glory, cruelty, treason, fraud, frenzy, divi-
siveness, discord, war and tyranny. Here, the inscription reads:

> Because each seeks its own good, in this city justice is subjected to
> tyranny; wherefore along this road nobody passes without fearing for his
> life, since there are robberies outside and inside the city gates.

There is no better way to understand what political philosophy is, and
why we need it, than by looking at Lorenzetti's remarkable mural. We can
define political philosophy as 'an investigation into the nature, causes, and
effects of good and bad Government'. Lorenzetti not only captures this
quest, but expresses, in striking visual form, three ideas that stand at the
very heart of what politics should be.

The first is that good and bad government profoundly affect the quality
of human lives. Lorenzetti shows us how the rule of justice and the other
virtues allows ordinary people to do those things that enrich human existence.

The other side of the picture shows tyranny breeding poverty and death. Clearly, it makes a significant difference to our lives whether we are governed well or badly. We cannot imagine that the way we are governed will not have profound effects on our personal happiness.

The second idea is that the form our government takes is not predetermined. We have choices to make. Why, after all, was the mural painted in the first place? It was painted in the Sala dei Nove – the room of nine – and these nine were the rotating council of nine wealthy merchants who ruled the city in the first half of the 14th century. The portrayal of evil government was not just an academic exercise, it was a reminder of what might happen if the rulers of the city failed in their duty to the people, or if the people failed in their duty to keep a watchful eye on their representatives.

The third idea is that we can know what distinguishes good government from bad: we can trace the effects of different forms of government and we can learn what qualities go to make up the best form of government. In other words, there is such a thing as political knowledge. Lorenzetti's frescos bear all the marks of this idea.

Lorenzetti, surprisingly, has no room for liberty! But justice appears twice. He wanted to convey the idea that justice is fundamental to the institutions that turn a mass of individuals into a political community in the first place. Justice is depicted as binding the citizens to one another and then all of them together to government. In these, he was following in a long-standing tradition that viewed justice as central to the justification of political authority. Saying that justice is central to good government is one thing, but saying what it means is another. The Roman emperor, Justinian, said: 'Justice is the constant and perpetual will to render to each his due.' Philosophy and justice seem appropriate issues on which to look at a different kind of Scotland.

Understanding the electors

Labour has to understand the electors and the people of Scotland. The last seven years have convinced many people that Labour has learned few lessons from the rise and success of the SNP. Miscalculations, mistakes and misjudgements and a barely believable sense of denial have given the SNP an easy run.

The world is complex and so are our politics. Despite the frequent assertions from political parties that they are now deploying the most modern election techniques with sophisticated voter analysis, borrowed in the main from the United States, why are the Unionist parties misreading the mood of Scottish electors and making such serious miscalculations in the referendum campaign? Political parties, especially Labour, are failing to understand the fragile politics, the volatility of the electorate, the breaking down of traditional political allegiances and loyalties, the multiple identities of people, the disillusionment with politics – especially of the Westminster kind – and nearly seven years of failing to understand the consequences of the seismic changes in Scottish politics or the remarkable rise of the SNP from the margins of politics to the mainstream. There is now a complex web or volatile cocktail of influences, insecurity, ideas, frustrations, anxieties, fears, hopes and aspirations influencing the hearts and minds of Scots as they approach the most important decision in our history. Politics and constitutional issues *do* matter and while there may be little direct public or at times political awareness of the issues, their influence will make a difference. The role of England in the emerging devolution story is hugely underrepresented in our debate, but that may prove to be the decisive factor in this unfolding narrative about the future of the Union. The narrow campaign, being acted out on the choice between being in or out of the Union, is deceiving and hardly captures or represents the deeper currents of public opinion now swirling around. What is going on? Why is a widely believed 'slam dunk' defeat of Independence in danger of turning into a nightmare? How can the Unionist parties, at least at this stage, have got the campaign so badly wrong? What does the Better Together Campaign need to do to understand the mood of a nation in transition and reconnect with a public that seems to be more in tune with their nation than the politicians and political parties that seek to represent and serve them? Why a campaign so mired in intolerance and political hatred and so lacking in intellectual, philosophical, inspirational and visionary approaches? Why are we avoiding the broader sweep of history, a deeper debate and the lessons to be learned from Europe? The answers to these questions are vital not just in terms of what is likely to happen on the 18 September, but a must if we are to move beyond that date, regardless of the outcome, and repair some of the collateral damage to Scotland and the Union as well as seeking some form of consensus on a way forward which avoids – for all of us – an unending period of uncertainty, recriminations and paralysis.

So far there has been little consideration given to what happens next. In or out of the Union, there has to be some form of sanity and settlement: the campaign has so far provided little reassurance on this front.

Alex Salmond is talking about building a consensus after the Referendum. And the leader of the Better Together Campaign hints that the English might get a vote on the question of the currency union! Since the turn of the year, two issues still trouble the NO Campaign. First, if there is a NO vote, what does it mean for Scots who want a more powerful Parliament in Edinburgh? Second, why is it proving so hard to convince NO voters to stay loyal to the cause? Sadly, these remain elephant in the room issues for Labour. There is little evidence to suggest they are being addressed with the urgency the current polling figures demand or generating any internal debate about the need for a change of tactics in the next five months. There is a great deal of mystery surrounding the Better Together Campaign and its apparent failure to understand the mood of Scottish electors. So what is going on? Does Labour need to have a better and more sophisticated understanding of Scottish voters? The battle for heads and hearts lies at the core of this campaign.

In this so-called age of reason and common sense, it would be reassuring if people voted rationally, based on evidence and facts. But this is not the reality of modern British or Scottish politics. People in many instances are not voting their economic interests but are voting their values, which in turn reflect identity. These identities are multiple – not single – and create a complex, less trusting, more questioning and volatile electorate. The issues of mood, heart and emotion, whether political traditionalists like it or not, are the key to understanding what is going on in Scotland and what is shaping voter intentions. Unless the Better Together Campaign can distinguish between head and heart, fear and hope, soft and hard politics and the emotional and the practical, the electoral consequences for the NO vote could be dire! In the world of modern election campaigns, this is not the territory of Albert Einstein. Understanding electorates is now a well-developed science in both the US and Britain, where Labour and the Conservatives are now 'segmenting' the electors in a new world of politics, where social class has lost much of its importance in determining voting behaviour. The squeezed middle of Ed Milliband is an idea drawn from this kind of new analysis.

Before looking at this issue in more detail, the Nigel Farage-Nick Clegg Euro battle provides some fascinating insights into how disillusioned voters

are thinking and how identity and nationality are influencing their political choices. Will Hutton writes in the *Observer*:

> Farrage's current bubble of support is because he has tapped so brilliantly
> into a wider mood. He would say it is because he is speaking the unpal-
> atable truth to the establishment. But his economic and social arguments
> are a farrago of half lies and on occasion arrant bullshit.

But in the run up to the European Elections, people are unconcerned
about the facts or evidence or hard truths. Their hearts and emotions are
inextricably linked to values, disillusionment and identity. That is why we
have to understand the different attitude, outlooks and values and not just
the traditional and dated dividing lines of electoral politics. Scotland is now
a platform for complex and different kinds of politics and if politicians and
political parties ignore these new realities they will further alienate themselves from the people they wish to represent. This is what is happening
in this campaign! Populus, the market research company, is doing work
in this area. The company argues:

> ... when the traditional class based, left-right, social democratic/Neo-Lib-
> eral model of British politics still have some relevance, our central argu-
> ment is that these need to be understood alongside a new politics of
> identity, culture and nation.

These are described as:

> ... [a] whole array of reactive movements that build trenches of resistance
> on behalf of God – mainly in the US – nation, ethnicity, family and locality.

We ignore the decline of capitalism, the challenges of globalisation and
powerful expressions of collective identity. In the paper 'Fear and Hope',
Populus responds to the current socio-economic class-based analysis of
AB, C1, C2 and DE and overlay a totally new way of thinking about
electors and their preferences. These segment breakdowns are described
as confident multiculturalists, mainstream liberals, identity ambivalent,
cultural integrationists, latent hostiles and active enmity. Significantly, 62
per cent of UKIP voters fall into hostiles and enmity –defined as pessimistic,
uncertain about the future, disengaged and ready to support people that
stand up for their country – whereas only 18 per cent of Labour voters are
in these two categories. Another notable figure: 42 per cent of Conservatives are recorded as cultural integrationists, while the figure for UKIP voters
is zero per cent! This simple comparison reveals the kind of voters who

are likely to support UKIP and explains that the overwhelming majority of their voters are opposed to integration, hostile to mainstream and active enemies of our current politics. A traditional social and economic class-based analysis would not have revealed this kind of information. Populus also do electorate by personality and this reveals that 67 per cent of Labour voters fall into the categories of calm persistence, long-term despair and hard-pressed anxiety! Much of this new analytical thinking starts to reveal the complex realities lurking in the minds of voters. Facts may not matter to those whose lifestyles, life chances and life experiences are so different from the class-based interpretations of the past. It is identity, stupid, and the NO Campaign should grasp this political reality.

The Common Good

Labour has to embrace the common good, not just as a comfortable sound-bite, but as a fully developed moral and philosophical basis for our approach to building a better and fairer Scotland, whether in or out of the Union. Once again, Labour should be better placed to influence the future. Setting aside the commitment to having another phase of devolution based on its own commission findings and a pledge to take a NO vote seriously, no overhaul of the politics of Scotland, post-referendum, is being considered. If it is a YES vote, the Labour Party, besides getting over the shock and humiliation, has no contingency plan and will find it difficult to gain any immediate traction or credibility in post-Independence politics. There is no reason why this should happen. Labour should accept now that, no matter what happens in September, Scottish politics have to change and that the UK Party must give full autonomy to Scottish Labour so that it can play a more open and less constrained role in shaping Scotland's future. From the era of the ancient Greek city-states through to contemporary political philosophy, the idea of the common good has embraced concepts of citizenship, collective action and active participation in the public realm of politics and public service. The common good rejects the idea that society merely comprises atomised individuals and instead accepts that people should live their lives as citizens, deeply embedded in social relationships.

With an eye to the Labour Party, David Marquand asked in the *Guardian* in 2010:

> Can it develop a coherent social-democratic governing philosophy, capable of guiding it through the inevitable uncertainties and contingencies of

Government? Can it breathe life into the ethic of citizenship and service which is fundamental to the public realm?

This remains the challenge for Labour, particularly in Scotland.

Michael Sandel, Professor of Philosophy at Harvard, said that we should bring morality back to the political debate and wants to return to the Aristotelian notion of the common good. And in his BBC 4 Reith Lecture, he argued for new politics of the common good and for moral and civic renewal.

The Jimmy Reid Foundation talks about the Common Weal.

The Fabian Society argues about the fact that for far too long progressive politics have ceded space for moral reasoning to those on the right of the political spectrum.

Michael Sandel's *What Money Can't Buy* and his four BBC 4 Reith Lectures talk about the politics of the common good and asks what it would look like. He outlines four aspects of the common good, outlined below.

Citizenship, sacrifice and service

A just society requires a strong sense of community. It must find a way to cultivate in citizens a concern for the whole, a dedication to the common good. It must find ways to lean against the purely privatised culture of the good life and cultivate civic virtue. This is how a democratic society can hope to cultivate the solidarity and sense of mutual responsibility that a just society requires.

The Moral Limits of the Market

One of the most striking tendencies of our time is the expansion of markets and market reasoning into spheres of life traditionally governed by non-market reforms. Markets are useful instruments for organising productive activity. However, unless we want to let the market write the norms that govern social institutions, we need a public debate about the moral limits of markets and market orientated thinking and reasoning. The point is made that a market economy is fast becoming a market *society*.

Inequality, Solidarity and Civic Virtue

In the UK, the gap between the rich and poor has grown in recent decades. Yet inequality has not loomed large as a political issue. There has been a lack of attention to inequality in contemporary politics. The key points being made by Sandel are that too great a gap between rich and poor undermines the solidarity that democratic societies need. As inequality deepens, the affluent secede from public places and services, leaving them to those who can't afford anything else. As a result, public services deteriorate and those who no longer use those services find alternatives that dissent from spending more money on them. The hollowing out of the public realm makes it difficult to retain that solidarity and sense of community on which our democracy depends.

A Politics of Moral Engagement

Our politics should be based on the model of mutual respect. The politics of moral engagement are not only a more inspiring ideal than the politics of avoidance, they are also a more promising basis for a just society.

The 'Politics of the Common Good' based on fairness, equality of opportunity, releasing potential, compassion, caring and inclusion, is actually a combination of traditional Scottish values. The party which reconnects with these values – and it may have to be a new coalition of shared political interests in Scotland – will win the confidence of the Scottish people. Our politics seem less concerned with searching for the truth and more willing to promote a diet of myth and fears, and to spin masquerading as objective truth. Creating a positive culture requires inspiring leadership and progressive political philosophy and simple, strong messages that communicate with individuals and groups.

Money, Markets and Morality

Within the context of the common good and the fairness, justice and equality agenda, Labour has to invest some time in a national debate about money and markets and the role of morality. These issues are not prominent in the contemporary debate in Scotland, and indeed the rest of the UK. The reach of markets as the market economy is in danger of becoming a market society. The role of markets in public life and personal relations, and which goods should be bought and sold are key questions that have to occupy the space around the quest to rethink our politics. Michael Sandel argues:

> ... some of the good things in life are corrupted or degraded if turned into commodities. So to decide where the market belongs, and where it should be kept at a distance, we have to decide how to value the goods in question – health, education, family life, nature, art, civic duties, and so on.

These are moral and political questions, not merely economic ones. This is a debate we didn't have during the era of market triumphalism. As a result, without quite realising it, we drifted from having a market economy to being a market society.

The Social Investment State

Labour needs to develop a model of the social investment state or nation that is the alternative to the market liberal strategy which dominates Coalition thinking at Westminster. Small countries can be very successful and there is real merit in distinguishing ourselves from what is happening in England. In his book *Small nations in a Big World*, Michael Keating describes the social investment state as an alternative strategy to market liberalism, in which public expenditure is seen as a contribution to the productive economy rather than a drain on it. There are references to this in the Independence White Paper and it reflects the work of the Jimmy Reid Foundation's common weal, the STUC and the Voluntary sector in Scotland. Michael Keating notes the contrasting experiences of the Nordic countries, which are closer to the social investment state, the Baltic states, which are closer to the market liberal model, and Ireland, which has attempted a hybrid of the two. There is clearly scope for Scotland to develop this model as it also contains a serious commitment to tackling inequality, which remains the most divisive issue in Scottish society. Again Scotland could pursue this model regardless of the outcome of the referendum. It provides a much better platform from which the links between social and economic policy can be established in the wider context of social democracy and social partnership. This approach rejects the market logic of low wages, low taxes and light regulation, which normally corresponds with low levels of public service. This is the road to ruin being pursued by the Conservative Coalition and lauded by the right of the Conservative Party. While a devolved Parliament provides protection in areas of education and health, which are fully devolved, we continue to be the subject of UK economic, fiscal and financial matters. The election of a Labour Government, in the eyes of a majority of Scots, is essential if we are to halt and reverse the onward march of the market liberal strategy. This assumes that the next Labour Government will want to imprint on policy a different political philosophy and a new set of ethics and values. Labour needs to construct a new narrative combining the values that fired Labour in its early formative period, the needs of a modern democracy, and the radical changes to how the party operates in a transforming constitutional structure.

A Social Democratic Party

There is a great deal to be gained by Labour reaffirming the fact that it is a social democratic party, in the mould of the Nordic countries and some of the other Western European states and regions. This also holds out the possibility of creating progressive alliances and coalitions in Scotland in line with other European nations and eventually moving to the point where broader sets of interests become the basis of politics rather than narrow, partisan manifesto-based party politics. In *The Crisis of Social Democracy in Europe*, Michael Keating and David McCrone describe its features. As a social philosophy, social democracy seeks to reconcile market capitalism with social responsibility. It is also a political tradition, a set of ideas about fairness and equality and a moral economy that refuses to accept the automatic primacy of markets over the need for equality. Social democracy is also a political practice, a way of governing which systematically seeks to include the needs of the deprived and to emphasise the public domain over the private, while being pragmatic about how this is done. For most of the 20th century it has been associated with an extensive state sector in both the economy and the public services, more as a means to an end, rather than an end in itself. Social democracy can also be defined as a group of like-minded parties across the world committed to the same political goals and ethics. Social democracy has also been a political and social sub-culture rooted in working class communities, bound by traditions of solidarity in the Trade Unions and has provided social boundaries defining 'us'.

Social Partnership

There is a need to overcome conflict and divisions in social, industrial and economic matters and to develop more consistency, inclusivity and understanding. Many of the small European countries use Social Partnership to get industry and other groups together, to negotiate key deals and think in the long term. There should be far more cooperation and consensus on strategic direction and priorities

The Nordic Experience

The Nordic experience is one model we could borrow from. There is a great deal of comment and practical experience to suggest that Denmark, Norway and Sweden have more 'happiness, humanity and hope' than we do. While much of this is very subjective, these countries do appear, on the basis of many international comparative indexes, to be more at peace with themselves than we do. Being part of a much larger UK makes Scotland different. The UK is still caught up in militarism, an interest still in global aggrandisement and a preoccupation with defence issues. The Nordic social democratic model offers Scotland a real choice in the event of a YES vote, but this alternative is not available to the UK, for obvious political and historic reasons as well as an enthusiasm for global adventure best illustrated by our invasion of Iraq with the US. Their quality of public life, level of political literacy, quality of public discourse, comprehensive education and welfare systems, and some of the best public services in the world all suggest that a new Scotland in or out of the Union could learn a great deal. It has been a downside of being part of the Union that, in Scotland, we have failed to establish more extensive links with European nations and, in particular, the Nordic countries. Independence would change that, but being part of a federal structure would also allow this to happen. The outcome of our date with destiny should not prevent Scotland continuing our journey forward.

Nation building

Are we in a position to adopt a more ambitious social investment approach? Do the pre-conditions exist or is there a great deal of nation or nation state building to be done to create the conditions in which a more progressive approach could be successful? Michael Keating argues that Scotland lacks the broad social partnership that characterises many successful small states. External change in the form of Independence would need to be matched by considerable internal change before it is fully equipped to face global challenges. Staying in the Union would require a much bigger effort to adjust the collective mindset because of the lack of any noticeable change or shock to the system. These questions have not figured to any great extent in the referendum campaign.

Change the way we do politics

Distinct from the philosophical, ethical, economic and social aspects of this political rethink, we also need to change the way we do our politics and in the process bring our political parties into the 21st century.

Politics has to renew itself. Public disillusionment intensifies, discontent deepens, disconnection grows, and more and more, people give up on voting as turn out tumbles, party membership collapses and trust and confidence remain at historically low levels. Our politics are broken. Only the SNP have been able to buck the international trends and stay in office for seven years, retain high levels of popular support and force a vote on the future of the Union. In the meantime the Unionist parties, in particular Labour, have failed to find any traction in the new political landscape of the post-devolution period. But the decline of our politics didn't just happen over the last seven years, more like the last 50 years, where the proportion of people in the UK voting for the two major parties started to decline dramatically, people started to lose respect for the ability of parties to tackle problems on their behalf and there has been a failure to attract a new generation of younger people. In addition, people are less clear as to what political parties stand for. Politics themselves look out of touch and appear soulless, managerial, uninspiring, technocratic, obsessed with the economy and increasingly unrepresentative of a population where political loyalties and allegiances are breaking down and the internet age is atomising society.

Faced with an overwhelming need for our politics to change, the response from the political parties has been disappointing, casual and lacking any sense of urgency. So what needs to be done? We need to change the mindset. This preoccupation with manifestos should end. People don't live in the envelope of a policy for everything in their lives. There should be more political tolerance and inclusivity. The minds of the public are not structured like a manifesto. No party has a monopoly of wisdom on every subject or issue. Manifestos in their current form don't fit a modern electorate.

This will require a realignment of our parties and our thinking towards the European models where coalitions and alliances are commonplace, Proportional Representation is introduced for Westminster elections, parties come together around a broader policy platform, and the public are offered a spectrum of ideas and policies around different political views or philosophies – not just a book of manifesto pledges, but something to show what a party or party grouping stands for. Progressive politicians and parties need to be attractive to young people whose ideals and interests are being expressed in a variety of non-party political ways. We need to capture their imagination. Politics is too defensive, too narrow, too intolerant, too controlled, too exclusive, too archaic in procedures and as a consequence has too many cadres of cheerleaders, often self-serving, with only a tenuous grip on what the purpose of politics is in a modern Scotland or UK. The political process and its current structure are letting down those who serve the public as elected officials. Overall they are doing some great work but they are trapped by a system which can be self-serving, which is hopelessly out of date and is narrow in its selection of candidates for elected office and often limited in the range of people who become involved. The old traditional party system is stifling MPs, MEPs and MSPs. They should be allowed to express their views more easily, be more open and less hidebound by the constraints of elected office, which stifle original thought and prevent cross party consensus on important public issues.

The public deserve more from their politics than they are currently getting. But it is only the political parties that can reform and renew themselves. The plight of Labour in Scotland and the outcome of the referendum may be the catalyst for change. A vote for Independence will be a shock to the system and Labour will have to change and adapt to the challenge of being a new State and working to become a Government! A victory for the Better Together Campaign could mean no change at all, if recent history is anything to go by. The Party in Scotland could remain a mere off shoot of UK Labour and this may cause, depending on the response of Scots to a NO vote, some political and practical problems in the elections of 2015 and 2016.

After nearly two years in which the referendum on Independence has dominated our politics, the hostility and bitterness between nationalism and unionism has deepened, and the nation is divided at a time when we are enduring unprecedented inequality, assaults on the welfare state and massive uncertainty about the future of public services. There is no consensus on the future of Scotland. This is in sharp contrast to the referendum in 1997 where people, parties and politicians overwhelmingly endorsed a new future for Scotland. The defeat of Independence – if that is the outcome – is likely to strengthen our crisis of national identity, not weaken it, and deepen our sense of frustration about the inability of our politics to rise above partisanship, and at times hatred, in discussing the future of Scotland. Adding further to our sense of drift is the complete lack of any inspiring Unionist alternative to the breakup of the Union, or indeed, the future of a Union with Scotland in it. 18 September 2014 could result in the answering of one question, but Scotland's constitutional future being totally unresolved because of the failure of the Unionist parties to have a deliverable alternative, any serious commitment to progressive ideas for Scotland's future and any real enthusiasm for reforming a Union in decline. The Unionist parties need to take the electors seriously in three important ways.

First, offer them some vision for the future of Scotland, in or out of the Union, which is based on the quality of life, not on endless threats and negativity. Second, engage with their national identity and pride in country. Third, talk more about political philosophy instead of dreary predictions of gloom and despair. For the Unionist parties there is political life after the referendum and the Union itself is in dire need of change. People are more than economic entities: they have feelings, hopes, aspirations, emotions and ambitions and want to know what kind of Scotland is on offer to them. So far the Unionist parties seem incapable of doing this. And on this particular point the YES to Independence Campaign need to raise their game as to what kind of Scotland they are offering. Talk of freedom, statehood and 'seats at the top table' of world affairs make little sense to people whose pride, ambition and self-worth will be more normally linked to the prospects for themselves, family and community. Throughout Scotland there is a need to have a wider discussion about what for nearly 2,000 years has been described as political philosophy, the concerns about the basic principles and values that underpin political life, and what is the best way of organising society in order to allow all its citizens to enjoy the good life. Many people are not aware that they are talking philosophy, but their ideas, their concerns, their views and their hopes and fears are all about the fundamental ideas that shape our lives and our society. The current referendum debate – in terms of philosophy, principles, values and ethics – is a philosophy-free zone and shows no signs of changing.

Political philosophy is about good government, morality and ethics and requires us to address key ideas such as fairness, justice, and the rights of individuals or communities to see how they are related to one another. Just as ethics requires us to give a rational justification for our actions as citizens, political philosophy examines the justification for political institutions and ideologies. From the ancient Greek world of Plato and Aristotle to the present day, these issues have occupied the minds of some of the world's greatest thinkers because they lie at the heart of what our lives and societies are all about. We need to debate political philosophy to decide how we shape our future. People, in this age of austerity and uncertainty, are looking for reassurance and for more meaning to their lives. Political arguments revolve around political philosophy and political ideas. Our politicians must recognise the fact that the public are sick and tired of uninspiring, managerial and technocratic politics, and seek instead a public discourse where big issues are more openly and honestly debated, and in doing so, our politicians acknowledge that there are tough choices to be made and priorities to be argued, but in a way which engages and informs the public and reframes the debate between parties and politicians.

Professor Michael Sandel used his 2009 BBC Reith Lectures to make the case for richer political debate, underpinned by the need to put morality back into politics. He highlighted the need to refashion the political debate in an era 'where the end of market triumphalism is in sight' and said, 'We should now challenge the doctrine of the idea of public services being run to emulate the competitive market.'

In this context a market economy is tolerable but a market society isn't.

In an *Observer* interview with Andrew Anthony in 2012, Sandel outlined how philosophy and politics should be a more prominent part of the public debate. This is compulsory reading for those who wish to reinvigorate our poltics. Sandel believes that philosophy is not 'distant and abstract', but instead a function of the 'hard ethical choices that life throws up'. What's more, he argues that it's vital for the democratic health of society to be able to identify the big questions that lie behind everyday conflicts and presumptions.

Sandel's overriding aim as a philosopher is to bring morality back into political debate. He wants to return the discussion to the Aristotelian notion of the common good. Our politics are devoid of this kind of debate.

Sandel, concerned about the common good, wants to push back the pervasiveness of markets, and seems most interested in stimulating a debate about the underlying moral impulses that determine how we view the world. 'We can't decide any of the questions we argue about,' he says, 'without implicitly relying on certain ethical ideas, certain ideas of justice, and certain ideas of common good. We can't be neutral on those questions even if we pretend to be.'

The signals and the noise

The Union politics of division and discontent, in the form of Tory extremism, are colliding with the Scottish politics of difference and diversity, seeking to build a new Scotland. This will be the new battleground of the referendum campaign. The Tories, and much of the Union, seem to be indirectly hastening the breakup of Britain. On the other hand, Scotland is enjoying difference and diversity and, heading in another direction, will want more freedom and change if the political menu being served up by Westminster becomes so unpalatable. Conservatism in London could be a much bigger threat to the Union than nationalism in Edinburgh.

Nate Silver is a political forecaster and election guru. Described as a 34-year-old Delphic oracle, he has written a remarkable book, *The Signal and the Noise*, in which he distinguishes between the noise and clutter surrounding major issues and the true signals we need to detect if we are to understand what is actually going on and to assess their long-term significance. Adopting this approach, what sense can we make, at least at this stage, of the ongoing referendum campaign and its likely impact on the nearly four million people eligible to vote next year?

The consistently complacent Better Together Campaign would be wise to heed the words of Nate Silver, who, when talking to the *Scotsman* said: 'Scotland will only vote for Independence if major crisis hits England.' Defining a crisis is never easy, but there are many issues currently circling the Conservatives and UKIP around populism and extremism. The issues identified in this book are linked to England. If there is a NO vote then the future of Scotland in the Union becomes heavily dependent on what happens to England in the constitutional debate, and in turn, what kind of influence England will exert on any further forms of devolution, including federalism. Taken together, they represent different kinds of politics from anything that is happening in Scotland. The strategy of distraction or scapegoating – demonising immigrants, humiliating welfare claimants, xenophobic anti-Europeanism and the commercialisation and franchising of the NHS and Education – is alien to Scots, and merely serves to reinforce the political divergence between Scotland and England. Could there be a game-changing scenario that could have a decisive impact on the result and decide Scotland's constitutional future? The last few months at Westminster have certainly created more headaches for the Better Together Campaign. What then, are the signals the political parties should have been picking up?

England, a crisis?

A crisis engulfing England is unlikely to happen. Instead, a series of smaller political shocks could coalesce and impact on Scottish voters and provide a real tipping point for those increasingly disenchanted with the political and ideological direction of the Union and the toxic politics that are fast becoming the hallmark of this Tory Government. The Coalition now exists in name only. The poisoning of Union politics is a real possibility. Scotland and England are diverging.

So what could happen? The hard edge of constitutional politics has dominated the first phase of the campaign. There are, however, sound reasons – practical, tactical, psychological and political – for the debate to switch gear and move in a new direction in a second phase. There is a softer, more nuanced, but potentially more deadly political scenario in the making, which will quietly gain ground and – out of reach and out of sight of the party machines – start to reshape how voters think and eventually act.

A perfect storm

This perfect storm of issues, events and toxic politics has been brewing, not in Scotland, but in London, Westminster and UKIP and Conservative Party HQ, which could impact the referendum campaign and the mood and mindset of a nation, change the political psychology of how Scots might vote and ultimately determine the outcome of the vote. Remarkably, the NO Campaign seems oblivious to what might happen and are simply ignoring the micro trends, tipping points and signals which could still blow the battle for Scotland wide open. A recent headline seemed to capture the scenario facing Scots: 'Independence is risky, but Union is even scarier.' There is little doubt that Scots would not like to see their future through the prism of the current Government's politics or ideology and their fear that this could be their shared destiny within the Union at Westminster. This is the nightmare scenario!

Hard politics

The Unionist Campaign throughout has combined the 'hard' and aggressive politics of Westminster with no vision, no narrative, no idea of Scotland, the nation, and no concept of how the role of Scots and Scotland could be enhanced within a modern Union. Scots are being treated largely to a Westminster perspective on the future of their own country. It is this level of frustration and anger which may lead them to turn their backs on an increasingly divided Britain; the rise of the political right; Westminster and Unionist politics; an English nationalism waking up and moving in the wrong direction; the toxic politics of the Tories and their 'Tea Party' allies UKIP; the tearing up of the post-war social and economic consensus; a Labour Party continuing to lack confidence; a Britain consumed by economic greed and inequality; a Britain that is increasingly intolerant and unfair; a Tory Government devoid of decency, compassion and beyond any notion of the common good; a Tory Party revealing their real disinterest in Scotland; and a Union in which there is a growing divide and where political and constitutional differences are widening. These are the issues that may determine Scotland's referendum. Why would Scots want to be part of this future when other choices exist? Do we want to be more like Denmark than England? What kind of Scotland do we want to live in? Would Scots not want to exit a Union that is incapable of reforming itself and instead seeks to frustrate the ambitions of others?

The reckless behaviour of the Conservative Government at Westminster could slowly but perceptibly be the catalyst for a shift in the public mood, especially at a time when Scotland is much more wrapped up in nationality and identity and less concerned with class and traditional political allegiances. Unionist politics in Scotland are in crisis. Labour is hesitant, lacking confidence and appears to be devoid of a narrative for Scotland's constitutional future and lacking a vision for Scotland in or out of the Union. Political disillusionment with Westminster is growing.

The SNP are the dominant political force in Scottish politics and face little opposition. Despite their populist and successful approach to Holyrood politics, they have failed to win over many more Scots to their cause of Independence. Could all of this be about to change if conservatism and a right-wing Government continue to reinforce political difference north of the border and continue to view with a contemptuous neglect the idea of Scotland the nation, not just another part of the north-south divide or an increasingly divided Britain?

The Prospects for Labour

The prospects for Labour will also figure prominently in the minds of Scots as we move closer towards the General Election in May 2015. The prospect of a Conservative Government or a Coalition with the Lib-Dems or UKIP remains a real possibility. Many Scots will be more reassured about the Union if Labour's prospects of victory in 2015 seem real, but will feel less positive if doubts remain about who runs Britain over the next five years.

So the big unknown in the debate is whether Labour can win the next election, can convince Scots that it can and that its policies will be radically different from those of the Conservatives. Will Labour be able to spell out clearly what it stands for? Labour has to reconnect with the electors and show willingness to transform a tired and dated Union and set out a new direction for a modern, federated, flexible and fairer Union where maximum powers are available to Scotland and the English question is addressed.

Above all else, Labour in Scotland has to engage with identity and nationality, difference and diversity and start to believe in Scotland as a nation, regardless of whether it is in or out of the Union. Labour should be arguing for a Union worthy of its name and where each country can work out its own destiny. Saving the Union by respecting Scotland's demands and ambitions is a small price to pay for stable politics. If this is not a price the Unionist parties can pay, then Scottish voters may have no other option but to vote to end the historic links and build a new Scotland.

What does a NO vote mean?

Scots want to know what happens on the day after the ballot. If Labour continues to drag its feet on this issue, then once again the SNP might offer their own alternative and campaign for them in the next two elections.

Unionist parties blocked a second question on the ballot paper and are now lumbered with a Union that shows some interest in minimalist change. The electors will be offered a choice of two extremes – Independence or status quo plus Unionism – and may, irritated by the fact that Labour, having not supported a second question, is showing little interest or urgency over providing an acceptable long-term alternative to Independence. The debate has gone well past this point where tinkering on the edges or bidding wars over more power and taxes or vague promises will address the deeper problems of a declining Union and Scotland role within it.

The advance of the right poses a real threat to the Union and Scotland's role in it. This scenario will likely embrace a lurch towards a form of English Nationalism combined with the fear, hate and scapegoat mentality being targeted at welfare benefit claimants, immigrants and foreigners. The issue of membership of the EU will be divisive and Scotland may wish to have nothing to do with this reckless adventure planned for 2017. Once again this will create instability in the minds of referendum voters, which will have been heightened by UKIP's strong showing in the European Elections in 2014.

The people of Scotland are well ahead of their politicians. Scottish electors may see softer, more intelligent politics where identity, nationality, humanity, fairness, equality, virtue, compassion, tolerance and diversity matter and feel that one nation politics might only be achieved in Scotland as the Union fails to deliver. The signals are clear, but is anyone listening?

In or out, a need for radical change

The 'scunnerisation' factor may also reach new levels as Scots bemoan the lack of inspiration and the endless intolerance and hatred between Labour and the SNP. Offers giving Scotland more powers – even if that can be agreed at Westminster, and this seems to be their intention after the announcement made by the three party leaders before the first televised debate – have been overtaken by history and the devolution years. The mood of the Scottish people may no longer be satisfied by a minimal response. The campaign is now well beyond warm words, a bit more tax and a few more powers for Edinburgh. This seems too little and too late. The campaign is now looking at a new start, embracing again social democracy, a better society, the dreams and aspirations of an emerging nation and building a more inspired future. So can all or any of this be captured by the Union or by Independent Scotland? Set against this real choice most Scots will by now be aware of the excitement, the sense of history and the importance of the decision they are about to make. One thing is clear, regardless of the outcome of the referendum, the Union has to be the subject of radical and transformative change if it is to survive. But there are few signs of the traditional parties understanding this. Other progressive European countries must see Westminster as frozen in time, out of touch and a divisive institution, incapable of reform and more concerned about hanging on to the faded glory of the past, always grudging in its concessions to the need for political and constitutional change and circling the wagons around the ridiculous idea of the absolute sovereignty of the Westminster Parliament as the weapon of last resort in its struggle to resist change.

Scotland and Germany

After the Euro elections a BBC commentator remarked that Scotland looked more like Germany than England. The debate so far has been incredibly narrow, with both sides unable to grasp a broader sweep of history or a wider appreciation of some of the big issues out with the economy. The Union needs to modernise now, regardless of whether or not Scotland becomes Independent. The political and constitutional reconstruction of the Union is nearly half a century overdue. The Unionist parties are still locked out of modernity and are the victims of their own failure to read the ruins and change. The YES Campaign still cannot believe their luck. The NO Campaign has, in a few months, turned what could have been a comfortable majority into a possibly narrow victory. That hasn't been achieved by the strength of Nationalism but by the weaknesses of Unionism. The incredibly volatile nature of the public reflects the disillusionment with political parties as the crisis at the heart of our politics and our democracy deepens. Why did nearly 70 per cent of Scots not vote in the European elections? Why has the average turnout in all other elections over the past decade been 50 per cent, meaning a shocking one in two of the population don't vote? Why is political party membership collapsing! Why is there little trust or confidence in Westminster politics? Why, against this decline in traditional Unionist politics, has the SNP remained in power at Holyrood for seven years, still come out top in the Euro poll, negotiated a referendum ballot on their own terms and are still viewed as the party that speaks for Scotland. No disrespect to the First Minister, but it is the accumulated weaknesses of the Union to blame for the seismic shifts in Scottish politics: a Westminster in denial, grudging every concession to keep Scotland in line, unable to see that constitutional renewal is urgently needed and ultimately possibly helping push Scotland out of the Union.

The decline of party politics

This political malaise and a whole raft of other factors are now intervening in the campaign and challenging the Union to respond. Traditional politics and attitudes are no longer fit for the 21st century. The recent Euro elections in Scotland have not changed our calculations as to what might happen in September. UKIP unfortunately scraped a seat at the expense of the SNP gaining another seat. Not surprising when you consider that they polled nearly 60,000 votes in 2009 and will have undoubtedly benefitted from the collapse of the BNP vote in Scotland and the general media mischief of trying to portray Farage as the beer swilling hero of the working man. What was important was the message coming from the EU elections in England and the implications for the General Election in 2015. The prospects of a Tory tie-up with UKIP will send shivers down the spines of most Scots who will view with revulsion the EU, immigrants, foreigners and welfare scroungers being used as scapegoats for a failing Union and a distraction from the real problems. The quality of public discourse in Britain and the level of political literacy, continues to decline to shocking levels. Also worrying is the prospect of an in or out vote on EU membership if this alliance of right-wing extremism and populism is able to hold a referendum in 2017. Scotland and England are politically diverging. The Better Together Campaign should see diversity as a powerful symbol of a new era rather than pretend it poses a threat or even worse, that it doesn't exist.

The debate has probably moved well beyond further constitutional tinkering, to the point that the Better Together Campaign must be bold and accept that it is the Union that is the problem, not Scotland. Scotland, win or lose, has started a remarkable debate that could help reverse the decline of the Union and enhance the prospects of the nation.

A new political enlightenment is long overdue and Labour will have to be part of this. From the margins of Scottish politics, to the mainstream and then to the majority party of the Scottish Government in seven years and possibly taking Scotland to Independence, the SNP have changed Scottish politics forever. Labour has to respond to this knowing its long-term future as a party is in doubt and that the new politics of Scotland are much more demanding and competitive.

Some other books published by **LUATH** PRESS

Scotland The Growing Divide
Henry McLeish
ISBN: 1-908373-45-8 PBK £11.99

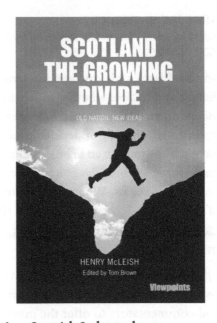

Is there a growing divide between Holyrood and Westminster? What does this mean for the people of Scotland, and for England?

Scotland makes a huge contribution to the United Kingdom: culturally, economically and through the numerous Scots who have led the UK in the fields of politics, business, academia and sport... The Coalition Government is firmly committed to Scotland's ongoing place in the UK.

UK Consultation Paper 2012 'Scotland's Consitutional Future'

This paper provides a vision of the further opportunities for Scotland if the Scottish Parliament's responsibilities were extended in order to allow for independence.

UK Government White Paper 2009 'Your Scotland, Your Voice: A National Conversation'

Had the SNP victory at Holyrood changed forever the mindset of Scottish politics?

As a Scottish Independence referendum fast approaches, *Scotland: The Growing Divide* returns to answer this question and more with a hard-hitting, incisive and informed look at where the devolution journey has taken us – from the heady days of the new Blair government in 1997 to the Independence referendum in 2014.

After Independence

Edited by Gerry Hassan and James Mitchell

ISBN: 978-1-908373-95-3 PBK £12.99

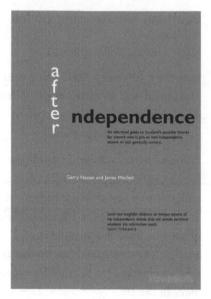

Scotland faces a historic and fundamental debate and choice: whether to become an independent nation or not. Whether for or against, or currently undecided, this will have a huge impact and consequences: on how we see ourselves as a society and how others see us. Whatever the outcome of this debate, Scotland and indeed the UK will be changed irreversibly and irrevocably.

After Independence draws together over two dozen leading thinkers, academics and commentators to offer the most comprehensive and detailed examination of the terrain and possibilities of Scottish independence and self-government both constitutionally and beyond.

Britain Rebooted

David Torrance
ISBN: 978-1-910021-11-8 PBK £7.99

Would federalism work in the UK? Wouldn't England dominate a British federation? How would powers be distributed between federal and home Nation level? What about the House of Lords?

In the run up to the historic referendum on Scottish independence there has been a plethora of tracts, articles and books arguing for and against, but there remains a gap in the literature: the case for Scotland becoming part of a 'rebooted' federal Union. It is an old, usually Liberal, dream, but one still worth fighting for.

It is often assumed that federalism is somehow 'alien' to the Scottish and British constitutional tradition but in this short book journalist David Torrance argues that not only has the UK already become a quasi-federal state but that formal federation is the best way of squaring the competing demands of Nationalists and Unionists.

He also uses Scotland's place within a federal UK to examine other potential reforms with a view to tackling ever-increasing inequality across the British Isles and create a more equal, successful and constitutionally coherent country.

DAVID TORRANCE

BRITAIN
SCOTLAND IN A FEDERAL UNION
REBOOTED

Details of these and other books published by Luath Press can be found at:
www.luath.co.uk

Luath Press Limited
committed to publishing well written books worth reading

LUATH PRESS takes its name from Robert Burns, whose little collie Luath (*Gael.*, swift or nimble) tripped up Jean Armour at a wedding and gave him the chance to speak to the woman who was to be his wife and the abiding love of his life. Burns called one of 'The Twa Dogs' Luath after Cuchullin's hunting dog in Ossian's *Fingal*. Luath Press was established in 1981 in the heart of Burns country, and now resides a few steps up the road from Burns' first lodgings on Edinburgh's Royal Mile.
Luath offers you distinctive writing with a hint of unexpected pleasures.

Most bookshops in the UK, the US, Canada, Australia, New Zealand and parts of Europe either carry our books in stock or can order them for you. To order direct from us, please send a £sterling cheque, postal order, international money order or your credit card details (number, address of cardholder and expiry date) to us at the address below. Please add post and packing as follows: UK – £1.00 per delivery address; overseas surface mail – £2.50 per delivery address; overseas airmail – £3.50 for the first book to each delivery address, plus £1.00 for each additional book by airmail to the same address. If your order is a gift, we will happily enclose your card or message at no extra charge.

Luath Press Limited
543/2 Castlehill
The Royal Mile
Edinburgh EH1 2ND
Scotland
Telephone: 0131 225 4326 (24 hours)
Fax: 0131 225 4324
email: sales@luath.co.uk
Website: www.luath.co.uk